JANE'S
MERCHANT
SHIPPING
REVIEW

Edited by A.J. Ambrose

Third year of issue

First published in the United Kingdom in 1985 by
Jane's Publishing Company Limited
238 City Road, London EC1V 2PU

ISBN 0 7106 0332 0

Distributed in the Philippines and USA and its
dependencies by
Jane's Publishing Inc
135 West 50th Street
New York, NY 10020

Printed in the United Kingdom by
Biddles Limited, Guildford, Surrey

TITLE PAGE PHOTOGRAPH
Newly delivered in 1984 as part of Furness Withy's
contribution to the newly inagurated EUROSAL
container services between Europe and South America,
is the 37,020 dwt *Andes*. She has a service speed of
18.5 knots and can accommodate a maximum of 3,130
TEU, and is one of a fleet of six new similar sisterships
to work the EUROSAL line sailings. (*FotoFlite,
Ashford*)

Contents

Acknowledgements

Every year, more and more people and organisations seem to get themselves embroiled in helping to produce this Review, and I should like to thank them all for their help, which, in some cases this year, has gone way beyond the call of duty. Where practicable, contributors have been credited independently, but special thanks is due to the following persons and organisations for taking time from their busy schedules to contribute in one way or another to this edition: Mr J Graham Day, Chairman and Chief Executive of British Shipbuilders; Mr James H Rand and Mr T A Meyer of INTERTANKO; Mats Enquist and the Salen Reefer Corporation; John Hill of Furness Withy (Shipping) Ltd; Dennis Mann of Lloyds Register of Shipping; Phil Neumann and Co of *FotoFlite* of Ashford; Cliff and Joan Porter and Ian Wells of the World Ship Society; Dennis Lambeth and Messrs Mun, Evans and Philips for their diligent and painstaking scrutiny of all proofs and communications, and lastly, but by no means least, I am extremely grateful to Alex Vanags-Baginskis and the others at Jane's Publishing Co Ltd, City Road, London, and to the uncredited 'other half' of the editorial team, namely my wife Rosemary.

Andrew J Ambrose

Introduction

by A J Ambrose

The Sad State

Overcapacity! One word, which, so effectively, summarises the whole – worldwide – merchant ship building and operating spheres of activity for 1984. There are other words, equally as applicable, and just as evocative of merchant shipping today: protectionism; liquidation; cut-backs; subsidy; rationalisation. And some phrases and clauses too: strikes; industrial disputes; retarded economic growth: shipyard closures; laid-up; part-cargoes; increased shipping fraud . . . All can be used adjectively when describing the industries' environment today. In summary, the situation is not a particularly good one. But neither is it *all* bad.

Without doubt the biggest casualty in the merchant sphere is the United Kingdom. From a fleet of over 50 million tonnes deadweight not too many years ago, the UK's fleet has now shrunk to around 18 million tonnes. This shrinkage has also added well over 50,000 people to Britain's expanding ranks of unemployed. From more than 1,600 British ships in 1975 the UK has lost from its flag over 1,000 ships, and is presently losing an average of two ships every week, with a forecast of a fleet totalling no more than 400 ships by the end of 1985. As an aside, the fleet of the Soviet Union will have expanded by 10 million tonnes in the same period.

Like Britain, Norway is also suffering badly, having lost 10 million tonnes of her fleet to competitors in the same period.

As for the United States of America, she has actually gained tonnage. But, before any solace be drawn from this fact, the expansion is almost entirely due to strengthened naval commitments and does *not* represent an increased merchant capacity as such. It is significant that the major fleet contractions are among the NATO members of western Europe, while the fleets of the Warsaw Pact countries continue to expand. To revert to Britain's sad case specifically, is it not significant, and frightening, that during the whole of the Second World War 12 million tonnes of British fleet were lost, whereas since the mid-1970s Britain has lost *well over twice* this amount of tonnage? And that, when nobody was actually shooting at it. Indeed, even during the Falklands' conflict the Argentinians could not dispose of British ships as quickly as did Britain's own politicians! There must be a moral somewhere.

Lemmings' Syndrome or Shrewd Investment in the Cruise Trade?

One of the brighter areas of the shipping world is the rapidly expanding cruise business. But can we not see some alarming similarities here? Consider all these new ships presently appearing and being ordered, with the tanker crisis, the bulk carrier overcapacity and, latterly, the cellular containership buying spree. All of these trades expanded their numbers and combined tonnage to such a degree that they may (and in some cases *have* already) put themselves out of business.

New ships for the cruise market are appearing from all directions. On 5 September 1984 the keel was laid for Home Lines new 35,000-ton vessel at the Meyer Werft yards in Papenburg, for delivery in spring 1986. Meanwhile, Norway's Royal Caribbean Line was announcing plans to order two large new vessels of greater tonnage than their largest and latest *Song of America*. Of around 45,000 grt each, with accommodation for 2,000 passengers and delivery in late 1986 and spring 1987 respectively, they are destined to enter the US trade with one based in the Caribbean and the other on the West coast, with one of their existing vessels re-deploying to Europe. Both these ships will probably follow similar lines to P&O's *Royal Princess* – on the subject of which it must be remembered that the *Princess* has two sister consorts under option at Wärtsilä right now.

Carnival's 1,420-berth *Tropicale*. (*Drawing: David Thorne*)

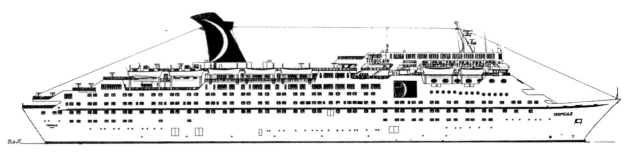

Lindblad Explorer. (DOT)

Then of course there is the Italian thrust, formerly associated with Norway's Sig Bergesen who has now dropped out of the deal but left it very much alive nevertheless. Two 50,000-ton vessels, to be built at Fincantieri's yards at a combined cost of $285 million, will be delivered in 1987 to a newly-formed company, Compagnia Italiana Crociere, who seem likely to charter one of these 2,000-passenger vessels to Carnival Cruise Line for operation under the Italian flag. The basis of the idea is to provide work for Italian ship-yards and ships' crews.

Next, there are two more vessels to be ordered shortly for Greece's Royal Cruise Line. These two 500-cabin ships for European and Scandinavian operations, costing an estimated $200 million for the pair, join a growing list of new orders, re-activations of liners and the like, scheduled for the future. And they are only those newly announced since the second article in this edition was completed a few weeks ago. Such is the pace of this market area at the moment. The cruise trade is a growth market today sure enough, but is the present level of expansion sufficient to sustain the unending list of new tonnage arriving over the course of the next few years?

It is truly depressing to survey the overall shipping situation from a commercial point of view, but, having said that, some encouragement can be obtained by comparison of this years' facts and figures with those of 1983 and 1982. Then, 1984 starts to look good, or at least marginally better, as some areas have witnessed up-turns in freight rates, profitability levels and the like, while even the lay-up situation has improved to a certain extent; at least, laid-up tonnage is no longer increasing, although it is not actually decreasing either! This is encouraging, but no signal to get excited yet.

Western developed countries, the so-called centres of economic commerce (!), with their massive operating overheads, top-heavy administrations, and lack of competitive edge over their Eastern competitors, are hard pressed to stay in the shipping business. Some more will, in the course of the next year, lamely accept defeat and drop out of shipping. This is unhelpful. What is necessary are fresh ideas. Sail power, nuclear power perhaps, and other examples of enhanced design and propulsion *should be* appearing on builder's slips, rather than the cheaply-built, heavily subsidised editions of vessels which can be built and operated at two-thirds of the cost in the Far East. Stock-building and subsidy (that advocate of inefficiency) should be discouraged on a worldwide scale. Tit for tat measures should be applied against fleets operating under protectionist and subsidised policies. Neither should developed countries dispose of their second-hand tonnage directly to their competitors. Such tonnage should be scrapped, or put in a National Reserve Fleet to await either a better economic environment or the needs of strategic exigency. Every vessel sold out of flag for further trading simply exacerbates the problem further and becomes *another* competitor, only ensuring that the day of reckoning and eventual collapse comes that bit closer to reality.

Note: Compilation of the next edition will have started by the time this work appears, and contributions in the form of articles, illustrations, and press information from both companies and individuals is welcomed. Please address it to: The Editor, Jane's Merchant Shipping Review, 238 City Road, London EC1V 2PU, England. The Editor regrets that he is unable to supply copies of photographs reproduced in this Review. Those appropriately credited can be obtained from *FotoFlite*, Unit APCL, Chart Road Industrial Estate, Godington Road, Ashford, Kent. Telephone 0233 37529; Telex 966152.

A Maritime Chronology of 1984

by R N Ambrose

In this chronological review of news items in the shipping world in 1984, it is sad to reflect that most of the news is bad. Casualties, missile hits, vessels in lay-up, and other negative items – in fact, a continuation of the pattern for 1982 and 1983.

But there are also some brighter spots in this bleak picture. Because of the very nature of 'news', things tend only to get reported when they are a problem of some nature. One should not forget, when refering to this chronology that literally thousands of other ships manage to get through the year without any problems, carrying out their normal, albeit even sometimes monotonous duties, with the very minimum of fuss and bother. These vessels do not make the news. Perhaps they should. When everything is going along normally, it is not considered newsworthy. Here then, are some of the problems of the shipping world, interspaced with the odd contrary snippet where something has gone right!

1 January

The 98,429 dwt 1967-built Greek-registered tanker *Ypatianna* is successfully refloated at Big Stone Beach Anchorage in the USA after some of her cargo of 23 million gallons of crude oil was discharged.

The roll-on roll-off vessel *Iran Hormuz* arrives in Port Khalid in the United Arab Emirates in the first

The final voyage of the former OCL container ship *Jervis Bay* (26,876 grt), seen here under tow by the West German tug *Hanseatic* bound for Taiwan. (*FotoFlite, Ashford*)

sailing of a twice-weekly passenger and cargo service from Bandar Abbas in Iran.

2 January
A new shipping corporation is established in Shanghai, China. Its fleet presently comprises four general cargo vessels and two reefers and they will carry freight bound for Japan and Hong Kong.

3 January
The 499 grt Danish-registered LPG carrier *Eva Tholstrup* is the victim of bad weather at Milford Haven in Wales, and is abandoned by her crew after she breaks free from her moorings. The vessel then runs aground on rocks but drifts off, and is taken in tow by two tugs. The only damage sustained is to her rudder.

The 29,262 grt container ship *Jervis Bay* breaks free from the tug *Hanseatic* while under tow from Antwerp to Taiwan to be broken up. A rescue team from Brest successfully anchors her in winds that are gusting up to 70 mph.

6 January
Crescent Shipping's 699 grt general cargo vessel *Vibrance* becomes the first ship to carry a commercial cargo into the newly-commercialised, ex-Royal Navy base of Chatham Dock in Kent. The cargo is timber, loaded at Kalmar for merchants in south-east England.

7 January
OCL's container ship *Botany Bay* causes extensive damage to a crane valued at £1.8m at Northfleet Hope Container Terminal on the Thames. *Botany Bay* suffers little damage.

8 January
Three die and three are injured on board the 176,053 grt Liberian-registered tanker *Brazilian Splendour* when an explosion occurs as a result of welding work being done while off the coast of South Africa.

10 January
British Shipbuilders sell Grangemouth Ship Repair Yard to the Company's managing director and two colleagues.

12 January
Swedish company Oskarshamns wins the contract to fit an additional bow thruster, modify rudders, and fit a skeg between the propeller shafts of the French nuclear fuel carrier *Sigyn* in an attempt to improve her manouvrability following the spate of collisions and groundings she has been involved in since her completion.

13 January
The keel of what will be the world's largest rail ferry, to be named *Railship II*, is laid by German shipbuilders Seebeckwerft, a subsidary of A.G. Weser. The ferry

The Liberian-registered general cargo vessel *Radiant Med* (ex-*Shusei Maru*) became the victim of Force 11 winds off the Channel Islands in January 1984. (*FotoFlite, Ashford*)

will be for service between Travemünde and Hangore in Finland.

17 January
The Soviet roll-on roll-off vessel *Inzhener Sukhorukov* (4,009 grt) and the Liberian general cargo vessel *Sun Castor* collide in Belgium's River Scheldte. *Sun Castor* sustains damage on her port side and goes to a Belgium yard for repairs.

21 January
The Radio Caroline ship *Ross Revenge/Imagine* breaks free from her anchor during rough weather. She is currently anchored seven miles away from her normal anchoring position, to which she will return when weather conditions improve.

22 January
The tanker *Ypapanti* (45,988 grt), which appeared in the news on several occasions last year (*see* Chronology 2nd edition), is sold at public auction in Greece for £866,000 by a Liberian company.

24 January
Sixteen crew members die when the 5,617 dwt general cargo vessel *Radiant Med* capsizes off the Channel Islands in Force 11 winds. She was bound for Ghent with a cargo of wheat and maize. Survivors are picked up by the St Peter Port lifeboat *Sir William Old*.

25 January
The container ship *Jervis Bay* breaks in two after running into rocks in the outer harbour of Bilbao

during heavy weather. She is now to be broken up where she is.

27 January
Australia has lifted her three-year ban on Russian cruise ships entering the country's ports.

29 January
The 5,986 grt *Contship Europe* and 2,541 grt *Ville de Bordeaux* collide at Felixstowe. *Contship Europe* develops a 10 degree list and sustains a 50 cm hole on her port side.

2 February
The British House of Commons announces Britain's first six freeports. They are to be Belfast, Birmingham, Cardiff, Liverpool, Prestwick and Southampton.

6 February
The Danish supply vessel *Gunnar Seidenfaden*, owned by the Danish Government, which had experienced problems with her underwater TV robot, resumes her search for 80 barrels of toxic herbicide that have been washed overboard from the *Dana Optima*.

7 February
The Panamanian cargo ship *Midnight Sun 1* sinks off the French coast during high winds. Eight of the 19-strong crew are lost.

9 February
Ben Lines 58,283 grt container ship *Benavon* which ran aground yesterday in bad weather close to Port Said, is successfully refloated and continues on her voyage to Singapore on her regular Europe–Far East Service.

11 February
An oil slick of 400 square yards is caused at Scapa Flow. The oil comes from the Finnish-registered 52,371 grt *Fanny* which has two fractured tanks.

15 February
Japanese trawlers *Anyo Maru No. 15* (349 grt) and *Kyowa Maru No. 11* (349 grt) collide in the Bering Sea during the transfer of an American from one vessel to the other. Fourteen are killed.

The 492 grt general cargo vessel *Camilla Weston* sinks after colliding with the West German-registered general cargo vessel *Larissasee* in fog off Britain's Norfolk coast. The crew are taken off the vessel by the UK-registered *Wegro*.

16 February
It is announced today that the UK–France cross-

P&O's new luxury cruise ship *Royal Princess* is towed to Wärtsilä's new fitting out complex. (*Wärtsilä*)

Giant 14 and her cargo of two cranes bound for Saudi Arabia under the tow of the tug *Eduard* sunk in the English Channel approaches. Crew from the tug abandoned their vessel and were picked up from liferafts. (*FotoFlite, Ashford*)

Channel hovercraft service Hoverspeed, owned jointly by British Rail and Brostrums, has been sold to its directors. Hoverspeed lost £4 million in 1982, and was in the red again in 1983.

17 February
Wärtsilä floods the dock in which they are building *Royal Princess*, and move her 15 metres astern for fitting of bow and stern sections.

18 February
Royal Princess is towed out ¼ mile by chartered ice-breaking tugs to berth at a new fitting-out complex.

The first commercial sailing ship to be built in Britain for almost 50 years is launched near Aberystwyth in Wales. The ship, a 100-foot clipper, will be used to carry cargo to the West Indies.

19 February
The Cypriot cargo ship *Tatiana* becomes the latest victim of fighting in the Lebanon when she is sunk at anchor off Tripoli. The crew of eight and three passengers are picked up by a US naval vessel.

21 February
The West German tug *Eduard* capsizes in bad weather off the coast of Brittany while towing the pontoon *Giant 14* with a deck cargo of two cranes. The *Giant 14* runs aground and sinks. She was being towed from Finland to Saudi Arabia.

26 February
An explosion on board the tanker *American Eagle* (20,520 grt) kills three of the crew in the Gulf of Mexico. The tug *Smit New York* takes the vessel in tow.

27 February

Tickets for the maiden voyage of P&O's new cruise ship *Royal Princess* are sold out within three hours of going on sale. Already there is a waiting list of several hundred.

28 February

American Eagle, formerly *Zenit Eagle*, and only recently acquired by the US military as a prepositioning ship for the rapid deployment force, has sunk, following the explosion of two days ago.

1 March

Iraq claims to have sunk eight vessels near to the Iranian coast. Three have been named as *Apj Ambika*, a general cargo vessel of 10,929 grt registered in India; the *Sema G*, a general cargo vessel of 9,675 grt and registered in Turkey; and the *Charming*, a bulk carrier of 19,210 grt registered in the UK.

6 March

Crew from the Royal Navy's fishery protection vessel HMS *Wooton* and the mine countermeasure vessel HMS *Cottesmore* go to the assistance of the Danish-registered liquified gas carrier *Anna Tholstrup* (1,113 grt) when fire breaks out in her engine room. The fire

is successfully extinguished and the ship continues her voyage to Northern Ireland.

9 March

Fire breaks out in a passenger cabin on the DFDS passenger ship *Scandinavian Sea* (10,736 grt) while she is on a day cruise off the coast of Florida.

11 March

The fire on board the *Scandinavian Sea* is successfully extinguished leaving 30 per cent of the ship gutted and an estimated repair bill of £685,000. The vessel is listing due to the water she has taken in, and may be declared a constructive total loss.

A hole is torn in the deck and 20 cars on board are damaged when the 1979-built Japanese car carrier *Toyo Fuji No 5* (4,177 grt) is hit in a disputed area of the Formosa Strait. China blames Taiwan for the incident.

12 March

The commencement of a new freight service between

Smoke billows from the tanker *Safina Al Arab* after she is hit by an Exocet missile. (*International Transport Contractors*)

Although operational in 1982, the Thames Flood Barrier was officially declared open in May 1984 by the Queen. In this view construction work is still in progress. (*R N Ambrose*)

Heysham in northern England, and Belfast in Northern Ireland, is delayed due to industrial action by seamen protesting that the vessel to be used, *Stena Sailer* (2,353 grt), is registered in the Cayman Islands and not the United Kingdom.

13 March

It is announced that shipbuilders Harland & Wolff have purchased the roll-on roll-off cargo vessel *Contender Bezant* (11,445 grt) which they will sell to the MoD after conversion to a flight training ship for service with the Royal Fleet Auxiliary.

Kuwait Oil Tanker's 210,068 grt ULCC *Al Rekkah* is taken in tow by *Smit Lloyd 120* and *Smit Lloyd 160* after a steam pipe bursts and she loses power off Vlissingen in the Netherlands. 100,000 tonnes of her cargo of crude oil will be discharged before she enters Rotterdam.

14 March

The Monopolies Commission announces that they will not allow Trafalgar House and P&O to bid for Sealink.

19 March

Traffic in the port of Alexandria is disrupted for two hours when the general cargo vessel *Salah el Din* catches fire with 300 tons of dangerous chemicals on board. Eight tugs tow her out of the port and successfully extinguish the fire.

The US-registered tanker *Mobiloil* (18,615 grt), owned by the Mobil Oil Corporation, runs aground due to steering problems in the Colombia River in Oregon, USA. 42,000 gallons of oil is lost causing a slick which threatens considerable pollution.

21 March

The Soviet tanker *Lugansk* (22,078 grt) is damaged when she hits a mine in Nicaragua's Puerto Sandino harbour. The Nicaraguan foreign ministry states that the mine was planted by anti-Sandinista mercenaries who are in the service of the US Government. Damage caused is minimal and she discharges her cargo safely.

DFDS announces the sale of one of their newer vessels, the 1978-built *Dana Optima* which had been on the Grimsby to Esbjerg route. The vessel has been bought by Ethiopian Shipping Lines.

22 March

The Belfast–Heysham roll-on roll-off freight service commences today with the docking of Belfast Freight Service's chartered *Stena Sailer* at Heysham.

27 March

Greek-registered tanker *Filikon L* (41,330 grt/85,123 dwt) is hit by a rocket 40 miles south-west of Iran's Kharg Island. The vessel was bound for Sicily with a cargo of crude oil. The missile hit the vessel's starboard side and penetrated the slop tank.

29 March

The Bahamas-registered cruise ship *Rhapsody* runs aground off Grand Cayman Island in the Caribbean with 1,200 passengers on board. There is thought to be no damage to the vessel's hull.

4 April

Cunard's cruise ship *QE 2* hits a quay at Gibraltar while docking. She was also damaged a few days earlier during berthing, and is due to enter shipyards in Lisbon for repair work.

5 April

The Panamanian general cargo ship *Raya Eclat* sinks after colliding with the South Korean-registered *Hwa Pyung Nam Jin* off Hong Kong. The crew of 28 from *Raya Eclat* (9,104 grt) are picked up by *Hwa Pyung Nam Jin* and police launches. The cause of the collision is unknown.

18 April

The 50,975 dwt Panamanian-registered tanker *Rover Star*, owned by the Grover Star Shipping Corporation, is hit by an Iraqi missile one mile off Kharg Island.

21 April

Fire breaks out on Cunard's 9,742 grt general cargo ship *Carmania* when she enters Gulfport near Mobile in the USA.

26 April

An explosion on board the tanker *Safina Al Arab* (178,808 grt/357,100 dwt) 120 miles off Kharg Island is thought to have been caused by either a mine or a missile.

30 April

Dover Harbour Board announces higher profits and plans for expansion. They plan to spend £10 million extending the Eastern Docks through land reclamation, £8 million on improving facilities for foot and coach passengers and £3 million on new tugs.

2 May

The *Balder London* (19,976 grt), owned by Lloyds Industrial Leasing and on charter to the British Government, joins the Royal Fleet Auxiliary and is renamed RFA *Orangeleaf*.

A missile hits the Liberian-registered general cargo vessel *Sea Eagle* (8,206 grt) in the Persian Gulf. It is thought that either the missile failed to explode or the fertilizer on board the vessel absorbed the blast. The ship continues to her destination, Banadar Khomeini, with relatively little damage.

The Turkish destroyer *Tinaztepe* (ex-USS *Keppler*) and the Turkish liquified gas carrier *Aygaz 3* collide in fog in the Bay of Izmit 60 km south of Istanbul. The *Aygaz 3* was bound for the Ipras refinery on the Marmara coast to take on cargo.

8 May

The Thames Flood Barrier is officially opened by the Queen. The barrier is designed to prevent flooding in London in the event of an exceptional surge tide such as took place in 1953. A particularly high tide of this nature is expected in the forseeable future.

9 May

ABC Container Line commences its Round-the-World service operations with the sailing of *Cornelis Verolme* (26,391 grt) from Felixstowe, England. Unlike Evergreen and US Lines, who will introduce new larger container tonnage for RTW service this year, ABC can carry both bulk and containerised cargoes.

13 May

The Kuwait-registered tanker *Umm Casbah* (55,620 grt) is hit by a missile in the Gulf while on her way from Kuwait to the UK with a cargo of 76,560 tons of crude oil. The blast causes slight damage in the middle section of the vessel's tanks.

14 May

The Iranian-registered tanker *Tabriz* (41,440 grt) and the Greek-registered tanker *Esperanza II* (32,668 grt) are attacked in the Gulf.

15 May

A man is rescued by North Sea Ferries' Ipswich–Rotterdam ferry *Norsea* after falling overboard from Sealink's *St Nicholas* which was heading for Harwich Parkstone Quay from the Hook of Holland.

16 May

The VLCC *Yanbu Pride* (109,165 grt/214,992 dwt) is attacked in waters that were previously considered safe off the Ras Tanura oil terminal in Saudi Arabia.

ABC Container Line's 1983-built 26,391 grt/42,077 dwt *Cornelis Verolme* which inaugurated a new service for bulk and containerised cargoes in May. (*FotoFlite, Ashford*)

North Sea Ferries 6,310 grt roll-on roll-off cargo ferry *Norsea* which operates the company's Ipswich–Rotterdam route came to the rescue of a Sealink passenger. (*FotoFlite, Ashford*)

It is confirmed that Greek shipowner Antonis Lelakis has bought the former DFDS ship *Scandinavian Sea* (10,736 grt). He intends to repair the fire damage caused earlier in the year and put her on the charter market.

18 May
Crew from the bulk carrier *Fidelity* are picked up by the Cypriot bulker *Cathy Mylo* and Iranian naval vessels after she is hit by a missile and sinks off Kharg Island.

21 May
The 1965-built UK-registered tanker *Southway* (39,011 grt/79,388 dwt), which broke her tow from the tug *Shamal* while on her way round the Cape of Good Hope to Taiwanese breakers five days ago, is picked up again by the tug after drifting unpowered and unmanned.

Royal Viking Lines' *Royal Viking Sky* (28,078 grt) catches fire in dry dock at Hapag Lloyd's Bremerhaven yard while undergoing a survey following striking a

coral reef on a voyage to the Virgin Islands. She is, however, expected to leave the yard on schedule.

23 May
Lifeboats from the LNG carrier *Aquarius* (19,869 grt), the Liberian-registered tanker *Felipes* (19,275 grt) and the *Rimba Dua* pick up the crew from the Liberian tanker *Casper Trader* (67,420 grt/142,317 dwt) following a distress signal in the South China Sea due to an engine room fire.

24 May
The Liberian tanker *Chemical Venture* (17,268 grt/ 29,427 dwt) is hit by a rocket off the Saudi Arabian coast. Two Saudi Arabian naval tugs go to her assistance.

A new pirate radio station takes to the air from the ex-Guardline vessel *Guardline Seeker*, renamed MV *Communicator*, broadcasting off the Essex coast.

1 June
The Greek courts declare the last of Hellenic Lines operations bankrupt. The affairs of the company will now be put into the hands of an official receiver.

3 June
The Turkish-registered tanker *Buyuk Hun* (80,683

grt/153,274 dwt), owned by Um Denizcilik ve Ticaret AS of Istanbul, is hit by a missile while heading for Kharg Island. Crew abandon the vessel and are picked up by tugs in the area.

5 June
Turkey announces that following the attack on *Buyuk Hun* her ships may be banned from entering the Gulf.

6 June
The Soviet cargo ship *Akademik Yuryev* rescues the crew from the Greek-registered general cargo vessel *Jennie S* (9,172 grt/16,074 dwt) after she sinks 500 miles off the coast of Newfoundland in heavy weather.

P&O announce that *Oriana* will be withdrawn from the Australian market in 1985 and cruise out of Southampton while *Pacific Princess* (20,636 grt), currently based in the United States, will be moved to the Mediterranean.

7 June
Sea Containers announces at their Annual General Meeting that they will be making a bid for Sealink.

10 June
Kazimah (160,010 grt/294,739 dwt), owned by the Kuwait Oil Tanker Company, is hit by a missile while heading for Kuwait in ballast. The subsequent fire is quickly extinguished; no casualities are reported. This is the most southerly attack to occur since the start of the Iran-Iraq war.

11 June
Iran takes delivery of a Japanese tug which is to be used for fire fighting and oil spills at the Kharg Island oil terminal.

13 June
Brazil's largest ship repair yard Renave is declared bankrupt following the default on a loan to buy a floating dock. Unless a buyer is found, the yard will be closed down.

14 June
Blue Star's reefer *Almeria Star* (9,781 grt/11,093 dwt) and Cunard's *Servia* (12,059 grt/12,182 dwt) collide in the mouth of the river Scheldte. *Servia* continues to Sheerness, while *Almeria Star* is assisted by tugs due to taking in water in two of her holds.

15 June
An explosion on board the UK-registered tanker

The *Guardline Seeker* in her new guise as the radio ship MV *Communicator*. (*FotoFlite, Ashford*)

Pointsman while undergoing repair in Milford Haven Docks in Wales kills three and injures 17.

The cruise ship *Rhapsody* is refloated after running aground two months ago off Grand Cayman Island. She is towed to a specially dredged channel for investigation of damage.

19 June

The tanker *Texaco Norge* (13,233 grt/21,539 dwt) runs aground in the Thames estuary. She is successfully refloated with the assistance of the tugs *Sun Thames, Sun Essex, Sun London, Sun Swale, Sun Kent, Hibernia, Watercock, Avenger* and *Burma*.

22 June

The 491,120 dwt tanker *Nanny* has been bought by a Saudi Arabian investment company to store oil outside the Persian Gulf as a safeguard against the area being closed to shipping.

The motor salvage tug *Salvageman*, the longest serving ship in the Falklands, arrives back in her home port of Hull for refit. After dry docking and refit she will return to the South Atlantic on a further six month charter to the MoD.

24 June

Ferry operators DFDS commence a seasonal ferry service between Cuxhaven and Harwich. The twice weekly sailings will be served by the 7,933 grt *Prinz Oberon*.

25 June

The Greek-registered tanker *Alexander The Great* (152,372 grt/325,645 dwt) is attacked by Iraqi jets in the Gulf. Damage caused is slight and there is no leakage of oil from the vessel's tanks.

27 June

The 260,150 dwt tanker *Tiburon* (ex-*Sea Scout*) is hit by an Iraqi Exocet missile in her engine room south east of Kharg Island only six days after being bought for £6 million by the Swiss consortium Suisse-Outremer Reederei.

28 June

Smit International's fire fighting tugs *Smit Colombo* and *Drado* take *Tiburon* in tow. Fire has swept through the engine room, accommodation and superstructure, and it is feared that her cargo of crude oil may ignite.

30 June

The Bahamas-registered 12,576 grt cruise ship *Sundancer* (ex-*Svea Corona*) starts taking in water and listing after running aground. The 780 passengers on board all disembark at Duncan Bay at the north end of Vancouver Island, Canada.

1 July

The South Korean general cargo ship *Won Jin* (10,205 dwt) is attacked by Iraqi jets near Bandar Khomeini and catches fire after being struck by two missiles. The ship, on charter to the National Iranian Shipping Corporation, was bound for Japan with a cargo of 9,000 tons of iron plate. Crew abandon the ship after attempts to extinguish the blaze fail.

The Cypriot bulk carrier *Alexandra Dyo* is attacked and badly damaged by the subsequent fire while en-route for Bandar Khomeini from Maputo with a cargo of iron ore.

The Panamanian bulk carrier *Erne* (15,178 grt/ 24,482 dwt) runs aground during an air attack in the Gulf but only sustains minor damage.

3 July
Finnish-based company Sally the Viking Line has chartered a Yugoslavian ferry, the 4,000 ton *Njegos*, to operate their Dunkirk–Ramsgate route. With Yugoslavian deck crew and French catering staff it is feared that there may be union difficulties.

5 July
The 276,424 dwt Japanese-registered tanker *Primrose* is hit twice during an Iranian air attack after loading oil at the Ras Tanura terminal. Dutch salvage company Smit Tak report that the vessel had two unexploded bombs aboard.

6 July
The newly privatised shipbuilding yard Tyne Ship-repair has won the MoD contract for the reconstruction work on the Royal Fleet Auxiliary vessel *Sir Tristram*. The work will involve lengthening the vessel by 29 ft (8.84 m), rebuilding the superstructure and constructing a heli-deck.

9 July
The arrival into the port of Felixstowe of the 1983-built, 1,599 grt/4,100 dwt ship *Akak Ocean* inaugurates a direct Felixstowe–Beirut container service. This fortnightly service is being offered by the Lebanese company Akak Lines.

10 July
Iranian aircraft attack BP's *British Renown* (261,011

The 1964-built Greek cruise ship *Royal Odyssey* which was involved in a collision with a Soviet cargo ship. (*FotoFlite, Ashford*)

dwt). She is hit by two missiles but not seriously damaged while en-route to lighten the 260,150 dwt *Tiburon* which had been seriously damaged in an attack two weeks before.

11 July
The Greek cruise ship *Royal Odyssey* (17,884 grt) is in collision with the Soviet cargo vessel *Vasya Alekseyev* (4,677 grt) in shallow waters between Denmark and Sweden today. *Royal Odyssey*, with 812 passengers aboard at the time, is holed forward but manages to reach Copenhagen unaided with no casualties.

The Soviet vessel is more seriously damaged and sinking by the stern in 30 feet of water, but prompt attendance by Danish tugs and a Soviet 'engineering' vessel saves the *Vasya Alekseyev* and she is later towed into Copenhagen.

17 July
The tanker *British Renown* is now alongside the tanker *Tiburon* despite being hit by two missiles while en-route to the *Tiburon* to transfer her cargo. *Tiburon* is anchored in the Dubai area.

18 July
It is announced that Sea Containers have bought the British Rail subsidary Sealink for £66 million, paid in cash through a newly formed holding company named British Ferries Ltd.

22 July
The cruise ship *Song of America* picks up the crew of the 82-year-old auxiliary motor vessel *Captain Morgan* after she catches fire and sinks south of Grand Turk Island bound for the Dominican Republic with a cargo of lumber.

24 July
P&O announces the placing of an order for a 170,000 dwt bulk carrier from Mitsubishi Heavy Industries. The ship is due for delivery in the first part of 1986.

26 July
Within three hours, three of the world's largest cruise ships, the *Norway* (70,202 grt), the *QE 2* (67,140 grt) and the *Royal Viking Sky* (28,078 grt) all berthed at Southampton. All three ships sailed on the evening tide.

27 July
An explosion while seamen were soldering an empty tank on board the Spanish tanker *Alcazar* (73,503 dwt) causes the death of four crew. The vessel was heading for Alexandria when the incident occured.

30 July
The Singapore-registered container ship *Gloria Express* (4,705 grt) runs aground near Iwojima Island after being caught in Typhoon Ed. The ship drifted for

several hours before running aground and is reported to be broken amidships.

Another casualty of the typhoon was the *Ilshin Glory* which sank while en-route for Nagoya.

The 57,375 dwt British-registered tanker *Alvenus*, owned by Lloyd's Leasing and managed by Silver Line of London, runs aground in the Calcasieu Ship Channel while en-route to her destination of Lake Charles, Louisiana, USA. The US Coast Guard reports that the vessel is leaking crude oil from at least one tank. An investigation is being called into the cause of the incident which occured in good weather conditions.

1 August

British and American merchant ships are today warned to proceed with 'extreme caution' while in the Gulf of Suez. This follows the confirmation of unexplained explosions damaging the Liberian cargo ship *Medi Sea* (14,136 grt), Japanese car carrier *Meiyo Maru* (17,380 grt) and Panamanian-registered *Big Orange XII* (855 tons).

2 August

Two more ships have become the victims of explosions in the Gulf of Suez and Red Sea. They are the Lauritzen-owned Bahamas-registered reefer *Peruvian Reefer* (6,010 grt), and the Spanish tanker *Valencia* (173,266 dwt).

5 August

The Liberian-registered 87,200 dwt tanker *Oceanic Energy* is damaged by a mine in the Red Sea. The Greek tug *Skyros* is heading to the southern half of the Red Sea to assist the tanker.

Crude oil from grounded tanker *Alvenus* has polluted a 15-mile stretch of the Texas coast line. US Coast Guards estimate 70 per cent of the vessels 4,500 barrels have formed a 6-inch thick sludge on beaches. The vessel's remaining oil is being pumped out in an attempt to refloat her.

The Norwegian tanker *Norske Barde* (31,995 dwt) carrying a cargo of gas oil runs aground on a reef in the Baltic en-route for Antwerp from Ventspils in the Soviet Latvia. The Swedish tanker *Tarnhav* (6,950 dwt) is to go alongside the larger vessel to offload some of her cargo in an attempt to refloat her.

7 August

An order for the world's largest ore/oil carrier is placed by Wah Kwong Shipping and Investment of Hong Kong. The vessel has been designed by Mitsui Shipbuilding of Japan and will be built by the China Shipbuilding Corporation of South Korea. The 305,000 dwt vessel is due to be delivered in 1987.

8 August

The cruise ship *Sundancer* is towed to Burrard Yarrows shipyards in Vancouver for drydocking following incidents earlier in the year when she struck rocks and

Alvenus, built in 1979 by Cammell Laird Shipbuilders, caused pollution problems on the Texas coast after she ran aground and lost a considerable amount of her cargo of crude oil. (*FotoFlite, Ashford*)

took in water and then on being towed to a dock owned by the Canadian company Crown Forest Industries she grounded and caused considerable damage to the dock on a shifting tide. Repair work to the vessel is expected to be in the region of US $10 million.

9 August

Atlantic Cartier, Compagnie Generale Maritime's new container ship and contribution to the Atlantic Container Line consortium, catches fire in the builders' yards in France. The vessel should have been delivered in September 1984 but this has been put back due to industrial action. The amount of damage to the vessel is not yet known.

11 August

The 8,644 grt Polish-registered general cargo ship *Jozef Wybicki* is struck by a mine in the mouth of the Red Sea while en-route to Jeddah from Malaysia. Repairs to the extensive damage caused in the engine room are underway and another Polish ship, the 9,782 grt *Leopold Staff*, is also providing assistance. No casualties are reported.

16 August

It is announced that Norwegian Caribbean Line has bought Royal Viking Line at an estimated cost of US $240 million.

18 August

An explosion onboard the dredger *Vlaanderen XVIII* (9,144 grt), which kills one member of the crew, halts traffic in and out of the port of Zeebrugge in Belgium for most of the day.

21 August

Fire breaks out onboard the DFDS roll-on roll-off ferry *Scandinavian Sea* which operates day cruises out of Miami. The vessel had just docked when fire broke out in the auxiliary engine room. The 700 passengers are evacuated with only three casualties. However, it is later discovered that two people had in fact died.

24 August

Townsend Thoresen's ferry *Free Enterprise III* (4,657 grt) which has been laid up in Southampton for two years, has been sold to Maltese company Mira Shipping Group and will be renamed *Tamira*. She will be based in Valetta and will possibly be used on freight/passenger routes to the Italian mainland or North Africa.

Iraqi aircraft attack the fully laden tanker *Amethyst* (53,425 dwt) south of Kharg Island. She was being used to shuttle oil out of the danger areas. The vessel is holed in a starboard tank causing an extensive fire.

25 August

The West German ro-ro passenger ferry *Olau Britania* (14,986 grt) outbound from Vlissingen (Flushing) for Sheerness, is in collision with the French ro-ro cargo vessel *Mont Louis* (4,210 grt) one mile west of the Akkaert Bank lightbuoy off the Belgian coast. The two vessels remain locked together following the collision, but are soon separated. Thereafter the *Mont Louis* sinks in 15 metres of water, while the *Olau Brittania*, which was only superficially damaged, proceeds to Sheerness. Shortly after the collision, the environmentalist group Greenpeace announces that the *Mont Louis* was carrying hazardous nuclear cargo. This consists of 450 tonnes of uranium hexafluoride, which was en-route for Riga, Soviet Latvia, for processing into low grade uranium 235 and 338, which is used for either nuclear power or armaments, depending on the degree of processing involved.

27 August

The Japanese-registered 35,730 dwt tanker *Cleo I* is

Salvage operations underway on the French roll-on roll-off Finnish-built *Mont Louis* (ex-*Bore Moon*). Operations were held up on several occasions due to bad weather conditions. (*FotoFlite, Ashford*)

struck by a missile fired from an aircraft while en-route for Ras Tanura from Sri Lanka. The ship's bridge is destroyed, but no casualties are reported.

28 August
Crew abandon the 3,713 grt Cypriot general cargo ship *Blue Falcon* approximately 550 miles off the Mexican coast after she was caught in Hurricane Lowell and started to take in water and lost power. Crew are picked up by another Cypriot ship, the *Josef Roth* which had been diverted to assist by the US Coast Guard.

29 August
Attempts to salvage the 30 flasks of radio-active material from the *Mont Louis* commence today. The salvage work is being done jointly by Smit Tak International and Remorguage et de Sauvetage.

31 August
The Dutch general cargo ship *Polaris* (1,000 grt) with a cargo of 1,500 tonnes of stones strikes rocks off Falmouth, England. The crew are picked up by lifeboat and the salvage tug *Caribic* attempts to save the vessel.

1 September
Attempts to salvage the roll-on roll-off vessel *Mont Louis* and her cargo have to be abandoned temporarily due to bad weather conditions.

4 September
DFDS have ordered a 7,000-tonne vessel for their North Sea services. The vessel will be built by Fredrikshvn Vaerft and delivered in March 1986.

6 September
Salvors of the *Mont Louis* have been experiencing more problems when floating debris smashes through the vessel's decks. Two empty barrels which break free are immediately picked up.

11 September
The Liberian tanker *St Tobias*, 115,025 grt/254,520 dwt, 1971-built, becomes the latest Gulf casualty when attacked 50 miles south of Kharg Island. She is hit in a ballast tank by a missile fired from an Iraqi aircraft.

12 September
The bulk carrier *Adib*, bound for Bandar Khomeini out of Geelong, is struck by a missile in her hold space while in the Khor Musa channel. The ship does not appear to be badly damaged, and is proceeding to her destination to unload.

13 September
The first full flask of radio-active material is lifted from the sunken *Mont Louis*. Meanwhile, in the Gulf, the West German-owned *Seetrans 21*, a utility supply

Sirius, an ex-trawler operated by the environment protection group Greenpeace, whose activities appear in the news from time to time. In October 1984 she was attempting to block the way of a Soviet whaling expedition. (*FotoFlite, Ashford*)

vessel with 11 persons on board, falls victim to Iraqi attack near Kharg Island. The vessel is sunk, with the loss of six lives.

16 September
Two more vessels are attacked and damaged in the Gulf. The 126,998 dwt tanker *Royal Colombo* is hit by a missile while carrying 120,000 tonnes of Saudi crude oil. One tank, containing 10,000 tonnes is holed, and a US Naval vessel is en-route to assist and patch the South Korean vessel.

In the other attack, on the Liberian tanker *Med Heron*, 123,597 dwt, about 30 per cent of the accommodation is destroyed, and three crew members are injured, when she is hit by a missile at around 09.20 hours while inward-bound to Ras Tanura to lift a cargo of crude. The *Royal Colombo* and *Med Heron* are attacked at around the same time.

18 September
Britain's dockers vote overwhelmingly to return to work, so ending the long-running series of stoppages which have plagued Britain's ports recently.

19 September
The Japanese 1950 TEU container ship *Kamakura Maru* is due to sail from Le Havre, France, with a cargo including two containers of re-processed enriched uranium bound for Japan. Moves by Greenpeace to harrass the vessel are expected. Meanwhile, the salvage of the nuclear flasks from the *Mont Louis* continues to provide problems for the salvors, as the ship has been battered by storms lately, causing the cargo to shift.

20 September
The Saudi Arabian ro-ro ferry *Belkis 1* is damaged by a mine 20 miles south of Suez City. The 3,114 grt

vessel is not seriously affected and is returning to Port Suez for repairs.

22 September
The UK's largest and most powerful ocean salvage tug *Salvageman* sails again for the South Atlantic following an extensive refit and a five-day visit to the Pool of London. The 20,000 hp tug was the longest serving member of the original Falklands Task force, despatched in April 1982 and spending more than two years on station during which time she was working continuously.

25 September
The world's largest operating passenger ship sails from Southampton, following a seven-week European tour and refit in West Germany. The 70,202 grt *Norway* is returning to her seven-day cruise circuit in the Caribbean.

26 September
The 128,255 dwt tanker *Burmah Legacy* is adrift with no power and a cargo of 68,000 tonnes of crude oil in the North Atlantic.

31 September
The tanker *Burmah Legacy* is now under tow to Halifax, Canada, from the tug/supply vessel *Taonui*, proceeding at 5½ knots, and is expected in Halifax in seven days time.

4 October
The last flask of uranium hexafluoride is removed from the wreck of the French *Mont Louis* today. However, a battle still continues around the wreck, as the French owners CGM refuse to pay the costs of the wreck removal operation. Even now, 22 empty nuclear-fuel containers, oil and other cargo remains on the broken vessel.

The tug Orla, which broke her tow from the jack-up rig *Interocean II* during bad weather conditions. She was en-route from the North Sea to the Irish Sea. (*FotoFlite, Ashford*)

5 October
Loading of 550 pounds of plutonium commences aboard the Japanese *Seishin Maru* (16,909 dwt). The consignment, bound for Japan's Joyo nuclear power station, is suitable for being used to produce atomic weapons and is being loaded in 'total' secrecy at the French port of Cherbourg. The voyage will be under escort from French, British and US warships.

8 October
Six crewmen are killed in the 92nd recorded attack on an unarmed merchant vessel in the Gulf since May 1981, when Iraqi aircraft bomb the Liberian 258,437 dwt tanker *World Knight* today. The tugs *Amsterdam* and Selco's *Salveritas* and *Salvanguard* are responding to extinguish large conflagrations aboard the ship.

10 October
Carnival Cruise Line has admitted that it is in the market for a new building 50,000-ton cruise ship which Norway's Sig Bergensen are contemplating having built as one of two sisters, in Italy. Due for probable delivery in 1987, these would be the largest purpose-built cruise ships ordered to date.

12 October
The tanker *Sivand*, 218,587 dwt, loaded with 190,000 tonnes of crude oil, is attacked and damaged south of Kharg Island shortly after sailing from the Iranian oil terminal, and the Panamanian 29,451 dwt LPG tanker *Gaz Fountain* is hit by three rockets about 150 miles north west of Dubai. Selco's *Salvanguard* and two other tugs are steaming to the scene to battle with severe fires that have broken out. The *Gaz Fountain* is loaded with 19,500 tonnes of propane and butane which she had just loaded at Ras Tanura.

Also attacked is the Indian tanker *Jag Pari* of 29,139 dwt, which is hit by four missiles from unidentified aircraft about 60 miles north of Bahrain.

15 October
The Iranian tanker *Sivand* is attacked and damaged again for the second time in one week. She is last seen near a small island about 60 miles south of Kharg and is expected to be lightened by another tanker which Iranian owners N.I.T.C. are trying to charter.

16 October
The 254,520 dwt VLCC *St Tobias*, hit by a missile on 11 September, has been purchased by the PR of China for breaking. This is the second VLCC purchased (the 262,316 dwt *Violanda* was acquired in September), and is a clear pointer to the development of a newly-enlarged Chinese shipbreaking organisation.

19 October
The diving support ship *Pacific Protector* is attacked by an Iranian F-4 Phantom II in the Gulf today. Four rockets are fired at the vessel, en-route from Ras

The British-registered tanker *Overseas Argonaut*, built by Gotaverken Arendal in 1975, went to the rescue of another British ship, the liner *St Helena*, when she had a fire in her engine room while off the coast of Sierra Leone. (*FotoFlite, Ashford*)

Tanura to Dubai and just east of Qatar when hit. The Captain, Chief Engineer and another crew member are killed, but a helicopter from the frigate USS *Stark* manages to rescue 16 crew members. The tug *Amsterdam* is now trying to salve the 1,530-ton vessel before towing her to Dubai.

The 18-year-old Panama flag tanker *Rover Star* (50,975 dwt) sinks 20 miles off the coast of Oman following a mystery explosion and subsequent fires while en-route from Aden to Kharg Island. The tug *Smit Rangoon* had towed her into deep water after being refused permission to bring the casualty into an Omani port.

The Spanish trawler *Sonia* sinks following an attack by the Irish Fishery Protection Vessel *Aisling*. The *Aisling* had requested the *Sonia* to heave-too for inspection, but the *Sonia* refused and tried to run away. She was chased by the *Aisling* for five hours when the FPV decided to put a shot across her bows. The *Sonia* then repeatedly tried to ram the FPV *Aisling* so the FPV opened fire expending 596 rounds of 20 mm and small arms fire on the *Sonia* before she sank.

19 October

Dutch heavy-lift specialists Mammoet and two West German heavy-lift companies, Sloman Neptune and Project Carriers, have merged their fleets to become the world's largest heavy-lift operator. It is announced in Amsterdam that the new operation would be known as Mammoet Heavy Lift Partners, and that a company called Mammoet Shipping will be formed to own the 14-vessel fleet.

23 October

New optimism over the future of the bulk cargo markets is voiced today, as improved freight rates are again recorded at the Baltic Exchange in London. Increased rates for grain cargoes between the United States, Europe and the Far East, coupled to increased Soviet time-charter activity, are held to be the major reasons behind the improvements.

The jack-up drilling rig *Interocean II* is in difficulty following the parting of a tow line from the tug *Orla* (8,000 bhp) while en-route from the North Sea to the Irish Sea. Gale conditions prevent the immediate reconnection of the tow, but the 6,600 bhp *Euroman*, assisting the *Orla*, manages to stay fast to the rig and by controlling the rig's drift, is able to drift the rig into the comparative shelter of Poole Bay on the southern coast of England.

25 October

Apparently having completely forgotten that his Government has decimated British Merchant Shipping since it has been in office, British Shipping Minister Mr David Mitchell brands 'protectionism' as the enemy of cost-effective sea transport in an address given to the Federation of National Associations of Ship Brokers and Agents. He makes no comment whatsoever about his Government's 'promise' to maintain a healthy British merchant fleet, and it is presumed that he had forgotten about it.

Meanwhile . . . A policy document issued by the Conservative Party's 'Centre for Policy Studies' published today outlines more than 30 recommendations for the future of British shipping. Unfortunately however, the document, misleadingly entitled 'British Shipping, the Right Course', is lashed severely from both the shipowners and operators' GCBS *and* the trade unions, and indeed almost anybody in the shipping industry asked to comment on it. Comments from both right and left of the GCBS and the NUS alone ranged from 'bureaucratic nightmare' through 'unhelpful', 'superficial and muddled', 'naive or wrong headed', 'untrue and unfair', to simply 'laughable'.

Environmental protection group Greenpeace states that its ex-trawler *Sirius* is attempting to block the passage of a Soviet whaling expedition bound through the Strait of Gibralter for the Atlantic. Headed by the *Sovietskaya Ukraina*, the fleet is equipped with 'cold-harpoons' which are totally illegal under the International Whaling Commission's agreement which came into effect in 1983.

29 October

Further problems continue to plague the *QE 2* this year, as following a series of faults, a fire breaks out while the vessel is 1,500 miles from Southampton on a New York–UK sailing. The fire starts in the engine room around lunchtime, and leaves the vessel without power. She is expected to arrive at Southampton on

4 November, completing her journey at 10 knots on just one turbine.

31 October
The Soviet Union has announced a ban on all fuel shipments to Britain, in a measure adopted to support the British miner's strike.

A crew member dies aboard the 35,420 dwt LPG carrier *Puerto Rican* which suffered a series of explosions shortly after leaving San Francisco. The US ship, which had been in union trouble lately, could have been sabotaged according to the FBI.

1 November
A fire starts in the engine room of 3,150 grt liner *St Helena* this morning while 275 miles south west of Sierra Leone. The vessel, en-route from Cape Town to the United Kingdom, has 35 crew and 40 passengers on board. The British flag tanker *Overseas Argonaut* (140,905 dwt) is standing by, and the West German tug *Fairplay 9* is expected to take *St Helena* in tow for Dakar by 3 November.

4 November
The stern section of the LPG carrier *Puerto Rican* sinks, after storms over the weekend caused the vessel to break up. A slick of oil one mile long and 200 yards wide has been created. The forepart of the vessel is still afloat and leaking, and the US coastguard has requisitioned tugs to dispose of the remaining parts of the vessel.

6 November
Figures released by Britain's GCBS show that total tonnage laid-up and idle at the end of September was the same as that for the end of August. A total of 65.8 million tonnes deadweight is without work. Approximately 14 per cent of the British fleet is laid-up; approximately 18 per cent of Greek, 17 per cent of Norwegian, 5 per cent of West German, 26 per cent of Danish, 20 per cent of French, 7 per cent of Panamanian and 15 per cent of Liberian fleets are laid-up. This compares with only 2 per cent of the Japanese fleet according to the GCBS.

9 November
South Korea's Trade and Industry Minister announced today that orders worth $623 million had been placed at South Korean shipyards during October. This volume of ordering represents the best monthly figure for the year and is approximately 280 per cent higher than for October 1983. Nevertheless, orders for 1984 as a whole show a decrease on those received during 1983, although prospects have improved in recent weeks.

12 November
Finland's Wärtsilä receives its biggest contract to date for icebreakers: the Soviet Union orders two nuclear-powered icebreakers, valued at around $325 million, for delivery in 1988 and 1989. The nuclear power unit will be installed in the USSR and will give the vessels a total power output of 52,000 hp.

13 November
Soviet-owned cruise operators out of the UK lost £12 million on their 1983 operations, if based on normal charter rates, claimed P&O and Cunard today.

15 November
The world's largest and most expensive purpose-built cruise ship, P&O's 44,348 grt *Royal Princess*, is christened by her Royal Highness, Princess Diana, Princess of Wales, at Southampton, England.

Irish Shipping, the state-owned Irish shipping group is put into the hands of the liquidators. This is the first time any Irish nationalised industry has been put in the hands of a receiver. Assets of Ir £23 million offset only a small proportion of the Ir £117 million liabilities. Serious legal threats exist, both criminal and civil, over whether Far Eastern shipowners were deceived into charters based on understandings where the Government would provide guarantees. It is reported that the affair may go as far as the International Courts in Europe before it is resolved. The Company was trading until FY 1982–83 when it suffered its first losses for 15 years.

16 November
The British flag 859 grt cargo vessel *Ramsland* is

Polish Ocean Lines cruise ship *Stefan Batory* (ex-*Maasdam*), a regular visitor to Tilbury, England, again experienced problems this year with passengers 'jumping ship' and defecting. (*FotoFlite, Ashford*)

23

Fred Olsen's 1966-built liner *Black Watch* (9,499 grt), became victim of bad weather off Plymouth when a wave caused damage to the vessel's forward superstructure. (*FotoFlite, Ashford*)

under arrest in the US port of Boston today, and is found to contain more than 30 *tons* of illegal drugs.

21 November

British Shipbuilders have announced plans to obtain another 2,890 job cuts. A total of 2,100 employees at Swan Hunter and 790 at Vospers are needed to accept voluntary redundancy by February 1985.

The Polish cruise/liner *Stefan Batory* sails from Rotterdam for Gdansk with only 406 of its original passenger list of more than 600 aboard. Apparently, the voyage was so good that many of the Polish passengers did not want to go home again, as 200 jumped ship at Hamburg and another 10 in Rotterdam. Most asked for political asylum. In addition, another 93 Poles jumped ship from the *Ragalin* at the West German port of Lübeck, it was announced today. On average about 10 passengers a week escape from Poland in this manner, while the *Stefan Batory* is notorious for its number of defecting passengers which, on occassions, have been in such large numbers that special refugee camps have had to be set up to accommodate them. A total of 14,900 Polish citizens have defected to West Germany since 1981.

22 November

A massive build-up of traffic is expected following the failure of a bridge on the St Lawrence Seaway. A total of 82 ocean-going vessels are now above the bridge. It is anticipated that some 200 vessels may be held up before repairs can be effected, and a decision to keep the Seaway open until 15 December has been taken in order to reduce the backlog of trade that will develop. It is not expected that the bridge will be opened again until 6 December.

24 November

The Fred Olsen liner *Black Watch* put into Plymouth, England after a wave reported to be 60 feet high smashed into the forward superstructure causing damage to the bridge and electronics equipment. The voyage is later continued after repairs had been effected.

29 November

Docks at Peru's 15 ports are closed as part of a 24-hour national strike.

30 November

British and French political leaders authorise studies for yet another attempt at a Channel Tunnel. The new plan will be privately funded in the initial stages, but certain Government incentives are expected to appear once work starts in earnest. Channel ferry operators say they will oppose the project and that it is financially unsound as its massive investment requirement will make it totally uncompetitive with existing air and sea links.

3 December

US Lines commence the first leg of its Round the World service when *American Maine*, 42,917 grt, sails from the Far East for Europe via the Panama Canal. *American Alabama* is scheduled to sail from Rotterdam on 6 December in what will be a regular 14-day RTW service.

The Gulf has errupted again after an apparent lull in the fighting when the 386,343 dwt VLCC *Minotaur* is hit by a single missile about 50 miles south of Kharg Island this morning. Selco's *Salvalour* and *Salviva* are

Selco Salvage's *Salvalour* (ex-*Ocean Jupiter*, ex-*North Sea*) was just one of the company's fleet of salvage tugs that went to the rescue of stricken vessels in the Gulf in 1984. (*Selco Salvage*)

The tug *Implacable*, under charter to the MoD, sank off the Isle of Wight while en-route for the Falkland Islands. (*FotoFlite, Ashford*)

already in attendance and attempting to extinguish fires in the engine room. The vessel is not believed to be seriously damaged.

5 December
Strike-bound Southampton docks receive another blow when P&O Ferries join a long list of companies which have left the port. They include US Lines, Dart Containerline, Med Shipping, European Ferries/ Townsend Thoresen, Scancarriers, Trio, SEACS Line, BHLR Line, and Polish Ocean Line. Felixstowe and Tilbury have gained most from these moves.

6 December
United States Lines lodge official application with the US Maritime Administration to take over Delta Lines and their operating subsidies.

Sig Bergeson quits its plans to construct two 50,000-ton cruise ships at an Italian yard.

The British Government confirms its intention not to sign the new Law of the Sea Convention.

8 December
The Kuwait cargo vessel *Tariq* is hit by a rocket fired by one of two Iranian F-4 Phantom II aircraft today about 70 miles north of Qatar. The *Tariq* is disabled in the attack, but not destroyed.

9 December
Another tanker, the 323,100 dwt VLCC *B.T. Investor*, is struck above the waterline by an Iraqi missile today. The Bahamas-registered vessel is not severely damaged and is proceeding under her own power to Bahrain for repairs.

10 December
The St Lawrence Seaway is opened for traffic again after nearly three weeks of closure due to a jammed bridge west of Montreal. At least four icebreakers are to be employed to keep the Seaway open for as long as is practicable in order to clear the backlog. More than 160 ships are waiting to pass the broken bridge.

14 December
The first Soviet-bound grain cargo to pass through Rotterdam in more than two years is trans-shipped from the Turkish bulk carrier *Anadolu Koparam* onto Soviet vessels. Although no publically announced boycott exists, it was only after the Dutch authorities' refusal of a Soviet Rotterdam Consulate that Soviet grain cargoes stopped arriving at the port in 1982.

15 December
The Greek 111,688 dwt tanker *Ninemia* is hit by an Iraqi missile in the latest break-out of Gulf warfare which has claimed three targets now in less than three weeks. Two of the *Ninemia*'s crew are killed in the latest attack, which took place around 100 miles from Kharg Island. The crew are picked up by another tanker, the *Calliope* (11,868 dwt), and by Iranian naval vessels in poor weather conditions. Salvage vessels are attempting to extinguish severe fires aboard *Ninemia*.

17 December
The British Government tonight announces that it will after all sign the UNCTAD 40:40:20 liner shipping code.

The Greek general cargo vessel *Aegis Cosmic* (12,498 grt) is attacked and damaged by Iraqi aircraft south of Kharg Island.

British MP and Chairman of a special parliamentary Maritime Affairs Group, delivers a scathing attack on successive British Governments regarding their total abandonment of the British Merchant Navy. He emphasises the point that the British fleet is declining by one ship every three and a half days, and at this rate the fleet would soon disappear altogether.

The UK's Department of Trade announces another loss to the British merchant fleet today. This one concerns the UK's international trade by sea figures, which show that British ships carry only 35 per cent by value and 24 per cent by weight of UK-generated international trade – a loss of 4 per cent compared to the previous years figures.

18 December
The final major hurdle in the re-activation of the SS *United States* as a cruise ship is overcome when the West German Economics Ministry announces that the FRG Government will provide export credit guarantees worth DM 364 million for H.D.W. to carry out the refit due to start in mid-1985.

21 December
The Gulf War claims yet another two casualities in the

The 1964-built Cypriot-registered general cargo vessel *Blue Spirit* (2,775 grt/4,130 dwt) caught fire in the North Sea with the loss of one member of the crew. (*FotoFlite, Ashford*)

shape of the 52,661 ton Liberian-registered *Magnolia* attacked 30 miles south of Kharg Island, and the Norwegian VLCC *Thorshavet*, outward bound from Kharg with a cargo of 230,000 tonnes of crude oil. Both vessels are hit by Iraqi missiles, set on fire, and abandoned by their crews. Two of the *Magnolia*'s crew are killed in the attack.

24 December
The tug *Implacable* sinks off the Isle of Wight following a capsize while en-route to the Falklands Islands to undertake an MoD 12-month charter. Ten of the crew are rescued by helicopter, but one seaman is still missing.

25 December
The Indian VLCC *Kanchanjunga* (276,744 dwt), with a full load of oil lifted from Ras Tanura, is hit in the latest attack in the Gulf. It is believed that Iranian

aircraft were responsible.

Yet another 112 Poles failed to return home from the West Germany port of Travemünde when the 7,800-ton ferry *Pomerania* sailed for Poland. More than 1,000 *one-way* journeys from Poland have now been made this year alone to this area of West Germany.

26 December
The Cypriot-registered general cargo vessel *Blue Spirit* catches fire in the North Sea off the German island of Borkum. Sixteen of the Spanish crew are rescued, but one is still missing.

The 122,582 grt/238,959 dwt Spanish flag VLCC *Aragon* is attacked with rockets fired from Iranian aircraft west of Qatar. The VLCC is set on fire but does not suffer serious damage and is likely to continue her voyage to Ras Tanura to lift a cargo of Saudi crude oil.

27 December
The Italian cruise ship *Eugenio C*, one of the large Costa fleet, collides with a Brazilian warship off Rio de Janeiro. None of the 800 passengers are injured and damage is minimal.

Shipbuilding – After the Recession

The State of British Shipbuilders and its Merchant Shipbuilding Prospects in a Static World Market

by J Graham Day

Graham Day, a Canadian lawyer, has been Chairman and Chief Executive of British Shipbuilders since September 1983. Following private law practice he was with Canadian Pacific Limited, later was Chief Executive of Cammell Laird Shipbuilders in England. Latterly he has been a Professor in the Graduate Business School and Director of the Canadian Marine Transportation Centre, both at Dalhousie University, Halifax, N.S., Canada. He retains a directorship with Misener Holdings Limited of Toronto whose interests include a Canadian flag bulk shipping fleet.

Industrial composition

British Shipbuilders, a state corporation, is by far the largest of the three elements of UK shipbuilding, the others being Harland & Wolff of Northern Ireland, also state owned, and 13 small, privately owned shipbuilders. British Shipbuilders' initial undertakings in 1977 included merchant shipbuilding, warship building, ship repair, both marine and general engineering and some unrelated businesses. Subsequent to nationalisation, the Corporation entered the large offshore structures market; this extremely costly experiment has been concluded recently.

Creation of ship designs with advanced computer colour graphics. Engineroom section of oceanographic research/survey vessel *Charles Darwin*, named by HRH Prince Charles at Appledore. (*British Shipbuilders*)

Application of robotics to shipbuilding processes is being actively developed – initially to grind bearing shells and similar components, and for small-batch manufacture of minor steelwork and outfit items. (*Swan Hunters*)

Experience in building high-speed naval craft made Vosper Thornycroft (UK) an obvious choice for construction of two 27.5-knot, 700-passenger ferries for Hong Kong. (*Vosper Thornycroft*)

In order to reduce losses, maximise the use of scarce resources and concentrate corporate effort, over the last 12 months British Shipbuilders has been withdrawing from, or disposing of, all businesses other than those of shipbuilding and marine engineering. In addition, in pursuance of declared government policy, the Corporation's subsidiaries engaged in warship building will be sold to the private sector by March 1986. British Shipbuilders then will comprise a mainstream merchant shipbuilding and marine engine building business.

Financial and employment facts

British Shipbuilders 1983/84 turnover was just under £900 million. While overall trading losses were sharply up again in 1983/84 at £161 million (1982/83 £117.5 million) due mainly to offshore structures contracts and a special depreciation charge, the underlying rate of loss on merchant shipbuilding in 1983/84 declined to £49 million, being considerably lower than the 1982/83 result of £85 million. The actions taken and in hand are expected to produce significantly better results for 1984/85.

As a consequence of merchant shipbuilding market conditions and business disposals, British Shipbuilders' employment declined by 22 per cent over the year ending 31 March 1984 to 48,550 of which under 15,000 were engaged in merchant shipbuilding and marine engine building.

Spearheading offshore oil ship technology, the two multi-role support vessels being built for a subsidiary of the Swedish Stena Group by Sunderland Shipbuilders are designed to meet future needs only now being identified. (*British Shipbuilders*)

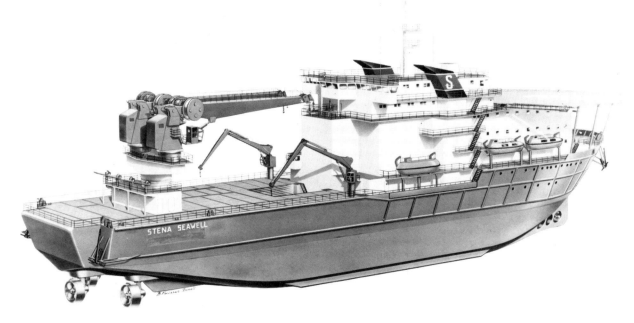

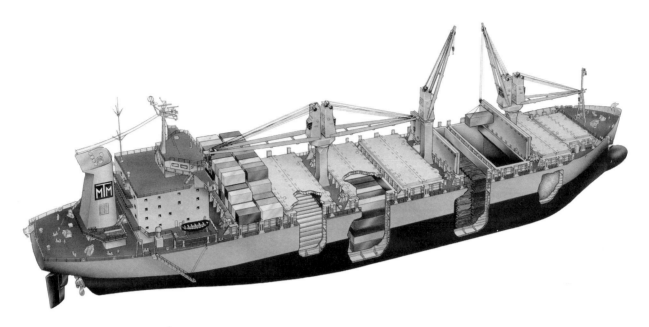

The 45,000-ton dwt Sunderland Container-Bulker, two of which have already been built, is the type of versatile ship owners will need to meet the stringent market conditions of the 'eighties and the 'nineties. (*British Shipbuilders*)

Order books and strategic shifts

British Shipbuilders' declining merchant ship order book 1977–1983 reflects both the lack of growth in the market and what is seen as a permanent structural market shift away from traditional European ship-building nations (Table 1).

Since 1977, the year British Shipbuilders was formed, annual world new merchant shipbuilding orders have failed to reach 15 million cgrt and future prospects are no better (Table 2).

This static, depressed market is dominated by Far East builders in Japan and Korea, the former in market share terms, the latter through pricing. With the major exception of Korea, the great majority of shipbuilding nations, including Japan, continue to shrink shipbuilding capacity in an effort to match likely new order intake.

Over recent months the composition of British Shipbuilders' merchant order book is reflecting these changes. For example, a largely stabilised order book now includes an increasing number of offshore vessels, including diving support, for both domestic and overseas owners.

Karisma, a 6,750 dwt roll-on/roll-off ship, was constructed to a new design developed by Smith's Dock Ltd for Brazilian owners, Kommar Companhia Maritima S.A. of Rio de Janeiro. (*British Shipbuilders*)

Selkirk Settler, one of three sophisticated 35,000 dwt bulk carriers built by Govan Shipbuilders Ltd, and operated by Misener Transportation of St Catherines, Ontario. The ships are designed for service on the Great Lakes, and internationally. Their specialised design and advanced features, including the ballasting system, permits them to lift greater tonnages than many other ships in the Lakes trades. (*British Shipbuilders*)

TABLE 1
BRITISH SHIPBUILDERS
MERCHANT SHIPBUILDING ORDER BOOK

Date	No. of vessels	Gross tonnes	Compensated gross tonnes
12/77	117	1,442,883	1,137,301
12/78	98	913,389	825,189
12/79	71	655,754	589,791
12/80	43	614,993	443,306
12/81	62	868,161	589,650
12/82	54	696,129	455,730
12/83	32	375,530	347,384

Source: British Shipbuilders

TABLE 2
WORLD MERCHANT SHIPBUILDING

Year	New orders (000 compensated gross registered tonnes)
1977	14,040
1978	10,796
1979	14,207
1980	14,357
1981	14,053
1982	11,533
1983	14,850

Source: Lloyd's Register of Shipping

Technology

The 'new' British Shipbuilders is deploying increasingly the most modern technology which can be made applicable to shipbuilding. Significant capital sums have been spent to accelerate the application of computer based technology across the Corporation. With the British Ship Research Association and in co-operation with both IBM and Computervision of the USA, British Shipbuilders considers it is at the forefront of Computer Aided Design (CAD) and Computer Aided Management (CAM) applications in shipbuilding.

Additionally, experimental work with robotics is indicating ways in which automation, particularly in steel work, can be advanced.

Education for change

Capital expenditures will have little economic relevance unless linked to appropriate managerial, supervisory and manual worker planning, methods and practices. An intensive programme of education and retraining is being undertaken to ensure that the benefits of technology and tradition go hand in hand.

Not surprisingly British Shipbuilders' overall best merchant ship customer are British flag owners. In 1983 British owners placed orders for 25 ships, 11 of which went to foreign shipbuilders. The 14 ordered from UK shipbuilders was ten fewer than in 1982. Of these 14, four were placed with British Shipbuilders.

These figures reflect not only the problems of UK shipbuilding in general and British Shipbuilders in particular but also the decline in the UK flag fleet.

Hupeh, a 44,600 dwt bulk carrier, built by Sunderland Shipbuilders Ltd for Taikoo Navigation Company of Hong Kong – part of the Swire Group. The vessel is of British Shipbuilders' B45 optimised economy design. (*British Shipbuilders*)

Jacqueline, 7,250 dwt roll-on/roll-off ship constructed for Hipermodal Transportes e Navegacao of Rio de Janeiro by Smith's Dock Ltd at Middlesborough. Launched in 1983, *Jacqueline* was the first Brazilian merchant vessel to be constructed in a UK yard for 11 years. (*British Shipbuilders*)

Fortunately at mid-year 1984 British Shipbuilders' order intake of British flag vessels was already more than double that of 1983. This change runs counter to the continuing decline of the British flag fleet and is considered to reflect the impact of positive change in consequence of British Shipbuilders' new strategies.

The new merchant ship and engine building concentration for British Shipbuilders is being accompanied by a progressive shift in product strategy. British Shipbuilders' world market share of 1.25 per cent dictates the requirement for concentration in discreet market sectors where direct competition with world price and volume leaders is reduced. For British Shipbuilders this means, essentially, a focus on certain domestic market sectors and upon those international prospects where price alone is not the determining sales factor and where particular trading relationships and product suitability may be associated.

As an early world leader in steel shipbuilding technology, the UK has suffered in latter years from a wide range of restrictive working practices on the part of many shipbuilding employees. Early in 1984 radical changes were agreed with the trades unions representing the majority of British Shipbuilders' employees. The retraining associated with these changes and the implementation of the changes themselves are currently under way.

Procurement

An important advantage enjoyed by some shipbuilding competitor nations is the cost reduction gained through purchasing effectiveness supported by significant volume. Among British Shipbuilders' new areas of operational emphasis is procurement.

Nationalisation of the shipbuilding industry in the UK initially combined in a corporate shell a number of fully serviced companies. Until recently these have been largely autonomous in procurement terms. Now, through co-ordination, British Shipbuilders' merchant shipbuilding group is moving to secure maximum advantage by a policy of total procurement. Techniques being deployed include the development of a common purchasing data base with attendant vendor assessments and moves towards supply and component standardisation. In the latter case these efforts are linked to the continuing development of CAD CAM technology.

Governments and shipbuilding capacity

While contraction in shipbuilding capacity continues in some countries, in recognition of the continuing market reality of slack demand, others see shipbuilding as a component central to the development of a national industrial base, as a significant employer of labour or as an essential earner of foreign currency. Nations in the latter category, regardless of market conditions, preserve or even encourage expansion of capacity and thus, to a marked extent, operate to offset the effects of capacity contraction elsewhere and hence exacerbate the costs of support for shipbuilding to all national

Mwokozi, one of four harbour tugs built by Ferguson-Ailsa Ltd for the Kenya Ports Authority. The tugs are for service at Mombasa. (*British Shipbuilders*)

governments, depress new vessel prices below full production cost recovery and, in turn, create problems for shipowners and their banks in terms of asset values.

It is only realistic to state that nowhere in the world is merchant shipbuilding capacity being sustained, or will be sustained, other than with some measure of governmental support. That support can range from the reservation of domestic markets, through price and sales finance subsidies to loss funding without limit. In the event, there are clear indications now that governments of many nations with shipbuilding industries are no longer content to provide continuing support at levels variously prevailing since the mid-1970s.

Market mini-view

Shipbuilding is merely the hardware supplier to the shipping industry. The fortunes of the former mirror the fortunes of the latter, usually with a period of delay. As noted, capacity problems continue to beset shipbuilding and these are being alleviated only in part as a result of restructuring and are then restricted to certain nations and regions.

The other side of the equation is demand – the shipping business, where there are some encouraging signs. Moderate trade growth is seen as contributing to a reduction in the volume of surplus tonnage as is continuing high scrapping rates, particularly of tankers. Certain market sectors, for example liner conferences, have been able to secure and maintain successive rate increases on certain routes. Analyses of both laid-up tonnage, the age profiles of certain sectors, eg. products carriers and a view of environmental factors, indicate

15,260 dwt SD14 cargo ship *Sunderland Venture* built by Austin & Pickersgill for the Shipley Shipping Corporation, part of the Wah Kwong Group of Hong Kong. The *Sunderland Venture* was the first new building ordered in Britain by these owners. (*British Shipbuilders*)

The *Isle of Arran* car ferry was constructed by Ferguson-Ailsa Ltd for Caledonian MacBrayne, and now operates on the Ardrossan-Brodrick route in Scotland. (*British Shipbuilders*)

that future trading potential of an important volume of shipping is limited.

Nevertheless, for the foreseeable future it is unlikely that the international merchant shipbuilding market will improve significantly in either volume or price terms. Contraction in capacity will continue, particularly in traditional shipbuilding countries as efforts continue to bring supply more in line with demand.

In conclusion

British Shipbuilders intend to continue in international merchant shipbuilding, probably preserving the market share which its restructuring, new strategies and current sales success are producing – about 1.25 per cent. While new order volume is important, particularly to absorb the overhead costs of doing business on a pre-determined scale, British Shipbuilders' corporate intentions are focussed on a return to profitability, not on sales volume *per se*. Only improving financial results coupled with quality and assured deliveries will engender the necessary confidence and hence support from government and customer alike.

The US and Caribbean Cruise Scene

by Russell Plummer and A J Ambrose

North America continues to be a magnet for cruise ship operators with extra capacity being provided all the time – much of it from completely new tonnage.

Not far short of 200 vessels are currently employed worldwide wholly or partly for cruising by more than 70 different companies, with the major market place centred on the US West Coast and Caribbean areas. Little consolation can be derived from figures which show only the shorter one to five day circuits attracting more customers, the demand for cruises of a week or more increasing only slightly.

There are obviously individual success stories in all sectors of this growth business yet, overall, the problem of excess capacity exists, and this situation is unlikely to change while older vessels continue in service despite the arrival of considerable newbuildings. Sale of earlier ships is often an essential ingredient towards the financing of the replacement tonnage but almost invariably the veterans are bought for further trading, and are often kept on almost identical routes.

This happened when Holland America Cruises off-loaded a trio of vessels in advance of delivery of their new sisters *Nieuw Amsterdam* and *Noordam*. Two of them, *Statendam* and *Veendam*, are still to be found on their old runs, *Statendam* on a Caribbean/Alaska mix in Paquet colours as *Rhapsody*, and *Veendam*, bought with sister *Volendam* by the CY Tung Group, now running on charter to Bahama Cruise Line between New York and Bermuda as *Bermuda Star*.

Of course, many of the long established ships have their own staunchly loyal bands of devotees who place individualism and character high on their list of priorities when selecting cruises and seem immune to the delights of modern uniformity in design and features such as all lower bed configurations. To them, the availability of genuine single-berth cabins, or traditional covered promenades – features conspicuously absent among recently delivered tonnage, or some ships extensively reconstructed – are of paramount importance.

It might not, therefore, be totally out of nostalgia that major companies such as Carnival or Sitmar continue to employ former liners of 1950s or early '60s vintage in spite of their enormous, and in Carnival's case, continuing investment in fresh tonnage. Carnival have not been alone in using their latest vessel, the 1,420-berth Danish-built *Tropicale*, on the West Coast of the United States while keeping the familiar trio *Carnivale*, and *Mardi Gras* – both originally Canadian Pacific units on the North Atlantic run – and *Festivale* – first *Transvaal Castle* and later *S.A.Vaal* on the UK/ South Africa service – on their established cruising routes in the Caribbean.

The two latest additions to Holland America Line's fleet. The *Nieuw Amsterdam* (*below*) was completed in 1983, and her sister *Noordam* (*left*) followed in 1984. Both vessels were built by Chantiers de l'Atlantique; They are seen here in Vancouver, Canada. (*David O Thorne*)

Statendam was sold by Holland America Line to Paquet Cruises prior to the delivery of *Nieuw Amsterdam* and *Noordam*. She has been renamed *Rhapsody* and trades from the US west coast. (*FotoFlite, Ashford*)

The Wärtsilä-built sisters *Sea Goddess I* and *Sea Goddess II* represent a new breed of cruise ship. Designed to cater to the very top levels of the market, they will no doubt draw their clientelle from the USA to a great degree. (*K Brzoza*)

Miami remains the cruise capital of the world and, with other developing Florida centres, offers an almost bewildering choice of cruise destinations and durations. With the influx of so much new tonnage filling unsold berths remains a problem and the trend towards companies offering 'stand-by' rates has accelerated to the extent that there are now, in the United States, the cruising equivalent of 'bucket shops' specialising in cut-rate cruise packages. Taken to its extreme, the situation in Miami is such that prior to Saturday departures, prospective passengers turn up complete with luggage and credit cards to negotiate for unsold berths literally at the gangway just before sailing time.

The 1984-built *Fairsky*, completed by French builders for Sitmar Cruises. She is seen here while on a cruise from San Francisco to Alaska. (*David O Thorne*)

The cruise scene is famous for some of its ex-liner vessels which are still trading well, even with the massive influx of newer tonnage. Sitmar's 21,619-grt 20-knot *Fairstar* is just one example. She is shown here in her former guise as Bibby's *Oxfordshire*. Built in the UK in 1957, she is trading under the Liberian flag and now serves the Australian market with cruises to the Pacific Far East. (*World Ship Society Photo Library*)

Carnival's expansion is by no means finished and a further three vessels are currently under construction at a cost of in the region of $500 million. The operator has returned to Denmark's Aalborg Vaerft for an enlarged version of *Tropicale* which is due to enter service in mid-1985 as *Holiday*, and this will be followed in 1986 by *Jubilee* and *Celebration*, a pair of vessels ordered from the Swedish Kockums yard at Malmo. The new trio are each designed to cruise world-wide but incorporate special features for the American market in the Caribbean and on the West Coast. Whether the conclusion of the building programme will spell the end for the existing steam powered ships remains to be seen, even though Carnival say they are additions rather than replacements.

Sitmar's *Fairsea*, built in 1956, formerly the *Fairland* (1971) and before that one of the Cunard fleet as the *Carinthia*. She left Cunard colours in 1968, and now serves the US market. (*World Ship Society Photo Library*)

Yet another old favourite still working in the Caribbean is Carnival's *Festivale* of 26,632 grt, shown here in her former guise(s) as the UK–South Africa liner *S.A. Vaal* and *Transvaal Castle*. She was extensively modernised in 1978 in Japan, when converted for her present role under the Panamanian flag. (*World Ship Society Photo Library*)

Sister to the *Fairsea/Carinthia*, is the 16,667-grt ex-Cunarder *Sylvania*, now trading as Sitmar's *Fairwind*. (*World Ship Society Photo Library*)

On the West Coast, the number of cruises available to Alaska in the summer and Mexico in the winter months rose to record levels during 1984 and the procession of new ships continued. Holland America Cruises have moved their whole operation to a new base in Seattle and took steps to ensure that their latest newcomer *Noordam* did not suffer the problems experienced when *Nieuw Amsterdam* made a delayed debut a year earlier. In a bid to eliminate the low-speed vibration in the earlier ship, the *Noordam* has been fitted with additional dampeners and counter-weights on the engine crankshafts and the kitchens have also been redesigned to improve meal service. Similar modifications will be undertaken on *Nieuw Amsterdam*.

Like the Holland America ships, Sitmar Cruises' *Fairsky*, delivered in April 1984, was built in France. After spending the summer on 14-day circuits from San Francisco to Alaska, *Fairsky* switched to seven and ten-day winter trips between Los Angeles and Mexico. Certainly the most interesting feature of the

vessel is its steam turbine propulsion with General Electric machinery taking steam from three Foster Wheeler boilers of which only two are needed in use for normal cruising speed.

Sitmar thus keep a steam powered fleet and have expressed confidence that *Fairsky* will prove more economical in operation than an equivalent diesel powered vessel. They also have the advantage of being able to draw on a substantial pool of steam experience from the engineering departments of their three existing ships, the US-based Clyde-built ex-Cunarder's *Fairsea* (ex-*Carinthia*) and *Fairwind* (ex-*Sylvania*) dating from 1956 and 1957, and the former Bibby liner *Oxfordshire* which now serves the Australian market on cruises to the Pacific Islands.

By no means all the expenditure in the cruise business has been reserved for new tonnage. Cunard has spent lavishly on the Norwegian American Cruises vessels *Vistafjord* and *Sagafjord* acquired in 1983, officially pronouncing them to be an excellent buy. *Queen Elizabeth 2* was not neglected either.

Cunard have invested $15 million on *Sagafjord* and *Vistafjord* with improvements including enlarged dining rooms and the construction of 25 luxury staterooms on each ship. *Sagafjord* has been kept in the American trade and was re-fitted at San Francisco while

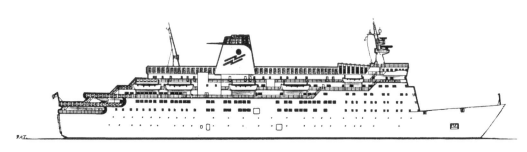

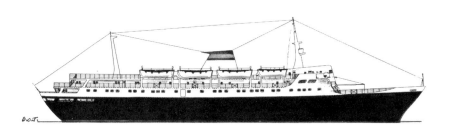

The variety of cruise ship tonnage afloat today caters to all tastes. From the 1961-built *Mardi Gras* (ex-*Empress of Canada*), a former dual role cruise liner of Canadian Pacific's (top); the former Baltic ferry *Sundancer* (centre), and the 3,963 grt *Stella Oceanis* (bottom), to the ships purpose-built for cruising such as the 1959-built dual purpose cruise/liner *Rotterdam* (facing page, from top), NCL's *Starward/Skyward* and RCCL's *Song of Norway*, examples of the 1970s-built generation, to the latest 1980s-built group exemplified by RCCL's *Song of America*. (*Drawings: David Thorne*)

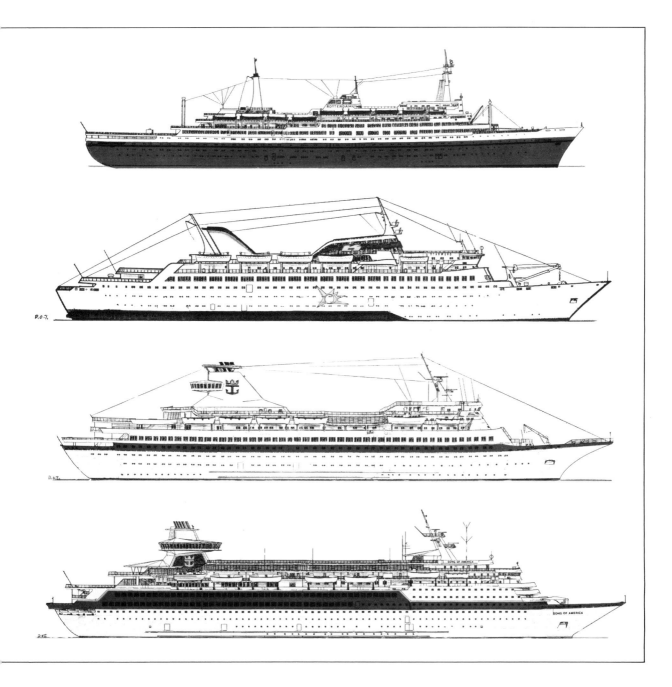

Vistafjord's work was carried out by Malta Drydocks. Some care has been taken to retain the Scandinavian flavour of the two ships and Cunard were encouraged by the level of bookings during 1984, a year in which the *Queen Elizabeth 2* also had increased loadings for both cruises and the summer season on the North Atlantic.

The *QE 2*'s one-time rival for Europe–United States traffic, *France*, now Norwegian Caribbean Line's

---

Vistafjord, now in Cunard colours, but retaining the Norwegian American Line charisma. *Vistafjord* and *Sagafjord* are still rated as the world's top cruise ships. (*FotoFlite, Ashford*)

Norway, also returned to the North Atlantic during the summer of 1984 with line voyage crossings before and after a cruise stint in Europe and Scandinavia that was really built around the 70,202 grt vessel's visit to Bremerhaven for a first major refit since conversion for cruising. *Norway* was not full on the positioning crossings and, significantly, there is to be no repeat visit to Europe in 1985, although another is expected when *Norway* receives her next refit in two year's time.

While *Norway* was in Europe, NCL completed the purchase of Royal Viking Line worth $240 million and now operates a total of eight ships with an aggregate capacity of some 7,200 berths. NCL acted quickly after it seemed probable that Royal Viking would go

The ss *Norway* again visited Europe in 1984. This time she operated a series of small North European cruises and liner sailings on her trips to and from her normal cruise grounds when positioning across the Atlantic. (*FotoFlite, Ashford*)

Royal Viking Star, one of the three Royal Viking Line ships taken under the NCL/Klosters fold this year. These three vessels trade to a higher pitched market than do the NCL vessels. (*David O Thorne*)

for three major vessels – two of them on the same day, 11 July. Royal Cruise Line's *Royal Odyssey* was in collision with the Soviet freighter *Vasya Alekseev* in the Oresund while *Funchal* ran into the small Norwegian cargo ship *Storhaug* outside Molde. Then, on 29 July, Costa's *Columbus C* struck the pier at Cadiz and sunk, and has since been declared a constructive total loss.

These incidents followed a more dramatic June grounding when what was described as an 'error of judgement' by a Canadian pilot resulted in the *Sundancer*, northbound on only the third in a summer series of cruises to Alaska, hitting a reef. Although the ship was turned round and made port at Duncan Bay where all passengers were landed safely, the vessel, originally *Svea Corona* from the Silja Line service in the Baltic, was declared a constructive total loss. Sundancer Cruises planned to follow summer trips to Alaska with a winter series to Mexico and was a joint venture between Silja Line partners Johnson Line, EFFOA and Princess Cruises founder Stanley McDonald. Since the loss of *Sundancer*, Sundace Cruises have acquired the ex-DFDS/Scandinavian World Cruises 27,000-ton *Scandinavia* from her Copenhagen–Oslo ferry service, and renamed her *Stardancer* for her second try at the US cruise trade. *Sundancer* meanwhile has been sold to Greek owners who intend to rebuild her for duties in the Mediterranean.

Possibly one of the most interesting developments in the US cruise trade (excepting the arrival of *Royal Princess*), is the news that the *United States* will, after all, be re-entering service as a cruise ship. This is

Sundancer (ex-*Svea Corona*) seen here in early 1984 as she headed for her new career following her conversion from a ferry. Chinese owners have also been buying up surplus ferries in recent months, with the intention of starting their own small cruise fleet to offer voyages in the Far East. (*FotoFlite, Ashford*)

into American hands, an agreement in principle having been announced with J H Whitney and Co. However, the NCL deal removed fears about the Royal Viking Line vessels *Royal Viking Star*, *Royal Viking Sea* and *Royal Viking Sky* staying under Norwegian ownership. They have continued with itineraries and marketing under the Royal Viking banner and NCL have no plans to amalgamate the two fleets.

Royal Viking Sky was one of the year's cruising casualties, grounding during a December 1983 call at St Thomas in the Virgin Islands. Although the vessel's Caribbean programme was completed, insurers insisted on dry docking and two Round Britain cruises were cancelled while *Royal Viking Sky* went to Bremerhaven in May.

July was a bad month for cruise ships with bumps

Sundancer in August 1984 after she ran aground off the US east coast. She has been sold for operations in the Mediterranean. Sundace have replaced her with the 26,747-grt *Scandinavia* purchased from DFDS in November 1984 and to be renamed *Stardancer*. (*Jim Galbraith*)

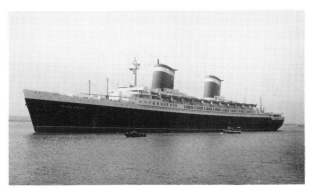

The *United States* is still surrounded with problems relating to the use of asbestos in her original construction. Shipyard unions maintain, with more than a little concern, that the conversion of this ship could prove hazardous to the health. Ironic really, the asbestos was included in the design for 'safety' reasons. (*World Ship Society Photo Library*)

interesting from a number of view points, as the 38,216 grt vessel does not, at the present moment, appear to be a particularly good investment! The market, suffering already from the strains of developing overcapacity, is such that one would consider that a conversion of a ship, laid-up for some years, would not now be as cost-effective as it was three or four years ago before the present new-builds appeared. Yet, the *United States* owners, US Cruise Lines, are going to spend possibly as much as DM 700 million (£106 m) on modernising the ship, which is significantly smaller than the brand new *Royal Princess* – which cost *less* to build and will also probably cost *less* to run!

The *United States* is due to cross the Atlantic to Howaldtswerke-Deutsche Werft's Hamburg shipyard in 1985, take 18 months to complete, and thus appear in trade sometime around mid-1987. Experimentation is presently taking place on new types of waste slurry

which may be used to power the vessel, and coupled to the reduction of machinery usage proposed, this could reduce the ship's fuel bills by a really massive amount. It is proposed that two of her four 60,000-hp turbines are de-activated entirely, and that the output of the remaining two is reduced to 10,000 hp each. This would reduce the vessel's total power output from 240,000 hp to just over 20,000 hp, and result in a reduction of the ship's top speed from 39 knots to 19 knots. A new-build would of course take longer to complete, but, even then, would it not have been cheaper? Time alone will tell. As the world's cruise operators continue their optimistic speculation, one wonders also whether the growth in this market will proceed as generally expected. Maybe the *United States* will trade on her name; maybe she will survive on a military subsidy provided for her alternative use as a troopship/hospital ship for the US Rapid Deployment Force. Either way, there will still be many who welcome her return, as she did indeed possess attractive lines. One hopes this will be so, however, when she emerges from HDW's yards in 1987.

In view of the fact that the USA provides the biggest market for cruising, it is, at first glance, surprising that US-flag ships do not figure strongly in the tonnage that actually serves this trade. With the exception of the *Constitution* and *Independence* (20,269 and 22,200 grt respectively) which trade to Hawaii, and a few very small coastal yacht-style cruise ships, the US cruise market is served entirely by foreign-flag vessels, principally from Norway and the United Kingdom.

Steps have been taken in 1984 to alter this situation however. Initially, an attempt was made to transfer two of Cunard's medium-size cruise ships under the US flag. These were the *Cunard Countess* and *Cunard Princess* (17,495 grt) but, due to the problems created by the 'Protectionism' of the US coastal trades, this move was eventually blocked at high political level. Nevertheless, other moves to provide an intrinsic US cruise fleet existed. Firstly, there is the Contessa project, in which US owners are to have built, in US yards, two 'handy sized' cruise vessels. Tenders for these vessels were invited in late 1983, and both are now under construction at the yards of the Marine Power and Equipment Company of Seattle. Of diesel-electric propulsion they are of 165.5 metres length, 24.38 metres beam and 5.5 metres draught, and are both due for delivery in 1986. Meanwhile, another new US cruise line was formed in late 1984 under the name of Gulf Pacific Cruise Line, which is based in Houston and intends to build an 800-berth vessel to be named *Galveston*. A provisional order estimated to be valued at around £100 million ($130 million) was placed with the Tacoma Boatbuilding Company in late October 1984, and Gulf Pacific have announced an intent to follow this with a second sister in the not too distant future. Being financed under the US-protectionism subsidy system (FMA Title XI Guarantees), the *Galveston* is scheduled for delivery in 1987.

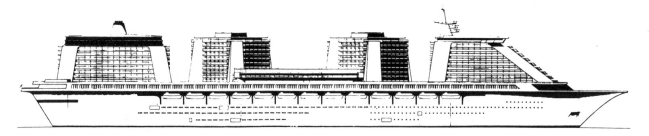

Tage Wandberg's design for a 210,000 grt cruise ship commissioned by Klosters Rederi. (Drawing: *The Motor Ship*)

Another new US project which will likely have significant effect on the US cruise trade is an ambitious plan by two US companies including World Ventures of New Jersey and another, as yet unrevealed partner. This project involves the construction of a series of various sized cruise vessels in Spanish yards for trading in the Mediterranean, probably out of Malaga. Although these vessels are, presently, not directed to the US and Caribbean scene, it is however intended that they will draw 60 per cent of their clientelle from the US market. Initially, the World Ventures operation ordered two 6,500 grt vessels, providing 400 berths each, and due for delivery in 1985 and 1986. They were ordered in early 1984 in a complicated deal in which Spain's Banco Central provided 90 per cent finance on the US $830 million required for the total building project which includes a total of nine vessels. The first two ships are due to be followed by three 900-berth cruise ships for completion between 1986 and 1988; three 24,000 ton vessels for completion between 1989 and 1991, and one larger vessel of between 30,000 and 40,000 tons for delivery by 1992. Union Naval de Levante will complete the first two of these ships, and probably most of the other seven too.

While not presently destined to trade directly in the US region, these vessels will certainly provide additional competition to the existing industry, which is already suffering from a few growing pains from various sources. In addition to the looming overcapacity expectations, the US National Maritime Union is working to increase the costs of established cruise operators trading out of the US ports such as Miami, with plans to create work for US seamen aboard foreign flag vessels. These plans, which will be introduced in the early 1985 sitting of Congress, will extend existing laws governing US flag vessels to most foreign ships trading primarily for US clientelle. Minimum wages, safety regulations and other legislations are intended to remove the advantages gained by operators who do not employ high-cost US crews, thereby opening the door to any US company to trade on an equal level with the others. Or, seen from the other point of view: *reducing* the efficiency and cost-effectiveness of foreign operators!

Nevertheless, 'foreign' operators such as Norwegian Caribbean Line (NCL) still feel able to compete with this kind of future, and even with the overcapacity expectations of coming years, Klosters Rederi, owners of amalgamated NCL and Royal Viking Line, have now commissioned Danish engineer Tage Wandberg to design the largest cruise ship (and largest passenger ship of all time) in the shape of their new 210,000-grt 'floating blocks of flats' type of ship. Hopefully Mr Wandborg will be able to remove the existing lines of the vessel and replace them with something cosmetically more appealing. There can be no doubt that the present artist's impressions and test model of this vessel can be best described as four blocks of flats on a barge!

Apart from the interesting 'wind trap' features of the vessel which should make life on deck fairly exciting, many sensible features are planned to be included in the design. The ship (if that is an appropriate title) is intended for the US and Caribbean trade, operating seven-day cruises such as those worked by the *Norway*. Obviously, as indeed is the case with the *Norway*, the 210,000-ton vessel would not be able to enter the cruise ports. As such, a complete wet-dock is to be included in the stern of the ship, from which launches will serve the ports while the 5,000 passenger ship anchors-off. The expected cost of the vessel is anticipated to be around $350–$400 million, and an order could well be placed in the very near future, with delivery around 1988–1990. Hopefully (and that does appear to be the operative word), the growth factors of the last two to three years will continue for the cruise trade, other operators will not have the same idea as Klosters, the world economy will improve, giving the cruise market clientelle the additional leisure spending power that is required to maintain this expanding fleet, and we shall not see the cruise ship follow in the wake of its illustrious forbears of the passenger liner field. Hopefully too, the optimistic and ambitious resilience of the cruise industry will prove to pay dividends. At present, in some areas it seems that it may. But *hope* alone is not a very tangeable substance.

Birth of a Princess

by A J Ambrose

On Monday 19 November 1984, a ship sailed from the English south-coast port of Southampton, at the start of her maiden voyage to Florida and thence to Los Angeles, her new home in the United States of America. This ship, conceived when the shipping world was facing its worst recession since the dark days of the 1920s and 30s, was heralded as something of a milestone in nautical history. This mammoth of the merchant fleet, having been named a few days earlier by Her Royal Highness The Princess of Wales, was the world's largest, most expensive, and most technologically advanced purpose-built cruise ship to enter service to date. This ship, the latest P&O leviathan, is *Royal Princess*.

The conception
Twenty years ago, it was inconceivable that the large passenger ship was a ship of the future; its heyday had been, and was now gone. The age of the mighty ocean passenger liners had passed. The emergence of the fast and comfortable jet airliner had all but killed long-distance ocean travel, and those ships which had not either been laid-up indefinitely or sent to an ignominious end at yards of the Far Eastern ship-breakers, were forced into the relatively new field of cruising. Cruising, however, was if viewed realistically, only considered by many owners at that time as a means of earning a last few dollars from their prematurely retired liners. It was small-bore business, simply a market place for the excess of unemployed and under-employed passenger ships still extant. The prospect, at that stage, of again building large passenger vessels

Royal Princess, **passing down the English Channel for the first time on Sunday, 4 November 1984. (***FotoFlite, Ashford***)**

The float-out of *Royal Princess* into the ice-covered waters of Helsinki harbour on 17 February 1984. *Royal Princess* was constructed in Wärtsilä's enclosed building dock, not on a slipway, thus technology is even dispensing with the traditional old term 'launched'. (*P&O Cruises*)

Royal Princess leaving Helsinki for trials on 15 June 1984. (*K Brzoza*)

such as the once-great North Atlantic leviathans, was now non-existant. No large new cruise ships were planned, and only a few smaller replacement vessels of below 20,000 grt were envisaged to emerge in the future, to take over the cruise trades from the many ex-liner cruise vessels that were to become due for their last voyage to the breakers' yards as their continued operation became totally uneconomic.

However, some companies were simply not content to phase out their liners yet. They had made massive investments in these ships, and felt that by marketing the cruise trade with aggressive advertising they could capture the upper levels of the newly emerging foreign holiday market. Initially, success was slow, but gradually the market developed. Growth was a term that was becoming more regularly used, as cruising developed into a respectable industry in its own right. The days of the passenger liner had passed, but the days of the cruise ship had arrived.

Now, some of the liners that had been laid-up for several years were beginning to show themselves again. This was perhaps best marked by the re-emergence, in 1981, of the former *ss France* from her protracted period of lay-up, into her new guise as the now heavily modified cruise ship *ss Norway*.

By this time, the cruise market worldwide was expanding rapidly. A number of owners, optimistic about the future, had started ordering cruise ships which were rising well above the envisaged 20,000 grt upper limit. The cruise ships *Europa* (33,819 grt), *Tropicale* (22,919 grt), *Song of America* (32,000 grt), *Nieuw Amsterdam* and sister *Noordam* (33,930 grt) and several other completely new purpose-built vessels started to appear. As the 1980s progressed, other operators became actively involved in seeking additional tonnage. Some ships were lengthened to increase their capacity, while other operators looked at the prospects for newer and larger vessels. By the time P&O placed their order for *Royal Princess* in April 1982, at least three other ships of comparable size were on the drawing boards for other operators. Further growth was predicted too, amounting to between 10 and 15 per cent per annum, with an estimated 5 million people expected to take a cruising holiday, each year, by 1985. The cruise market had come of age.

P&O took the plunge. On the 17 February 1982, the decision to build the 45,000-ton *Royal Princess* was announced. Eight weeks later, the order for the world's largest purpose-built cruise ship was placed, with the Helsinki shipyards of Wärtsilä, in Finland. Construction was soon underway.

A budget of $150 million was put aside for the new vessel, or Hull Number 464 as she was then known.

She was towed out of her building dock (behind the ship in this view) on 17 February and then towed into the harbour (in the background) where she was turned before being towed into the fitting out berth shown. On the other side of quay is the 4,000-ton *Sea Goddess*, one of two sisters being built by Wärtsilä for Norske Cruise. (*P&O Cruises*)

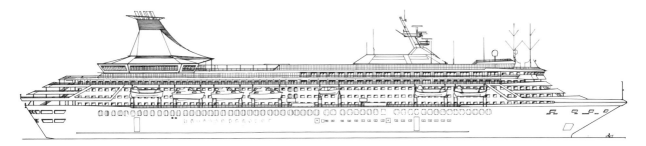

Profile view of *Royal Princess. (Drawing: Michael J Ambrose)*

Planning and design work had progressed well. Designed for worldwide cruising, but particularly intended to become the flagship of Princess Cruises, P&O's United States-based operation, *Royal Princess* was aimed directly at the Company's southern California market place. There, three of Princess Cruises' ships were already catering to 100,000 passengers a year, while the US market as a whole had been rising annually: from 1 million in 1978 to an estimated 1¾ million for 1984. Future potential was obvious, and thus Hull 464's design was evolved to pitch her directly into this trade.

From their Los Angeles base, Princess Cruises were operating their three ships *Pacific Princess* (20,636 grt), *Island Princess* (19,907 grt) and *Sun Princess* (17,370 grt) to a market which consisted in the main of adults of above 45 years of age with above average incomes. This represented a fairly high-pitched market place in

This schematic cutaway view illustrates the unique arrangement of *Royal Princess*. The shaded areas represent the cabins, most of which are situated in the superstructure. (*Wärtsilä Helsinki Shipyards*)

which the new ship was to cater, but allowed an expected daily income of around $300 per passenger, thus providing a $90,000 daily working income for the vessel thereby giving the justification for the high, $150 million, capital involvement. This was, of course, dependant on P&O being able to attract a market share of up to 9.5 per cent of the total US market.

In fact, the arrival of *Royal Princess* in late 1984 represented an increase in capacity of around 60 per cent for Princess Cruises and, furthermore, an increase in pitch over the already fairly high market pitch of the three existing vessels. As such, while filling the new vessel should prove no problem, keeping all three of the older vessels active in the short term will be no easy task. Nevertheless, the appeal of a new ship, the expanding nature of the market place, and the massive promotional campaign for the new *Royal Princess* – centred around the operator's catch phrase '*Royal Princess* – The Most Exciting Resort in the World' – should all help to develop new business. Coupled to P&O's high degree of passenger loyalty (an average, worldwide, of 25 per cent of cruise clientele sail regularly with the same company, whereas P&O achieve the astounding figure of 60 per cent!), and a series of improvements and renovations to the older vessels, should help the Princess Cruises operation to

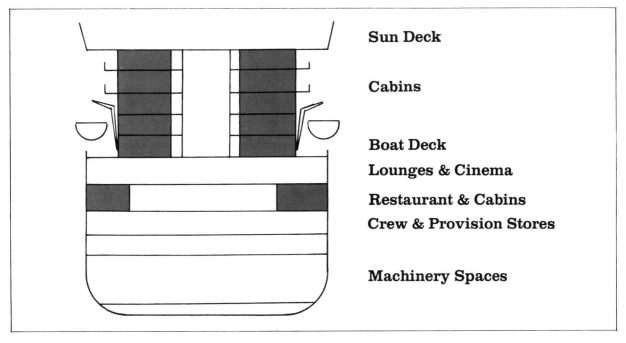

Sun Deck

Cabins

Boat Deck

Lounges & Cinema

Restaurant & Cabins

Crew & Provision Stores

Machinery Spaces

Royal Princess during fitting out in June 1984. (*K Brzoza*)

accommodate the increase in capacity, without removing any of the existing vessels to other parts of the world. Such are the circumstances into which the new vessel is born.

The ship

The design of *Royal Princess* was evolved jointly by P&O and Wärtsilä and is unique in many ways, as was the case with the P&O's former flagship, the 44,807 grt *Canberra* when she first entered service back in 1961. With only 1,200 passengers in 600 cabins on a 45,000 grt vessel the low density *Royal Princess* possesses an uncluttered, open and restful air, which is immediately apparent as the vessel is boarded. Entering the ship into the Purser's lobby located on the main deck will bring a surprise to the most ardent of European cruise ship passengers, as instead of the high-contrast decor commonly found aboard ship, the intererior of *Royal Princess* bears more similarity to that of a modern hotel. This impression is created by the use of soft pastel colours, various works of art, and some 1,700 plants in 175 tubs which are blended in to the hotel-style design of the ship's interior. It is in fact significant that one of the firms of consultants used in the interior design of the ship was the US company Hirsch-Bedner & Associates, who are best known for their skills in the interior design of hotels.

The Purser's lobby (or perhaps, hotel foyer) uses two decks, with an opening in the middle leading down into the restaurant below, and is designed to be the ship's central meeting area and focal point. It is set off with a central statue commissioned by P&O from David Norris, which is surrounded with running water further enchancing the soft and fresh atmosphere of the vessel's interior.

The principal consultant in interior design was the Norwegian architect Njal R. Eide. His task was to provide the ship's interior with an atmosphere of casual elegance and the feel, type and style of decor as would be found in a reasonably luxurious Californian family home. This has most definitely been achieved, as the vessel has both a distinctive US West Coast image and feel to it.

Nevertheless, one can still find examples of teak (veneer) and brass, and the wash basins in the cabin's private bathrooms are mounted in solid marble surrounds. Primarily, formica is well in evidence, but fairly tastefully so, and with US fire regulations now so rigourously enforced, it is not perhaps surprising to learn that great efforts have been made to ensure that as little as possible aboard the ship is made of flammable material.

Other public rooms include a startling show lounge and casino, a cafe, library, card room, children's play room, shopping precinct, boutiques, a night club, cinema/conference room, an observation lounge aft which doubles as a lively discotheque at night, and a fully equipped gymnasium and sauna.

The entertainments provided in the public rooms are varied and cater to a range of tastes with Broadway-style shows, classical music orchestras, modern rock and popular groups and dancing of both ballroom and modern styles, while the cinema will be

The accommodation is extremely well appointed. These two views show (*upper*) one of the 152 de-luxe cabins which have their own verandah, and (*below*) one of the standard cabins which would itself be classed as a de-luxe cabin on many ships. (*Wärtsilä*)

The Plaza, dominated by the 'Spindrift' sculpture, is the main foyer of the ship, overlooked by a circular balcony on the deck above where the Princess Court is located. (*P&O Cruises Ltd*)

The naming ceremony on 15 November 1984. HRH The Princess of Wales immediately prior to the naming with the P&O Chairman, the President of Finland and the Bishop of Southampton. (*R Ambrose*)

showing the latest in film releases to add to the extensive range of both indoor and outdoor activities available.

Outside, the cruise clientele have two acres of open deck space around which to promenade (more than any other cruise ship afloat, according to P&O), or just lie in the sun and bask, or take a dip in one of the four separate swimming pools or two jacuzzis.

The internal arrangement of *Royal Princess* is, in many ways, unique. The main air-conditioning ducting, electrical wiring and plumbing, is positioned in a central core which runs through the middle of the ship, around which the passenger cabins have been constructed so that all are outward facing. Most of the cabins are positioned in the superstructure, and thus the hull has been utilised for many of the public rooms where the extra width has allowed the designers much greater flexibility and originality of design.

The ship has 600 passenger cabins to accommodate 1,200 persons, and *all* of these cabins rank as first-class by any conventional measurement standard. Not only are all cabins outward facing with their own double-glazed picture window giving panoramic views of sea, sky and ports of call, but additionally all have en-suite bathroom, twin or double-bed facilities, private refrigerator, independently controlled air-conditioning, 24-hour steward service and, among other things, an interesting multi-channel television set. This TV system can relay four local shore-based television transmissions, two separate video channels, a teletext service giving various information on numerous items from the day's menu to the historical background of the next port of call – plus another channel which is used to relay live broadcasts from on-board ship, ranging from the performance in the main theatre to a view of the coastline and the water on either side of the ship! Thus can the discerning

Royal Princess returns to Southampton on 18 November 1984 after a short cruise to the Channel Islands. She is seen here being manouvred into her berth. (*R Ambrose*)

passenger, even a lazy one, know what is going on aboard ship at all times.

Of the 600 passenger cabins, 152 are ultra-comfortable suites with their own private verandah. Indeed, a measure of the standard to be found aboard *Royal Princess* is that even the 500 crew are accommodated in either one or two-berth individual cabins with their own toilet/bath or shower. However, probably the *most* significant aspects of the ship, from the readers point of view, are to be found in the vessel's machinery spaces.

The main propulsion machinery of *Royal Princess* consists of four air-start Wärtsilä-Pielstick 6PC4-2L medium-speed diesel engines, arranged in pairs and driving (through two sets of reduction gearing) two heavily skewed controllable-pitch propellers. Each engine develops 7,290 kW (9,900 bhp) producing a total power output of 29,160 kW (39,600 bhp) giving a service speed of 22 knots.

From a power-take-off through the main reduction gearing each engine also drives a 7,500 kVA shaft-generator. These are backed up by two Wärtsilä-Vasa 6R22 stand-by alternators each developing 950 kW at 1,200 rpm mcr. Considerable efforts have also been made to harness waste energy too, and the two oil-fired boilers used for heating are backed up by a heat-exchanger mounted in the ship's funnel to make use of the heat from the main engine exhausts. In addition, the water produced by the non-recirculating air-conditioning plant is used in conjunction with the exhaust heat exchangers to power the ship's twin 300-ton per day evaporators, providing the ship with fresh water direct from the sea.

All four main engines are fitted with economisers, and *all* the vessel's machinery can be operated on just one type of high-viscosity fuel oil of up to 600 cSt. *Royal Princess* can in fact be operated on extremely low quality fuel, of poorer grade than is presently found on the market, and with the declining standards of bunker fuel nowadays this aspect is of prime importance. Great advances have been made in engine and machinery building of late due to declining bunker quality and rising fuel costs, and to this extent at least, *Royal Princess* must be considered a masterpiece of modern engineering technology when compared to her running mate, the former P&O flagship *Canberra*. Whereas the 44,807 grt *Canberra*'s fuel bills represented 25 per cent of her total operating overheads, on *Royal Princess* this figure has been reduced to as little as 5 per cent!

To aid manoeuvreability independant of tugs, the ship's two individually-controlled rudders are backed by two 750 kW bow thrusters. Stability is catered for with a pair of Sperry-Gyrofin stabilisers, each fin weighing 77 tons and controlled by a 90 bhp drive

motor, giving 80 tonnes lift at 18 knots – which is predicted to reduce rolling by as much as 90 per cent.

Other items on the ship's machinery inventory include: the high-economy rotary heat exchanger air-conditioning system; a biological sewage treatment plant and a comprehensive, two-incinerator garbage treatment system. To maintain the vessel in top structural condition for the whole of her life span she is also fitted with an automatic corrosion protection system. This involves the application of an electrical charge over the whole underwater surface of the hull, preventing the electrolytic reaction which causes rust. The hull is also finished with the relatively new SPC anti-fouling paint which works on the basis that as marine life forms on the immersed surface of the hull the coating gradually wears away so the 'barnacles' and other fouling just drops off. The combination of these protective systems can have quite a large effect on the ships economics, as the reduction of water resistance reduces the energy requirements and thus to a certain extent reduces fuel costs – sometimes by a substantial margin.

The machinery arrangements on *Royal Princess* are monitored by a RACAL ISIS 400 on-board computer system. This provides the engineer with details on 850 significant separate sensor points located throughout the ship's machinery, and provides an alarm system in the control room should any item not be working as it should.

The Purser is equipped with a computer in his department too. This unit, a large IBM management system, is used to monitor and control the ship's commercial aspects, and handles such information as accounts, passenger and crew data and various other 'hotel' management functions. Computers are also to be found in the other area of the ship-operating triad, namely in the deck branch, where one can find such examples as Satellite navigation and communication equipment, the arbitrary ARPA (Automatic Radar Plotting Aid) and numerous other sophisticated navigational and communications devices.

Initially, the itinery of *Royal Princess* features the Princess Cruises former runs to the Mexican riviera, the Panama Canal zone, the Caribbean, Canada and Alaska (the latter being fly-cruises with the ship based temporarily at Vancouver). But *Royal Princess* has been designed and built to cruise worldwide, and cruises to the South Pacific and the Far East are also planned: to Hawaii, Australia, New Zealand, Fiji, Tahiti, Hong Kong, Singapore and Japan.

This ship is full of technology, designed to make her a more viable proposition than the present surfeit of ex-liner cruise ships. *Royal Princess* is presently unique, and the world's largest purpose-built cruise ship to date. However, as these words are written, larger cruise ships are already on the drawing boards. The cruise ship, as a significant individual type in its own right, has come of age. The halcyon days of the cruise ship are here, and it seems increasingly predictable that more is yet to come.

Bow and stern views of *Royal Princess* bound for the port of Southampton. (*FotoFlite*)

Far East Shipbreaking

by J H Rand

Mr J H Rand is President, Marine Transport Lines, Inc, New York, and Chairman of International Association of Independent Tanker Owners (INTERTANKO).

Tanker and combination carriers reported sold for scrapping between 1 January and 10 October 1984, total 15.6 million dwt, including 37 very large and ultra-large crude oil carriers (V/ULCCs) aggregating 8.8 million dwt. The end scrapping result for 1984 may, however, not reach the world-record peak of last year, totalling 26.6 million dwt of tankers and combination carriers. *(See Fig 1 – Tankers and combination carriers sold for scrapping 1973–1983)*

The main shipbreaking centre of the world is located in the Far East, where Taiwan continues to hold its leading position as the largest demolition centre of its kind in the world. The second table shows the scrapping figures which include all type of ships scrapped in the period 1976–1983. *(See Fig 2 – Ships scrapped at main demolition centres)*

An INTERTANKO delegation visiting the shipbreaking industry in the autumn of 1982 concluded that Far East breakers could scrap more than 100 V/ULCCs per year, provided such tonnage could be purchased at low and attractive prices. With a workforce of more than 10,000 specialised labourers at

Ulsan, South Korea, where a very capable shipbreaking industry has developed in a very short space of time. (*T A Meyer*)

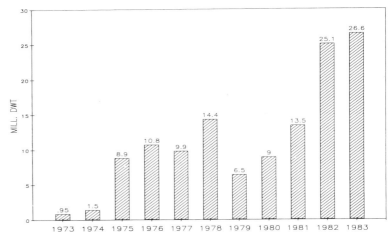

TANKERS AND COMBINED CARRIERS
SOLD FOR SCRAPPING 1973 – 1983

SCRAPPING 1976 – 1983
ALL TYPES OF SHIPS
FIGURES IN THOUSAND DWT.

YEAR	1976		1977		1978		1979		1980		1981		1982		1983	
TOTAL	10,986		11,038		20,034		10,341		10,074		15,003		28,342		33,381	
Major Countries:																
Taiwan	6,409	(58%)	6,964	(63%)	12,806	(64%)	6,528	(63%)	7,860	(78%)	9,736	(65%)	17,110	(60%)	16,924	(51%)
Spain	2,301	(21%)	1,637	(15%)	2,196	(11%)	1,432	(14%)	-		558	(4%)	847	(3%)	997	(3%)
Korea	416	(4%)	677	(6%)	1,493	(8%)	748	(7%)	305	(3%)	1,934	(13%)	5,320	(19%)	8,750	(26%)
Pakistan	286	(3%)	536	(5%)	908	(5%)	224	(2%)	550	(5%)	1,312	(9%)	2,935	(10%)	2,168	(6%)
India	-		-		-		57	(½%)	-		248	(2%)	227	(1%)	1,014	(3%)
China	-		-		-		-		-		-		253	(1%)	1,429	(4%)
Thailand	-		-		-		-		-		-		-		288	(1%)

(Source: A.P. Møller)

J H Rand, Chairman of Intertanko.

Kaoshiung harbour in Taiwan. The buildings to the left are the homes of many of the workers. The derricks are those taken from ships. (*T A Meyer*)

the shipbreaking berths in Kaohsiung harbour, Taiwan, one may understand the potential. The efficiency of the Taiwan breakers enables them to reduce a 30,000 long-ton light-displacement VLCC (about 220,000 tonnes dwt) to a pile of sheet plate and component parts in less than six weeks. Members of the Shipbreaking Association of Taiwan and the private steel mill enterprises carry out the demolition business with professional skill.

The performance of ship demolition in South Korea is no less impressive. Inchon Iron and Steel Company Ltd, which commenced operation of a new scrapyard in Ulsan, can dismantle a lot of five VLCCs in less than 40 days with the assistance of heavy lifting and other equipment generally unavailable in Taiwan. With a workforce of some 600–800 labourers, the results achieved after only a few months operation demonstrate how efficient scrapping can eliminate the surplus tonnage. Less sophisticated, but still effective, is the method adopted by shipbreakers in Pakistan, India and Bangladesh where vessels up to VLCC size are beached at full speed, instantly creating a 'natural' shipbreaking berth. Gadani Beach, (Pakistan), when operating with full capacity, employs 20,000 workers spread over 130 plots, each capable of accommodating two–three vessels for demolition simultaneously.

The 37,792 grt *Pindos*, Panamanian and built in 1964, an Esso VLCC and two other vessels lie awaiting the cutter's torch in Koahsiung. (*T A Meyer*)

Shipbreaking – Taiwanese style. There has been considerable competition of late between South Korea and Taiwan, with China looming large on the horizon, having purchased her first really large tanker this year. (*T A Meyer*)

However, it can still take some 10 months to scrap a VLCC. The demolition area spreads over a distance of some 8,000 metres. The labourers are living in sheds close to the beach, erected by wooden debris from dismantled ships. The infrastructure needed for scrapping such as winches, derricks, etc, is taken from the vessels being scrapped.

The fact that Far East breakers have managed to stay at the forefront of a market plagued by uncertainties, fluctuations in demand and widely swinging prices is largely due to three factors: (1) the capacity to handle all sorts of vessels, including VLCCs; (2) the ability to demolish them quickly and relatively cheaply due to low labour cost; and (3) a good local and regional demand for ship scrap material. Industrialised countries are hampered by high labour costs and by rigid standards on steel material for the building and construction sectors, which limits utilisation of re-rolled material. Another limiting factor is that ship scrap material competes with imported domestic scrap re-cycled after melting. Without a local market for re-rolled material, it is difficult to stay in a highly competitive shipbreaking industry.

Scrapping is one of the few credible solutions to restore the equilibrium in shipping services, where severe over-tonnaging exists, and is urgently needed to rectify the acute imbalance in supply and demand in the tanker sector, most particularly for the VLCC/ULCC market. Scrapping of super-tankers has increased consistently since 1978 and has accounted for some 60 per cent of all tanker tonnage broken up. Most of the VLCCs scrapped were less than 13 years old. The most significant deal was probably the sale, on 'as is – where is' basis, of the *Pierre Guillaumat* to Hyundai in Korea. At 565,000 dwt and only seven

years old, she was the largest and youngest vessel of her type to be sold for demolition, although she has yet to be broken up. Overall, the average age of tankers scrapped is some 18 years or more.

International regulations on marine safety and pollution (SOLAS and MARPOL) have produced variable rates of scrapping as vessels not in compliance with international regulations face the choice of going for demolition or upgrading at high cost. In light of the uncertain market, the obvious choice for most owners is to sell for scrap. However, this process is painful for owners and their financial institutions when vessels' book values far exceed the net proceeds from demolition.

Tankers are superior scrapping candidates since they contain large proportions of high quality plates suitable for re-rolling; as a consequence tankers generally command higher scrap prices than other ship types.

Since the ship scrap material is difficult to transport and receives competition from other sources of ferrous scrap, there is no established international market for ship scrap material. Countries such as Taiwan and South Korea do, however, have a definite local requirement for plates suitable for re-rolling. Other markets are nearby Far East countries which import

steel and ferrous scrap, in addition to iron ore and coal, for steel production. Ship scrap can be used as a melting material or in solid form for steel bar production. Notwithstanding the current depression in the steel market, it appears likely that future increases in production as well as the transition to energy-efficient electric arc furnaces, will have a favourable impact on the demand for ship scrap material.

As long as the tonnage surplus exists, there can be no market recovery. Those owners who retain obsolete and uneconomic ships should remember that this scenario will persist indefinitely unless increased scrapping takes place. Holding back a sale for demolition in the hope that the market will improve is unlikely to be successful, and the same may be said for buying VLCC against a rise in the charter or second-hand market. When a VLCC is sold for further trading it will be a competitor for tomorrow. The folly of such action was discussed at INTERTANKO's Annual General Meeting. Buying a secondhand VLCC for $4.5 million and putting the ship into lay-up (annual cost US $1 million) for three years, will require a scrap price of around US $350 per light dwt in order to cover the cost of the voyage to the Far East breaking yard and a net 15 per cent return on the investment.

Shipbreaking at Gadani beach, Pakistan. ULCC/VLCC-sized ships commenced being scrapped here in 1982–83. Ships are simply 'rammed' up the beach, cut up, winched further up the beach, etc. The work is highly labour-intensive here. (*T A Meyer*)

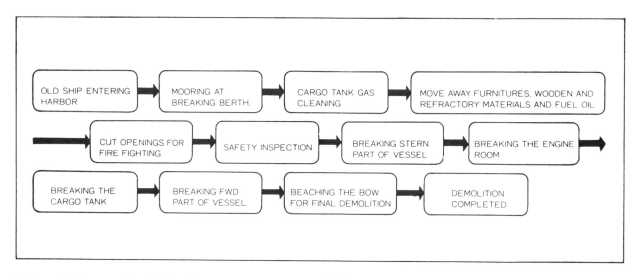

Schematic diagram of the shipbreaking process.

Access to local re-processing plants such as steel mills is an important part if not vital part of the whole shipbreaking operation. Contrary to the old saying that old ships become razor blades, ship steel is usually of good quality and can be re-rolled into new plate. Perhaps its greatest use is in the construction industry however, where ship scrap is used to make reinforcing rods for use in concrete buildings, roads, and other structures. (*T A Meyer*)

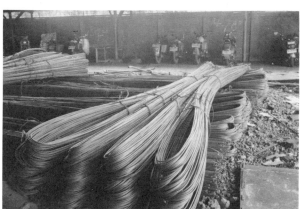

In contrast, the owners may, once a decision is taken, sell the ships for scrapping 'as is – where is' in lay-up in Northern Europe for some US $70–80 per light dwt. Another option for owners is to trade the vessel in ballast, or with a cargo, to the Far East. After unloading, the tanker has to be cleaned and gas-freed and sold to a breaker where obtainable prices can be in the range of some US $130–140 per light dwt.

The difference between the 'where is' price at the lay-up site and the delivered price at the breaker's yard has encouraged some shipowners to develop the technical staffs and expertise necessary to specialise in vessel reactivation, delivery and predemoliton cleaning. Such specialisation enables them to deal with the risks most shipowners are hesitant to accept, and the purchase of laid-up tonnage for subsequent resale and delivery to ship breakers has become a small but increasingly important facet of the demolition scene.

Ships in lay-up and sold for demolition on an 'as is – where is' basis need not be reactivated for delivery, under their own power, to Far East scrapyards. Long-haul ocean tows of single and multiple units are now commonplace, and sophisticated towing and salvage companies have improved their performance in response to the demands of the market. An excellent example of these increased capabilities is a recent single tug 'gang tow' of two VLCCs from Norway to Taiwan. Where vessels are sold 'as is – where is', owners obtain an immediate, fixed price and have no further responsibility or risk for the vessel's delivery to its demolition yard. INTERTANKO has successfully encouraged owners to sell vessels on an 'as is – where is' basis and has also encouraged Far East breakers to co-operate with ship traders and delivery organisations so as to enable all the parties involved to share in the benefits of such arrangements.

This page and overleaf: The most sophisticated of the Far Eastern breakers are those of South Korea. In these views, the strict contrasts can be seen between the levels of technology employed, and the differences in labour-intensity, use of cranes and premises. (*T A Meyer*)

The legal and commercial arrangements which normally govern the sale and demolition of a tanker are highly complex, and it is perhaps not unusual that specialists have entered the field. For example, the vessel must be delivered on time and sufficiently clean and safe for cutting work. A late delivery may expose the ultimate buyer – the shipbreaker – to unacceptable economic risks if the resale value of the scrap material has simultaneously declined. An improperly cleaned ship can be both dangerous and illegal to break, exposing either or both seller and shipbreaker to legal sanctions or costly remedial cleaning. Failure to properly address this myriad of complexity can cause a sale to fail or be subject to financial renegotiation. Finally, or perhaps to begin with, there is the question of getting the ship from lay-up to demolition site, particularly when a voyage under the vessel's own power is indicated. Reactivation, recertification, repair and operation of a vessel which has been laid-up for any length of time is something of an imponderable for the large majority of shipowners since it falls far outside the normal scope of vessel operations.

Shipbreakers have their own local commercial and technical regulations to deal with. Regulations covering safety and pollution prevention require gasfree certificates by local chemists, certifying that the ship is safe for cutting work. Import taxes and license fees can add substantially to total dismantling costs. (*The graph, Fig 3, shows the various sequences in a ship demolition operation.*)

Tanker cleaning and gas-freeing represents a continual problem for Far East breakers since it is a costly and time consuming process. A new cleaning centre has been set up in Manila to accommodate tankers en-route to local demolition yards. This facility is ideally located for vessels coming to the Far East from Europe, the Middle East and South East Asia. Due to stringent anti-pollution rules, construction of a land-based cleaning facility was refused by the authorities in Kaohsiung, Taiwan. INTERTANKO has suggested that floating facilities be utilised and this has prompted a search for alternative solutions presently being conducted by the local shipbreaking industry.

In recent years the tanker owning industry, independent and oil company alike, has scrapped some 225 VLCCs. A rough estimate of the original cost of these vessels falls in the neighbourhood of US $9,000,000,000 while the proceeds from the scrap sales of this fleet is unlikely to have exceeded US $1,000,000,000.

By October 1984, there were about 50 million dwt of tankers laid-up, representing some 20 per cent of the total tanker fleet. Of this figure, some 40 million dwt were tankers over 200,000 dwt. It is a sad fact that a large proportion of these idle vessels, especially those fitted with steam turbine propulsion, will never see service again and are destined only for the breaker's yard. This may be a substantial sacrifice on the parts of owners, but may be necessary to avoid even heavier losses if the decision to scrap is postponed.

It is promising to see that all ships offered to scrappers are being sold and there are some signs on market improvements. My sincere wish is that more and more obsolete vessels be sent to scrap yards. Profit lies in scrapping ships at present, not building them.

Heavy-Lift Shipping

by Dag Pike

Dag Pike is a marine journalist writing for many leading shipping magazines. He is an ex-ships' captain who now specialises in writing about the heavy-lift market.

The heavy-lift sector of the shipping industry has two unique distinctions. It contains what are probably the most specialised of merchant ships, and at present it probably has the highest level of overcapacity in the merchant fleet today. These two factors are not entirely divorced and to a large degree it is the very specialised nature of the heavy-lift shipping industry which gives it a different trading pattern from general shipping and which has created a different time scale for the effects of the shipping recession to filter through. However, it now seems as though the worst of the overcapacity situation is over, with the last vessel of a big ordering spree now delivered and with the market very slowly improving, but it still looks like a long road ahead to restore equilibrium.

The overcapacity came about through optimism of a boom in heavy-lift shipping, which in turn led to operators in this field ordering new vessels to expand their fleets, while at the same time a number of new-comers were attracted to this market sector creating a threefold increase in the size of the fleet in as many years. The boom in heavy-lift shipping arrived at much the same time as the general shipping recession started to bite but, because of the long lead times involved in many of the specialist shipments with which heavy-lift ships were involved, particularly those with project cargoes, the effects of the general recession were not immediately apparent. It took about two years for the real effects of the recession to hit the heavy-lift market and this coincided with the delivery of a number of new vessels with greatly increased

The most versatile of today's heavy-lift ships is the *Dock Express* type.

One of the latest generation of lo-lo heavy-lift ships, the *Jumbo Challenger*, capable of handling unit loads up to 1,000 tonnes.

Ro-ro handling is gaining in importance for onward transportation.

capacity. The inevitable results of this equation were plummeting rates and a large overcapacity. But while the general shipping sector is slowly climbing out of the recession, the time delay in the heavy-lift sector means that the recovery is likely to be much slower, with most operators now looking to 1986 before increased performance can be expected.

Optimism is generated from the fact that there are an increasing number of enquiries for cargoes to be carried in 1986, and the long lead times involved with these cargoes point to an upturn in both the project cargo and offshore oil industry cargo markets which are the lifeblood of the heavy-lift industry.

The overcapacity in the heavy-lift market was created not just by the sheer number of ships ordered for this sector but by the greatly increased capacity of these ships. It takes some time for the market to catch up with the increased capacity, particularly when one

is talking about single unit loads. Where a manufacturer might have considered project cargo units up to 500 tonnes and is then offered ships with a capacity of handling cargo units up to 1,000 tonnes, it takes time for the adjustment to be made because it means upgrading all the handling facilities from the manufacturing site through to the construction site.

This highlights the integrated nature of many of the heavy-lift transportation movements and many of the specialist companies now offer a complete turnkey package for cargo movements which can include installation at the delivery end as well. This isolates the heavy-lift sector even further from the general shipping industry and in many respects makes it a part of the construction industry. The long lead times are incurred because the heavy-lift specialist is brought into the project right in the early planning stages.

The same increase in handling capacity has taken place in the submersible ship sector of the heavy-lift industry. This sector is aimed particularly at the offshore oil industry for moving drilling rigs and other very large pieces of equipment. In this case the ordering boom for new ships coincided with the offshore drilling boom, and the virtual collapse of the rig market two years ago created particular difficulties for the heavy-lift companies specialising in this sector.

Here again the increased capacity of individual ships is only now being recognised as owners start to appreciate the advantages of transporting semi-submersible drilling rigs by means of the submersible heavy-lift ship. This new market is in some respects counteracted by the fact that these very large submersible ships can carry two or even three jack-up drilling rigs at any one time. While this is good business for the shipowner involved, it actually reduces the overall number of shipping movements in this market sector.

Presently, the average employment of the very large

The *Dyvi Swan* carrying floating equipment to the Falklands.

The *Mighty Servant 3* with the semi-submersible rig *Benreoch* as deck cargo.

Mammoet's new heavy-lift carrier ms *Happy Buccaneer* equipped with two HUISMAN-ITREC Heavy Lift Mast Cranes (HLMC's) with 550 tons SWL. Each crane undergoes testing with 1,200 tons at 36 m radius.

submersible heavy-lift ships can be as low as 50 per cent of their available time. Thus few ships can theoretically be operating at economic level and it is suggested in some quarters that owners are accepting rates as low as 50 per cent below what would be economically viable, simply to keep their ships employed.

Many heavy-lift ships are currently operating on the spot market, and shippers are conscious of this and therefore tend to delay placing contracts until the last minute, in the hope of negotiating low rates from owners desperate for work. This is a situation which cannot last indefinitely.

As far as can be ascertained only two heavy-lift ships have been laid up recently. This has helped to ease the market situation very slightly, but the general consensus among owners is that things should start to improve during 1985.

One of the big problems facing owners of the new generation of heavy-lift ships is the high cost of re-positioning these ships to pick up cargoes. Most heavy-lift ships operate on a worldwide basis and the cost of re-positioning can make a ship uncompetitive for a particular cargo when another owner with a ship close at hand can offer a lower rate. Such situations tend to play into the hands of those owners with larger fleets who have a better chance of picking up cargoes on the spot market. This is becoming an increasing feature of the current heavy-lift market.

Although an integral part of the industry, the use of barges for heavy-lift transportation has always been considered a separate entity. At a time when cargo owners are looking for the lowest possible rates on movement of heavy-lifts, barge transport can often prove more attractive than the ships which have to charge high rates but offer a quicker service. In the current market, barges are picking up a better share of heavy-lift cargoes, particularly when transporting equipment for the offshore and dredging industries. However, the heavy-lift ships are also in a position to offer competitive low rates at times when cargo is available on routes where they have to be re-positioned. In this situation, any cargo is better than nothing, and barge owners and tug operators are also feeling the pinch in the current tight market. A number of barges having been laid up because there is no employment.

Competition for the dedicated heavy-lift ship is also coming from the liner companies which have been the traditional carriers of heavy-lift cargoes. A large number of cargo ships built today are still fitted with

Built in West Germany in 1982 by Martin Jansen Schiffswerft and owned by Blaesbjerg & Co K/S of Denmark, the 6,908 grt *Thor Scan* has heavy-lift capabilities as well as being able to carry 20 ft containers. (*FotoFlite, Ashford*)

57

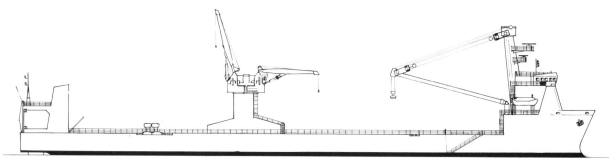

Drawing of *Project Europa*. (*Drawing: M J Ambrose*)

Another heavy-lift vessel belonging to the Blaesbjerg fleet is the 1982-built 6,000 grt 10,000 dwt *Project Europa*. (*FotoFlite, Ashford*)

heavy-lift derricks. In the halcyon days of shipping some two or three years ago, speed and schedules were all important to liner operators and specialised heavy-lift cargo tended to be ignored. Today there is a greater willingness in the liner companies to divert or delay in order to pick up these cargoes and this is creating increased competition for the specialised heavy-lift companies. In particular, there is competition for project cargoes which entail carrying both large and small pieces of equipment in the one overall package.

The heavy-lift sector of shipping has tended to be dominated by European owners in terms of specialised ships but there is now a growing investment in heavy-lift ships in Japan. In the past, Japanese owners have tended to concentrate on large cargo ships which can handle individual cargo units up to 500 tonnes in weight but, now, Japanese owners are investing in specialised ro-ro ships which can handle individual units of much greater weight. This emphasis on handling cargo only by ro-ro method is in contrast to the European attitude which tends to look for versatility in cargo handling, with most European ships on the market being able to load cargo by at least

two alternative methods. The Japanese owners have decided to concentrate only on ro-ro loading and discharge, aiming their ships particularly at the project cargo market. Here, very heavy modules are first transported by ship and then have to be transported onwards by road. This road transport demands putting the cargo on wheels and if this is the case the same system can be used for discharge.

Dan Mover is a semi-submersible heavy load ship owned by J. Lauritzen A/S and registered in the Bahamas. Built in 1982 at the Nagasaki yard of Mitsubishi Heavy Industries, the *Dan Mover* is 10,282 grt and 13,310 dwt. She is powered by twin MAN 6-cylinder engines giving an output of 9,000 bhp (6,620 kW), and has twin controllable pitch propellers and two CP thwartship thrust forward. (*FotoFlite, Ashford*)

The semi-submersible heavy-lift ship *Ferncarrier* is seen here transporting the drilling rig *SF 140* owned by the Santa Fe Group. (*FotoFlite, Ashford*)

Wijsmuller's *Super Servant 3*, a semi-submersible heavy load vessel built in Japan in 1982 by Oshima Zosen. Her sister *Super Servant 4* was completed in the same year by Sumitomo Heavy Industries, also of Japan. Powered by two Stork-Werkspoor engines, she is 10,135 grt and has a speed of 13 knots.

These Japanese ships are also characterised by a very shallow draught enabling them to enter some of the small ports which have to be used for project cargo deliveries. The shallow draught and very wide beam necessitates fitting three propellers to absorb the required power output within the shallow draught. This concept gives the large clear deck space required for modern heavy-lift transportation. These comparatively simple ships are also much cheaper to build than the complex designs being developed by European

owners and this must give an advantage in today's highly competitive market.

This comparatively late Japanese entry into the specialised heavy-lift market is probably the result of seeing the *potential* profitability in this shipping sector. It would appear also that the Japanese heavy-lift operators, both ship owners and barge owners, are cushioned to a certain extent from the overcapacity in the heavy-lift market by virtue of an element of protectionism.

Some European operators claim that preference for heavy-lift cargoes originating from Japanese manufacturing yards is being given to Japanese shipping companies to the detriment of the European operators, but this is not a surprising development and probably only reflects the Japanese increasing their involvement in the heavy-lift sector rather than any overt act of protectionism. There is also the attraction of turning to an operator in this specialised field who speaks the same language and who is located on the doorstep rather than based half way around the world. European heavy-lift shipping companies have recognised the growing problems of the Japanese market which is a very important source of cargo, and most have been at considerable pains to establish good representation in Japan and other Far East countries.

Many of the orders for heavy-lift cargoes from Japanese yards and manufacturing industry were, until recently, placed by the major American construction companies, and with the transport of these cargoes being arranged under the auspices of the Americans the European heavy-lift operators could, in most cases, compete on equal terms with the Japanese. Now however, it appears that there is increasing Japanese and South Korean competition in the major construction markets, as both the manufacture and transport of these cargoes is being concentrated in the Far East. This change comes at a time when there is also a change in emphasis for the destination of many of these heavy-lift cargoes. Over the past few years this concentration has been in the Middle East, to meet the seemingly insatiable demand for manufacturing and process plants in this region and although some projects are still being developed here, this specific market is running out of steam to a certain extent and is being replaced by developing markets in South East Asia.

With both the offshore oil industry and the downstream process and manufacturing plants still comparatively buoyant in South East Asia, it is anticipated that this region will see much of the heavy-lift shipping over the next few years.

China is another potential market which still remains to be developed as far as heavy-lift shipping is concerned. There is little doubt that the developing offshore oil industry in China will generate new markets and there is also a growing trend for China to import specialised manufactured products such as railway locomotives and port equipment which are

Owned by Jan-Erik Dyvi Skipsrederi of Oslo Norway and built by Kaldnes M/V A/S of Tonsberg, the 19,216-grt, 32,650-dwt *Dyvi Tern* is a tanker/heavy load deck cargo carrier. She has two heli-pads, is powered by a single B&W 6-cylinder engine and has an output of 13,100 bhp (9,636 kW). (*FotoFlite, Ashford*)

ideal for transportation on heavy-lift vessels. Because the Chinese tend to concentrate as much as possible on the manufacture and construction work in their own yards, it appears likely that they will have to turn to outside help for the transportation expertise and European heavy-lift operators are nibbling hungrily at this opportunity.

Joint ventures between Chinese and foreign heavy-lift operators would appear to be the logical development and there seems particular scope here for Japanese and Singapore operators to obtain part of this lucrative market because of their close location.

The offshore oil industry worldwide is likely to provide increased custom for the heavy-lift shipping companies in the future. Apart from transporting drilling rigs on a worldwide basis, heavy-lift transportation is being increasingly used for the movement of modules and jackets. The trend in the past has been for these items to be constructed fairly close to the installation site to minimise the transportation problems but, with the increased capacity available on heavy-lift ships today, contractors are now tending to shop on a worldwide basis for the lowest construction costs for these modules and jackets, using heavy-lift transport to bring them to the final site. This trend is justified on the basis that many of these modules are very large and comprehensive and the saving in building costs more than compensates for the transportation costs.

Protectionist attitudes by some companies in respect of their offshore oil developments may restrict this market to a certain extent, but in many cases construction work is being put out to tender on a worldwide basis and South Korea is rapidly developing as a new centre for this type of work largely due to low labour costs. Many European shipping companies see this market sector as offering considerable potential for future cargoes. A sign of this development can be seen in a contract which has just been placed for the transportation of jackets and modules across the Pacific. These units are being built in Japan and will be delivered to the oil fields of South California for installation; the first time that this trans-Pacific route has been developed for oil industry cargoes.

From the technical side, ships have been developed with great complexity and versatility to meet the prospective requirements of shipping heavy-lift cargoes in the future. There is no consensus of opinion as to the optimum concept for heavy-lift ships and thus a great diversity of vessel types has been introduced in recent years. The conventional heavy-lift ship is still seen as a cargo vessel fitted with heavy duty derricks, and has been developed by companies like Jumbo Navigation into their latest 10,000-tonne dwt vessels equipped with twin 500-tonne derricks, which can also be developed to handle cargo by ro-ro methods.

Jumbo Navigation have concentrated on building up a versatile fleet of smaller ships with the emphasis on handling cargoes by lo-lo methods and the flexibility of the fleet has enabled them to remain active in the current difficult times.

Dock Express have opted for the maximum versatility in the design of their heavy-lift ships with the ability to load cargo by all three of the conventional methods. This highly sophisticated fleet can submerge the cargo deck for floating cargo aboard, and cargo can be handled with equal facility by ro-ro methods whilst lo-lo cargo can be handled by the twin 500-tonne gantry cranes. The latest vessel was added to their fleet last year with even higher handling capacities and these sophisticated ships are in direct contrast to the stark simplicity of the Japanese heavy-lift ships. Ships of a similar type are operated by the Dutch company Mammoet and by the Russians.

The submersible ship was a development originated from submersible barges. The Dutch company Wijsmuller were the first to fit power units to submersible barges with their *Ocean Servant* category, and from this concept they developed into the fully powered submersible ship, firstly with the *Super Servant* class and latter with the *Mighty Servant* vessels. The last of the *Mighty Servant* vessels was delivered early this year and the capabilities of these vessels have recently been demonstrated by their first transport of a semi-submersible drilling rig. These ships can also handle cargo by ro-ro methods and are fitted with a 250-tonne capacity derrick which plumbs a sealed lower hold below the main cargo deck.

Submersible ship concepts have been followed by a number of other companies, notably Dyvi from Norway. This company has a fleet of four very large submersible ships and have recently taken over the management of the converted VLCC *Ferncarrier*. The

Ferncarrier is one of two vessels of this type which were converted from VLCCs into submersible heavy-lift ships, taking advantage of the low state of the tanker market to develop a comparatively cheap submersible heavy-lift ship. The *Ferncarrier* and its rival the *Sibig Venture*, operated by the Dutch company ITC, are the largest ships of this type in the world and the *Ferncarrier* was the pioneer in the first transportation of a semi-submersible drilling rig.

The latest ships to enter the heavy-lift market this year are two complex vessels which can handle heavy cargoes by lo-lo and ro-ro methods. The Danish company Blaesbjerg have a fleet of vessels primarily developed for the project cargo market but also able to handle a wide variety of other cargoes efficiently. The Blaesbjerg vessels are typified by a large clear cargo deck in addition to a lower hold, plumbed by twin heavy lift derricks, also served by a large stern ro-ro ramp. The latest vessel to be added to the fleet is a 20,000-tonner completed this year by Bremmer

Two of Rotterdam-based Dock-Express BV's fleet of vessels. The company owns and operates heavy-lift and container/dock ships. *Dock Express 20* (5,495 grt, 7,071 dwt) is one of the newer additions to the fleet, having been completed in 1983. (*FotoFlite, Ashford*)

The heavy-lift vessel *Starman Anglia* is owned by Starman Ltd which is part of Blue Star Line Ltd. She was built in 1978 by Swan Hunter and is 2,776 grt, 1,970 dwt and has a maximum draught of 4.5 metres. (*FotoFlite, Ashford*)

Vulkan in West Germany. This vessel is equipped with the largest heavy-lift derrick ever fitted to a ship, which has a lifting capacity of 800 tonnes and is mounted forward, just aft of the accommodation block on the forecastle head. The vessel is also equipped with twin 75-tonne cranes mounted on a gantry which can span the whole cargo deck, while the stern ro-ro ramp can handle unit loads up to 2,000 tonnes. This vessel, named *St. Magnus*, is owned in West Germany and will be operated by Blaesbjerg.

The latest heavy-lift vessel to be commissioned is the *Happy Bucanneer* completed for the Dutch company Mammoet who are a subsidiary of Nedlloyd. This vessel is built somewhat along the lines of the Dock Express ships, featuring a deep cargo hold with access by a heavy duty ro-ro ramp. However, this vessel is not of the submersible type and is designed for handling cargoes by ro-ro and lo-lo methods only. Twin fully revolving cranes mounted on the starboard side of the vessel give a combined lifting capacity of 1,000 tonnes and cargo can be handled from either side of the vessel.

The feature of both of these latest ships to enter the heavy-lift market is their ability to handle conventional cargoes equally as efficiently as heavy-lift cargoes. This perhaps reflects the poor state of the heavy-lift market in that owners are looking to equip their vessels to handle more conventional cargoes as a hedge against the current and possible future difficulties in the heavy-lift sector. Versatility has become an essential part of heavy-lift ship design in the eyes of European owners and the four Dyvi Swan ships are capable of conversion into product tankers as an alternative to carrying heavy-lift cargoes. One of this class of ship has been operating as a product carrier for several months this year, again reflecting the poor state of the heavy-lift market.

Most heavy-lift ships can be adapted to handle alternative cargoes as a hedge against difficulties in the heavy-lift market, but whether they can handle these alternative cargoes in a sufficiently efficient manner to compete with specialised ships is another matter.

However, Wijsmuller have found alternative employment for some of their heavy-lift ships in the current difficult times, as salvage vessels, and the *Mighty Servant 2* underwent considerable modification earlier this year to equip her for salvaging the remains of the *Ocean Ranger* drilling rig which sank off Newfoundland in 1981. The conversion involved the installation of a 350-tonne ringer crane and the fitting of a diving moonpool as well as additional temporary accommodation. This conversion and the employment of the vessel on this task demonstrates the versatility of modern heavy-lift ships which could point the way to the future employment of ships of this type as workhorses for the offshore oil industry.

The current difficulties in the heavy-lift market are seen by most observers as a transient phase in the continuing development of heavy-lift transportation. The shipping companies involved now recognise that the rate of orders for new vessels which took place two or three years ago was too high to be absorbed by the developing market and it is now likely to take another two years before the overcapacity is fully absorbed. One bright spot in the current dismal picture is the fact that designers and manufacturers of process plant are increasingly recognising the growing capabilities of heavy-lift transportation and will be designing their plant to match these capabilities.

If you add to this this increasing use of heavy-lift transportation by the offshore oil industry, then the long term prospects for heavy-lift shipping must be good. Provided of course, that shipowners do not use this optimistic forecast to order further heavy-lift ships for the fleets of the world.

Completed in August 1982, *Sibig Venture* was converted from a VLCC to become the world's first submersible heavy-lift ship conversion. Originally built as the 117,710 dwt tanker *Venture España*, she was transformed into a heavy lift ship with a cargo deadweight of 44,000 tonnes over a period of about seven months at Astilleros Españole's Cadiz yard. She is seen here on a rare passage through the English Channel carrying the self-elevating drilling rig *Andros* from Singapore to Rotterdam. (*FotoFlite, Ashford*)

The Supercarriers

by A J Ambrose

As we step into the second half of the 1980s, the part ro-ro combination container carrier is entering a new generation. Since the early days of this decade, many significant new designs have emerged from the builders' slipways and, in 1984, the developing trend towards larger, more efficient and consequently more profitable vessels, has continued apace.

This new breed is particularly exemplified by two types which have appeared this year, namely Atlantic Container Line's new 'G3' design, and Barber Blue Sea's $200 million trio: *Barber Tampa*, *Barber Texas*, and *Barber Hector*. Innovatory new cargo-handling systems, a reduced complement, greater standards of safety both in port and at sea, and highly-efficient machinery and hull forms providing considerable fuel economies, represent the hallmarks of this significant new type of ship.

The Barber trio

It was the Barber Blue Sea consortium who entered 1984 proclaiming the arrival of their three new vessels under the banner of 'The Supercarriers'. An appropriate title for the Hyundai-built *Barber Tampa*, *Barber Texas*, and *Barber Hector*, all completed during the year to join the Consortium's existing fleet of 14 ships, operating services which are basically round-the-world, connecting Canada and the East and West coasts of the United States, with the Middle East, Far East, and South-East Asia.

The design parameters of this new trio were based

Barber Blue Seas' *Barber Tampa* on sea trials after completion by Hyundai Heavy Industries Ltd of South Korea. She was delivered to her owners on 14 February 1984. (*D H Mann*)

Two views of *Barber Hector*, the third vessel in the class employed on the Barber round-the-world roll-on/roll-off service. (*Ocean Transport & Trading*)

to a large extent on the consortium's earlier *Barber Tonsberg* class ships, but incorporate greater stowage space in a hull that allows maximum economic advantage in respect of propulsive energy, while offering enhanced stability in a collision situation. Watertight integrity and the reduction of the fateful 'free surface effect' has been, and indeed still is, a serious problem with the wide and open cargo areas of modern ro-ro tonnage. Thus, the design has included two transverse watertight bulkheads extending across the stowage space (in addition to the normal compartmentalisation of machinery spaces etc) in order to alleviate this problem to some extent, thereby offering greater survivability if the vessel's outer skin is punctured.

As for the three vessels' main *raison d'etre*, three basic cargo loading systems are provided, intrinsic to the design, to serve the total available stowage space of 72,500 cubic metres in a total deck area of 15,300 square metres. Design deadweight is set at 30,400 tonnes, with a scantling deadweight of 44,000 tonnes in a gross of 25,000 tons. Within these constraints, the Barber vessels can accommodate up to 2,464 TEU (Twenty Foot Equivalent Units), or the equivalent in palletised cargoes, or all forms of roll-on roll-off freight including cars, commercial vehicles, trailers and any moveable object which does not exceed the parameters of either the impressive starboard three-quarter stern ramp – which is visually the most significant feature of the class – or the 15.25 metre high by 12.5 metre wide main loading portal. The ramp itself, a MacGregor-Navire (Centrex) design, has a length of 45.1 metres, a minimum clear lane width of 12.5 metres, and can accommodate heavy

and outsize single unit loads of up to 420 tonnes, or 220 tonnes if the load is concentrated.

For normal operations with containers and trailers, the ramp would be used for two-way loading/unloading and is totally organic to the ship, allowing complete freedom from prepared berths or link spans. In addition, a portable ramp is carried aboard, to serve a loading port on the vessels' starboard side. This facility is provided mainly for the export car trade, allowing independent and simultaneous loading of up to 630 private cars onto two hoistable car decks, without interuption to the normal flow of traffic over the main stern-ramp.

Loading via the stern-ramp is performed by shore-based tractor units aided by seven fork lift trucks of various sizes and capacities, which are carried aboard. Transit between decks is catered for with fixed ramps which can also be used to load ro-ro traffic to the upper deck. Normally, however, the upper-deck cargo would consist of stacked containers loaded by

Forerunner of the modern Supercarrier ship type, the 31,460 dwt *Boogabilla* was completed in Japan only four years ago. The whole after-body of the new ACL class was based to a large degree on this vessel. (*FotoFlite, Ashford*)

means of shoreside gantries and cranes, and the vessels own 40-tonne-lift crane, mounted forward. This crane can only reach about 40 per cent of the upper-deck area however, as it is limited by its maximum 32 metre outreach. Theoretically though, there is no reason why containers stacked aft on the upper deck could not be handled by fork lift trucks should lack of port facilities so demand.

To cope with the large requirement for electrical power needed for lighting and ventilation of the cargo spaces in addition to the ships normal power demand, six large generators are provided, including one 1,000 kW turbo-alternator, three 1,900 kW and two 900 kW generators, giving each ship a total electrical supply of 8.5 mW.

The main propulsion machinery, situated directly beneath the aft superstructure, is a single Hyundai-B&W 8L90GB diesel, providing a maximum continuous rating (mcr) output of 36,600 bhp at 97 rpm. This is reduced by 10 per cent in normal service to develop a normal continuous rating (ncr) of 32,940 bhp at 94 rpm, giving a service speed of 19.5 knots at maximum design draught. At this level fuel consumption is estimated to be around 105 tonnes per day, the equivalent of 78 grammes of fuel per deadweight-tonne mile (gftm), or 1 kilogramme of fuel per TEU mile (gfcm).

For independant manoeuvreability, two 'thwartships thrusters of 1,910 kW are fitted, one forward and one aft, both thrusters and all primary engine controls being duplicated on the ship's bridge. This allows unmanned engine room operation and assists to a certain degree in the reduction of the ships' complement to 22 on the British-flag vessel, and 20/21 on the Scandinavian sisters.

All three ships are classed ✠ 100A1 ✠ LMC ✠ UMS and represent an impressive extension to the Barber fleet. Being among the largest of their type afloat, *Barber Tampa*, *Texas* and *Hector* well qualify for their 'Supercarrier' title. With their flexibility and efficiency these vessels will undoubtedly provide the Barber consortium with competitive trading well into the future.

Atlantic Container Line's third generation

In recent years the steam turbine engine has been in a process of decline, due to the rise in fuel costs and the economic advantages of the slow speed diesel. As a result, numerous owners with costly turbine vessels in their fleets, have been searching for alternatives and considering the pros and cons of either re-engining or replacement tonnage. When ACL were confronted with this problem, their first intention was to refit the

Atlantic Conveyor seen here immediately after launching at British Shipbuilders' Swan Hunter Shipbuilders Ltd. (*British Shipbuilders/Swan Hunter Shipbuilders*)

Atlantic Companion in the English Channel. Of the five ACL G3 class vessels she was one of the three built by Kockums of Malmo in Sweden. (*FotoFlite, Ashford*)

ACL's first generation. One of four sisterships, the *Atlantic Song* is seen here working cargo at Liverpool. It was with one of these G1 class vessels, *Atlantic Span*, that ACL first experimented with the use of on-deck cell guides in 1982. (*Atlantic Container Line*)

Messrs Trans Consultants AB. Three of the new ships were ordered from the Swedish Kockums of Malmö, one was ordered from the French Chantiers du Nord et de la Méditerranée of Dunkirk, and the fifth from Britain's Swan Hunter shipyard of Wallsend.

In many ways, these five G3 class vessels are very similar to the three Barber vessels, and one can thus be forgiven for drawing comparisons. Both types can effectively be termed Supercarriers, but the operational requirements of the two classes differ in a number of ways.

ACL's routes basically connect Europe with the USA. Much of the traffic on this route is containerised and the most economic manner of handling containers between geared ports is to use the cellular concept. As such, to transport containers still on trailers on the highly competitive North Atlantic routes would not be

ACL's second generation G2 ro-ro container ship *Atlantic Champagne*. It was from a proposal to re-engine these steam turbine vessels with diesel engines that the G3 concept eventually developed. (*Atlantic Container Line*)

ACL's *Atlantic Companion*, first of the G3s to enter service. The massive stern ramp and aft superstructure/garage block gives these ships an individuality not yet mirrored by any other type. She is seen here entering New York, one of ACL's regular ports of call. (*Flying Camera Inc/ACL*)

G2 class ships with diesel engines. However, as planning progressed, it soon became clear that the best answer was to build anew. Twenty different designs were scrutinised, and by mid-1982 the consortium had decided on the basic design for the new G3 class. This embodied many of the innovatory concepts first used in the *Boogabilia* ro-ro vessel from the design stable of the Swedish naval architects

(Diagrams not to scale)

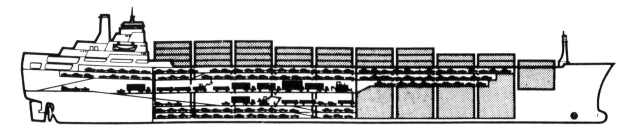

Atlantic Saga, Service, Song, & Star

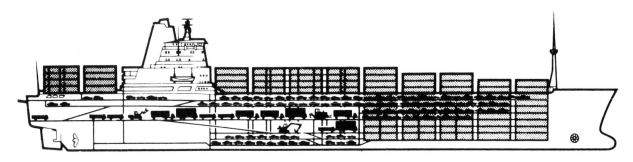

Atlantic Causeway, Champagne, Cognac, Crown & Cinderella

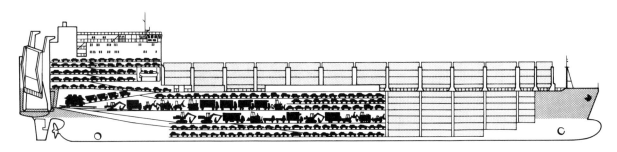

Atlantic Companion, Concert, Compass, Cartier & Conveyor

These sectional views of the three generations of ACL fleet show the gradual expansion in the size of the ships. These diagrams are not to scale, but still show fairly clearly that the G3 vessels are nearly twice the size and have twice the capacity of the earlier ships. (*Drawing: Atlantic Container Line*)

the most effective form of business for ACL to adopt, and thus, unlike the Barber ships, the new G3 vessels have neither crane nor ro-ro access to the upper-deck, all upper-deck space being allocated to containers handled by shoreside gantry equipment. In addition, the G3 class are fitted with hatches to permit gantry-loading of containers to the decks below, and this ability coupled to the use of full cellular guides both above and below decks is perhaps the G3's most significant aspect.

These cell guides offer considerable advantages in that loading and unloading operations are speeded up, and allow containers to be loaded four high without weight restrictions. The cell guides are similar to those fitted on ACL's G1 vessel *Atlantic Span* in 1982, but a major innovation of the G3's system is their ability to be used in conjunction with deck hatches, whereas previously cell guides would only be used above ro-ro spaces. The cell guides above and below deck are vertically aligned and a hydraulically operated section at the hatch level is hinged out to provide clearance for the movement of the side-rolling hatch covers. By use of the deck cell guide system synchronised with hold guides, the need for complicated and time consuming lashing systems and the positioning of stacking cones between containers has been dispensed with entirely. This new system allows easier sequencing of containers

The massive MacGregor Navire three-quarter starboard stern ramp is intrinsic to the vessel, needing no special port facilities such as link-spans in order to work the cargo. It is the most distinctive physical feature of this unusual ship type. (*Atlantic Container Line*)

and fewer problems at ports where complex loading and discharge patterns occur, in addition to providing less labour-intensive cargo handling and consequently greater safety both in port and at sea.

A total capacity exists for up to 2,139 TEUs (150 of which can be reefer units) and 614 cars simultaneously. Ordinarily however, only about 1,500 TEU containers will be carried, all of these gantry-loaded, with the remaining spaces aboard being used for ro-ro goods. The ro-ro spaces can be divided into two types,

basically 'car' decks or 'trailer' decks. The 4.5 metre high trailer decks are used for a variety of cargoes, with a surprisingly small proportion of space actually being used for road trailers.

Much of the cargo on these decks consists of block-stowed goods, heavy-lift items on terminal trailers, and all forms of wheeled traffic. The two trailer decks also house hoistable car decks, these being deemed necessary in addition to the three car decks in the hull and the five car decks in the aft superstructure block.

For ro-ro traffic a maximum all up weight of 420 tonnes can be accommodated. The loading deck has a threshold width of 25.5 metres, although maximum cargo width is limited to 12.5 metres by the clear lane width of the starboard quarter stern ramp.

The complete superstructure block aft is effectively a development of the superstructure of the purpose-built car carrier, bearing marked similarities to the inside of a multi-storey car park. Above the car spaces, is the accommodation for the crew of 18 who are well catered for with a restaurant, bar, library, TV/video room, a gymnasium (which is also equipped with a projection room for use as a cinema) and a fully heated swimming pool with adjoining sauna.

Although the five new G3s are almost twice the size of the earlier ACL ships, their real triumph in commercial terms is however the economy of their

This diagram of ACL's new G3 type shows the cell guide container loading arrangements and is indicative of the variety of ro-ro cargoes typically carried on the North Atlantic routes.

operation. Even though large vessels such as these have enormous propulsion requirements and heavy power demands for lighting and ventilation etc (the extractor fans to remove exhaust fumes from the ro-ro decks, for example, alone requiring 1,000 kW!), the use of efficient hull design and machinery installations has reduced operating costs per ton carried by a substantial degree.

The main propulsion machinery consists of a single six-cylinder turbo-charged Gotaverken-B&W 6L90GBE developing an mcr of 17,500 kW (23,800 bhp) at 97 rpm, coupled to a five-bladed propeller. In service this is reduced by 15 per cent to an ncr output of 15,750 kW (21,330 bhp), giving a service speed of 18 knots at design draught and accounting for a fuel consumption figure of between 60 and 70 tonnes per day. Maximum deadweight is 36,500 tonnes with a design deadweight of 28,736 tonnes. Based on these figures, fuel consumption can be estimated at around 50.3 gftm or 75.7 gfcm giving the ACL ships a slightly better efficiency figure than the Barber Blue Sea vessels. However, the differences in both their trades and service speeds does not make such a comparison particularly significant, as both types are highly efficient designs if compared to earlier steam turbines operating the equivalent routes.

Another economy incorporated in the ACL vessels is the use of both bow and stern thrusters, reducing the dependence on tugs during docking operations. A 1,500 kW 20 tonnes thrust unit is fitted forward, with a 1,900 kW, 25 tonnes thrust unit aft. Both thrusters are driven by electric motor and are fitted with variable pitch propellers. Naturally, with the requirement for

Atlantic Companion enters Liverpool, England. Although the funnel is mounted to the starboard side on both the ACL and BBS vessels, the engine is mounted centrally. Directly beneath the main entry-deck upward interdeck fixed ramp on both types. (*Atlantic Container Line*)

considerable electrical supply the ship's auxiliary machinery is quite extensive. Two Wärtsilä-Vasa 8R32 and two Wärtsilä-Vasa 6R32 diesels, driving NEBB alternators each developing 2,310 kW and 1,722 kW respectively, give a total power supply availability of 8.06 mW. Further economies are achieved by *all* the ship's machinery being designed to

Profile view of Barber Blue Seas' *Barber Hector.* (*Drawing: Michael J Ambrose*)

Barber Blue Sea

BARBER HECTOR

Profile of the ACL G3 class *Atlantic Conveyor,* **showing clearly how the upper deck cell guides lend themselves well to the aviation support ship role for which this ship was partially subsidised by the British Government. The flight** deck, laid directly on top of the containers, is a derivation of Fairey Engineering's Medium Girder Bridge. (*Drawing: Michael J Ambrose*)

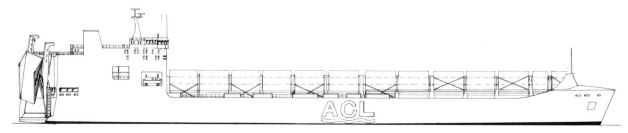

ACL

PRINCIPAL PARTICULARS OF THE SUPERCARRIERS

The Barber Trio

Hull	Name	Flag	Completed	Owner/Operator	Builder
H248	*Barber Tampa*	Nor	Early 84	Barber Lines/BBS	Hyundai HI
H249	*Barber Texas*	Nor	Early 84	Barber Lines/BBS	Hyundai HI
H250	*Barber Hector*	UK	Early 84	Blue Funnel Line/BBS	Hyundai HI

Dimensions: 262 m (oa) × 246.40 m (bp) × 32.26 m beam (Panamax) × 21 m depth × 47 m height
× 9.75 m (design)/11.7 m (scantling) draught
Capacities: 44,000 (scantling)/30,400 (design) deadweight; 25,000 grt; 2,464 TEU
Range: 40,000 nautical miles
Service speed: 19.5 knots

The ACL Quintet

Hull	Name	Flag	Completed	Owner/Operator	Builder
593	*Atlantic Companion*	Swed	5/3/84	SAL/Transatlantic	Kockums
594	*Atlantic Concert*	Swed	25/5/84	Wallenius Lines	Kockums
595	*Atlantic Compass*	Swed	21/9/84	Swedish America Line	Kockums
321	*Atlantic Cartier*	French	Due July 84	CGM	Chantiers du Nord
121	*Atlantic Conveyor*	UK	Due Dec 84	Cunard	Swan Hunter

Dimensions: 250 m (oa) × 233.6 m (bp) × 32.26 m beam (Panamax) × 20.24 m depth × 9.75 m (design)/
10.88 m (scantling) draught
Capacities: 36,500 (scantling)/28,736 (design) deadweight; 25,362 grt; 2,139 TEU
Range: 17,280 nautical miles (40 days)
Service speed: 18 knots

The MacGregor-Navire 'Stackcell' on-deck guide system as fitted to ACL's G3 class vessels. (*MacGregor-Navire*)

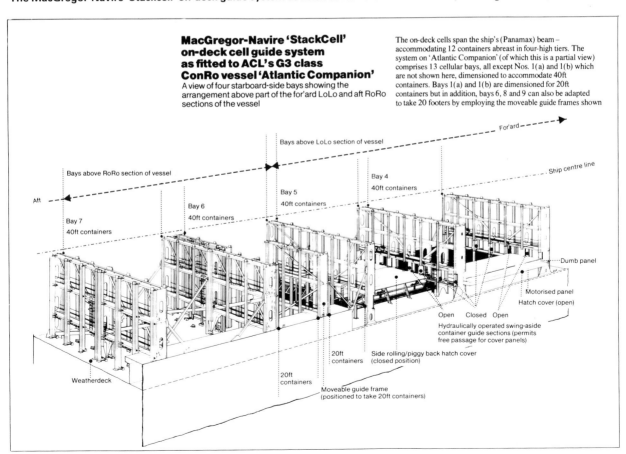

MacGregor-Navire 'StackCell' on-deck cell guide system as fitted to ACL's G3 class ConRo vessel 'Atlantic Companion'
A view of four starboard-side bays showing the arrangement above part of the for'ard LoLo and aft RoRo sections of the vessel

The on-deck cells span the ship's (Panamax) beam – accommodating 12 containers abreast in four-high tiers. The system on 'Atlantic Companion' (of which this is a partial view) comprises 13 cellular bays, all except Nos. 1(a) and 1(b) which are not shown here, dimensioned to accommodate 40ft containers. Bays 1(a) and 1(b) are dimensioned for 20ft containers but in addition, bays 6, 8 and 9 can also be adapted to take 20 footers by employing the moveable guide frames shown

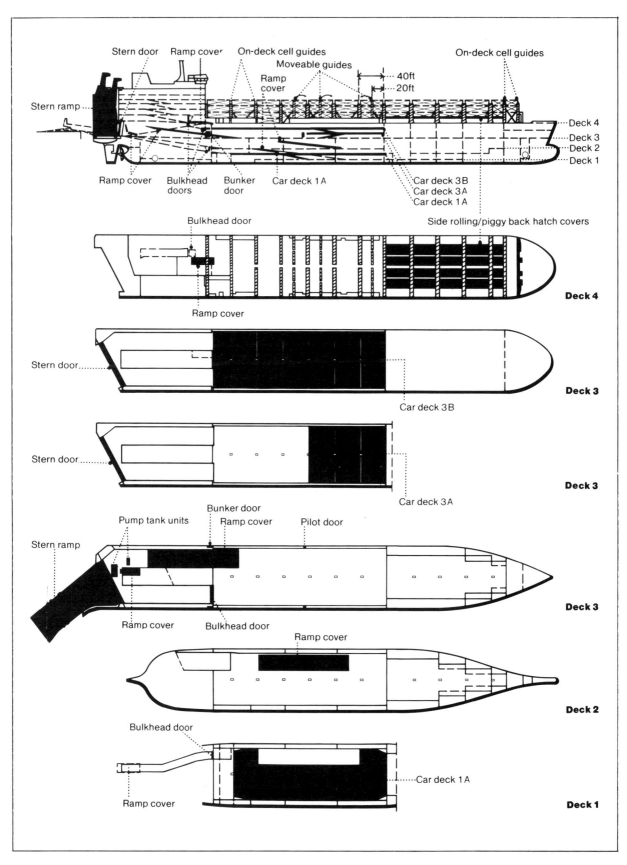

Internal deck and ramp arrangement of the ACL G3 class. (*MacGregor-Navire*)

burn a very low grade of fuel of up to 600 cSt at 40 degrees, thus avoiding costly multiple fuel installations as well.

ACL's trading on the North Atlantic routes consists of regular weekly sailings to and from New York, Baltimore, Portsmouth/Virginia, Halifax/Canada, and Gothenburg, Bremerhaven, Rotterdam, Antwerp, Le Havre, and Liverpool, with various feeder and pick-up services throughout Europe and North America. The consortium consists of Compagnie Générale Maritime (CGM) of France (22.2 per cent), Cunard of Great Britain (22.2 per cent), Wallenius Lines of Sweden (22.2 per cent), Swedish American Line (17.2 per cent), The Transatlantic Shipping Co of Sweden (11.2 per cent), and Incotrans-Intercontinental Transport (ICT) of the Netherlands (5 per cent).

The combined cost of ACL's five new ships was around $300 million, with the three Swedish vessels *Atlantic Companion*, *Atlantic Concert* and *Atlantic Compass* costing 1.3 billion Swedish Kroner or around £43 million each ship. This compares favourably with the cost of Cunard's vessel, the famous *Atlantic Conveyor* replacement, reported to have cost £45 million, although this figure includes a degree of subsidy from the British government for military features included in the ship's construction. These military features will allow the new *Atlantic Conveyor* to be rapidly converted into an aviation support ship in times of mounting tension, allowing her to operate Sea King ASW helicopters and Sea Harrier aircraft, as detailed in the previous edition of this Review.

Originally, Cunard had intended to order their vessel from a South Korean builder, as was the case with the Barber consortium. This would have reduced the cost of the ship to around £35 million. However, with the loss of the first *Atlantic Conveyor* during the Falklands conflict, and the fact that all of the other four G3s, including the French *Atlantic Cartier*, were to be built domestically with some form of incentive subsidy from their respective governments, the British government was eventually forced to intervene to secure the work for British Shipbuilders. Coupled to local problems at the shipyard, the British vessel's completion was consequently delayed somewhat.

The French vessel also suffered from late delivery, following a fire in the ships' accommodation block while she was being fitted out. This exacerbated earlier delays caused by industrial (in)action at the shipyard which effectively delayed her launch by two months. Nevertheless, when the five ships finally appeared, they were able to offer considerable advantages and economies over the earlier vessels, and are destined to help secure ACL's future in the North Atlantic trades well into this new age: the age of the Supercarrier.

Arctic Navigation

by Graham Stallard and David Thorne

Introduction

It is a fact of physics that at −2°C salt water begins to freeze, and as temperatures drop the sea turns from a pliable transportation medium to a barrier with a consistency akin to armour plate! It is a fact of geography that the Arctic Ocean has a number of strategic characteristics similar to those of the Mediterranean – it faces major continents, offers short and direct routes between these continents, and has few exits to other oceans. From a climatological point of view these two bodies of water could not be more different. In contrast to the benign Mediterranean the greater part of the Arctic Ocean is covered with pack ice throughout the year. Coastal areas are ice free in summer, usually for no more than two months. For the remainder of the year ice close to the coast is from one to two metres thick. First year ice rarely exceeds 2½ metres in thickness, but multi-year ice can be much thicker, and stronger.

Latitude 75°N runs just off of the Soviet Arctic coast, and the only significant land masses that it

The Arctic.

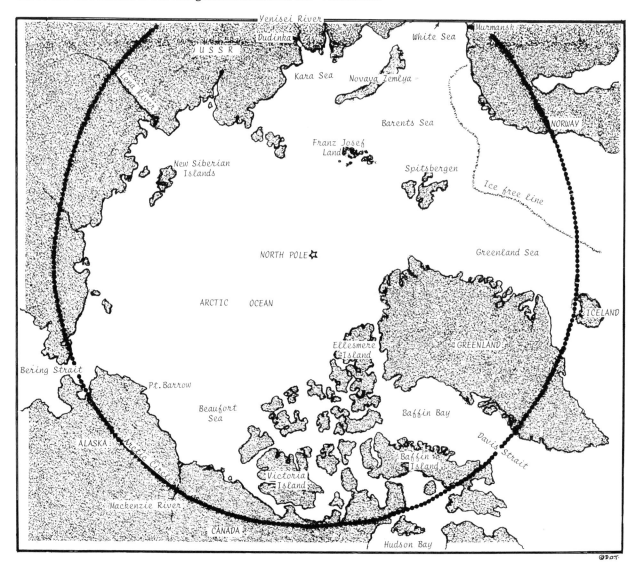

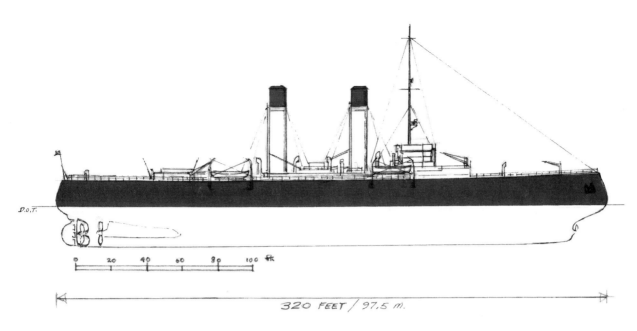

D.o.T.

0   20   40   60   80   100   ft.

320 FEET / 97.5 m.

(All drawings by David Thorne)

Yermak was the prototype of the modern icebreaker. She was built in 1898 by Armstrong's Elswick shipyard and lasted until 1965.

crosses are Greenland and Novaya Zemlya. At this latitude the world is approximately 9,000 km in circumference. The Soviet shoreline accounts for 45 per cent of this distance. By contrast the US Alaskan coast covers only 12 per cent. Both of these coastlines are simple in structure, and are exposed to the Arctic ice pack. The Canadian High Arctic accounts for 25 per cent of the circumference at latitude 75°N, and is a tortuous mass of islands, sounds and bays. The Norwegian Arctic shoreline is short, and virtually ice free. Greenland can physically be considered with the Canadian component.

Explorers have long been intrigued by Arctic 'short cuts' to the Pacific. The North-West Passage around North America was sought in the 16th Century, but had only been achieved half a dozen times by the mid-1960s. Czarist Russia was painfully aware of the strategic significance of the Northern Sea Route, but the first merchant ship convoy did not pass from the Atlantic to the Pacific until 1934, with the first warships following a year afterwards. Transportation over shorter distances has been far more common, with the summer supplying of military and scientific outposts being the most common activity. However the Soviet Union has long had a pressing need to develop the important resources of Siberia, and was the first to devote considerable attention to the need for a large-scale Arctic marine transportation system.

Icebreaker development
All vessels have some degree of icebreaking capability, but it is normally very limited. Merchant ships

designed to trade into ice prone waters are often ice strengthened, but they usually require the assistance of a specialised icebreaker at some point during their voyage. This may only be to enter harbour, or it could be for virtually the whole journey. Until recently icebreaking capability was only provided in specialised vessels with a unique role and distinctive characteristics. In some respects they are akin to tugs, but are usually much bigger. Their role has similarities to that of a naval escort, but with a few exceptions icebreakers are civilian manned and operated. Yet as with naval vessels it is customary to consider their size in terms of displacement tonnage.

The first vessel intended for icebreaking was put to work in Hamburg Harbour in 1871. The problems of providing a winter ferry service to ice-bound Prince Edward Island led to the construction of two special vessels. Despite making better progress through ice while going astern the first ship was not a success! The second, the *Stanley* introduced the concept of riding up on the ice and crushing it, and worked quite well. However, the near optimum combination of strength, weight and power came together in 1898 when W. G. Armstrong's Elswick shipyard completed the Russian icebreaker *Yermak*. This most significant vessel had a displacement of 8,000 tons and measured 97.5 m × 21.8 m × 7.6 m. She had three sets of triple expansion machinery driving three propellers aft, and one forward. The total power output was 9,500 ihp. The original *Yermak* was as wide and powerful as most contemporary battleships, but was shorter and lighter. She was also to prove remarkably durable, lasting for a total of 67 years.

It was even more remarkable that the *Yermak* could not really be regarded as obsolescent until the final decade of her lengthy career. Her size was not exceeded to a significant extent until the late 1950s, and her power had been greatly exceeded only once by then. Steam reciprocating machinery had proven to be particularly suited to the demanding conditions facing an icebreaker, providing high torque at low revolutions. Such machinery was being installed in new vessels as late as 1959, when the Canadian light icebreaker *Wolfe* was commissioned with Skinner 'Uniflow' engines (the latter have remained in production for static use, but are once again being installed in ships for Third World countries with cheap labour and adequate coal supplies).

Only recently has technology enabled direct-drive diesel machinery to be a practical form of icebreaker propulsion. However the use of diesels to generate power for electric motors was introduced in 1932 in the Swedish icebreaker *Ymer*. Diesel-electric machinery has since become dominant, but it was not until the mid-1950s that a significant increase in power was achieved. The American vessel *Glacier* was introduced in 1955, with a power plant of 21,000 shp.

Operating economics have virtually ruled out the steam turbine where diesels are practicable. The only conventionally-fired turbo-electric icebreaker, the Canadian *Louis S. St. Laurent* is regarded as very uneconomic, and plans are afoot to re-engine her with direct-drive diesel machinery (three Sulzers totalling 22,500 shp, replacing a turbo-electric plant of 24,000 shp). Turbo-electric machinery was featured in a number of design studies for large vessels, as there was a practical limit to diesel-electric machinery of approximately 45,000 shp. However recent advances have considerably raised this figure, and thus turbo-electric power plants are unlikely to go to sea, except when mated to a nuclear reactor!

Nuclear-fired steam turbines first moved a ship, the American submarine *Nautilus*, in 1954. Four years later this remarkable vessel made an historic trans-

Polar voyage under the Arctic ice. One assumes that such naval activity is now common place. Civilian use of nuclear submarines in the Arctic has long been advocated, and is probably technically feasible. However the capital cost is formidable, and steady improvements in icebreaking technology and economics are likely to render such spectacular concepts uncompetitive for the foreseeable future.

In 1959 the Russians completed a vessel that has proven to be just as revolutionary as USS *Nautilus*. The icebreaker *Lenin* was the first nuclear-powered surface ship in the world. She has a standard displacement of 15,940 tons (19,240 tons full load), and measures 124 m × 26.8 m × 10.5 m. Not only was she significantly larger than her predecessors, but at 44,000 shp she was twice as powerful as *Glacier* and four times as powerful as the average large icebreaker. She was the first vessel solely intended for Polar use, and her great endurance and power marked a turning point in the development of Arctic shipping. In her early years she was highly experimental, and she was to undergo protracted reconstruction between 1966 and 1972. However she paved the way for the very impressive 'second generation' vessels of the 1970s and 1980s, has been invaluable for operational research and training, and has proven to be a very capable icebreaker in her own right.

Enter Wärtsilä

By the late 1950s the large Soviet icebreaker fleet (25 vessels) was ageing rapidly, more vessels were needed in addition to replacements, and Soviet shipyards were preoccupied with the naval expansion programme. Most of the new icebreakers would have to come from abroad, but relatively few yards were experienced in building these specialised vessels. The first new Soviet icebreakers were intended for Baltic operations, and Wärtsilä had just completed the *Voima*, which the Soviets considered to be a satisfactory design. An order was therefore placed for three sister ships – the 'Kapitan Belousov' class, completed between 1955 and 1957. This order was the start of Wärtsilä's specialisation in icebreaker design, development and

Lenin **was the world's first nuclear-powered surface vessel. This impressive ship has served as a research and training unit for the second generation nuclear powered vessels, and is a very capable icebreaker in her own right.**

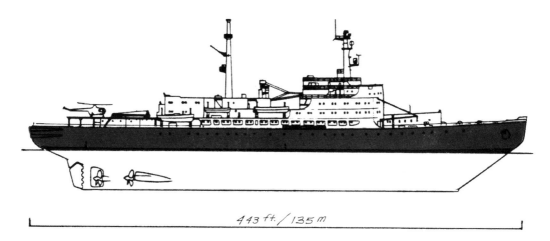

443 ft. / 135 m

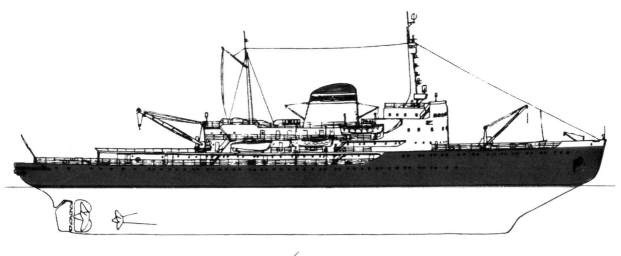

122.1 m/400.5 ft.

construction. Three decades later half of the world's icebreaking vessels are Wärtsilä-built, and most of the remainder have benefitted from Wärtsilä's concepts, equipment and/or consulting services.

While primarily intended for Baltic use the 'Kapitan Belousov' class have been used for limited operations in the Arctic. Apart from their restricted power the main drawback is that the bow propellers that are so useful in the Baltic, are very prone to damage in the heavier ice of the Arctic. A class of large vessels solely intended for Arctic operations was soon laid down. *Moskva* was completed in 1960, and four more were to be completed by 1969. Standard displacement is 13,290 tons, and these large and powerful vessels measure 122.2 m × 24.5 m × 10.5 m. The first three have diesel-electric machinery of 22,000 shp, but the last two have an output of 26,000 shp.

Up until the late 1960s icebreaker design was a pragmatic, 'trial and error' process. The results were remarkably good, but Wärtsilä felt that there was a lot to be gained from a scientific approach, and opened a research facility that was centred around an ice testing tank. This proved to be a very well timed initiative. The 1970s were to see a great increase in interest in Arctic development. On-shore resource development required efficient transportation. Off-shore development would need entirely new ice-capable vessels and structures, and rising fuel costs provided an incentive to 'improve and breed' that not even government agencies could afford to ignore.

The first vessel to benefit from the work of the research facility was the Baltic icebreaker *Urho*. A revised hull form, and twin rudders for better manoeuvrability were not immediately apparent to a casual observer. However, the relocation of all accommodation from the hull in a 'block' super-structure (in order to reduce the shocks, noise and vibrations of icebreaking operations) was quite noticeable and established a new 'fashion' in icebreaker design.

The five vessels of the 'Moskva' class, built by Wärtsilä in the 1960s, were the world's first purpose-built Arctic icebreakers.

The list of new concepts, inventions, improvements and refinements that have emerged from the Wärtsilä research facility is lengthy and impressive. It includes new hull forms adapted to specialised types of operation, hull coatings to reduce friction, and the Wärtsilä Air Bubbling System. This generates a 'curtain' of compressed air bubbles along the hull to reduce friction with adjacent ice. This system has been adopted by most ice-going ships around the world in recent years. There have been a number of other research facilities opened since 1969, and the overall result is steady improvement of the efficiency and operating economics of icebreaking.

Wärtsilä applied the Air Bubbling System to the next class of Arctic icebreaker. The initial ship was named *Yermak* in honour of the 'grand-daddy' of modern icebreakers, but she is a very impressive vessel in her own right. The three vessels of this class were completed between 1974 and 1976. Displacement is 20,241 tons and they measure 135 m × 26 m × 11 m. The shaft output of 36,000 shp is by far the greatest for diesel-electric machinery to date.

The 'Moskva' and 'Yermak' classes are very capable of keeping the main channels open, but their considerable draught makes them unsuitable for clearing the shallow mouths of the major Siberian rivers. Four special vessels have been built to keep these important waterways open. A pair was completed in 1977 and 1978, the lead-ship being *Kapitan Sorokin*. A slightly modified pair emerged in 1980 and 1981. They are as long and as wide as the 'Yermak' class (131.9 m × 26.5 m), but have a draught of only 8.5 m. The power rating of 22,000 shp matches that of the early 'Moskva' class vessels.

Creating a transportation system into the heart of Siberia posed more problems. In some respects the

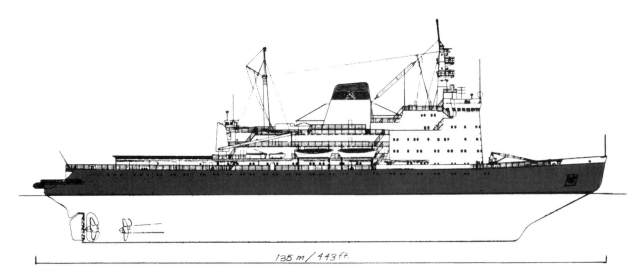

The three-ship 'Yermak' class of the early 1970s are the world's most powerful diesel-electric icebreakers. They were built by Wärtsilä for the main channel operations on the Soviet Union's Northern Sea Route.

'Yermak' class icebreaker *Krasin*. (*Wärtsilä*)

rivers were the most difficult challenge. To keep these waterways open most of the year small, manoeuvrable vessels were essential. The climate is severe and the ice can be formidable. 'Big is beautiful' as far as icebreakers are concerned, yet these important vessels would have to be quite small. The six vessels of the 'Kapitan Chechkin' class were completed in 1977 and 1978. They displace only 2,240 tons, and measure 77.6 m × 16.3 m × 3.25 m. The diesel-electric machinery is rated at 4,490 shp. A new class was

Kapitan Nikolayev of the 'Kapitan Sorokin' class was the first of four similar vessels built by Wärtsilä in the late 1970s for operation in the shallow approaches to the major Siberian rivers. The accommodation block superstructure and rather 'stiff' appearance are very apparent.

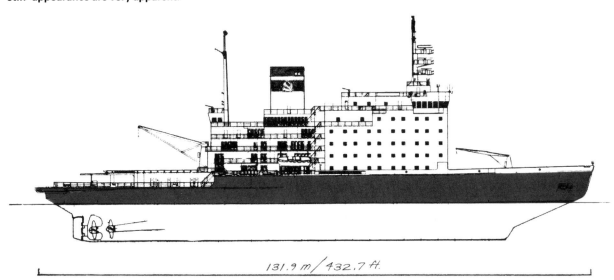

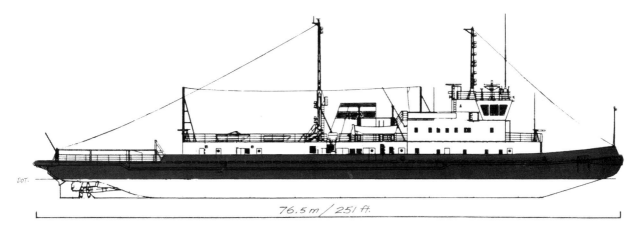

76.5 m / 251 ft.

Below: Shallow-draught Arctic icebreaker *Kapitan Dranitsyn* of the modified 'Kapitan Sorokin' class. (*Wärtsilä*)

Above: Wärtsilä has built 14 small, powerful icebreakers for operations on the Siberian rivers. There are two different designs, *Kapitan Yevdokimov* being the lead-ship of the most recent class. In addition to coping with extreme cold, heavy ice and constricted waters, these vessels need folding masts to pass under bridges.

ordered in 1980. The first of eight, the *Kapitan Yevdokimov* was completed in 1983, and all will be delivered by late 1984. They are marginally smaller than the previous class, but are more powerful. Their draught has been considerably reduced. (Displacement of 2,150 tons. Dimensions: 76.5 m × 16.6 m × 2.5 m. Power: 5,170 shp.)

Mention should be made of a new class of three vessels – the lead ship being the *Mudyug*, that are intended partially for operations in the Barents Sea, at

Below: Siberian river icebreaker *Kapitan Yevdokimov*. (*Wärtsilä*)

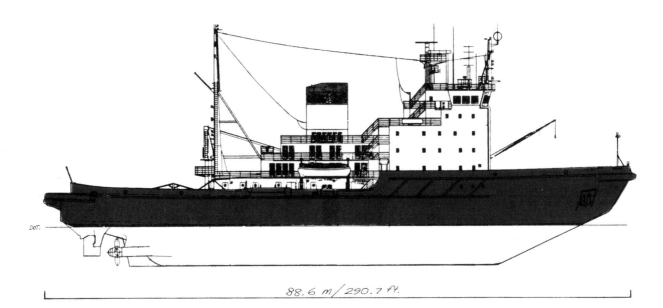

_88.6 m / 290.7 ft._

Mudyug is a sub-Arctic, multi-purpose icebreaker, intended to operate in the Barents Sea at the western end of the Soviet's Northern Sea Route. This vessel and two sister ships, are Wärtsilä's first use of direct-drive diesel machinery.

the western end of the Northern Sea Route. They can function as tugs, and salvage vessels. Their displacement is only 5,560 tons, but they are technically interesting in that they are Wärtsilä's first icebreakers to use diesel-mechanical machinery, as opposed to diesel-electric. The power output is 12,400 shp.

The Second Generation nuclears
In 1972 the *Lenin* was recommissioned with a new powerplant. Later that year the first of a new class of nuclear-powered icebreaker, the *Arktika* was launched by the Baltic Shipyard, Leningrad. She became operational in 1975, and proved to be considerably larger and more powerful than the *Lenin*. Standard displacement is 19,300 tons (23,460 tons full load), and dimensions are 136 m × 28 m × 11 m. The power output is 75,000 shp – over double that of any other icebreaker except the *Lenin*, and an increase of 30,000 shp over that powerful vessel. *Arktika* has recently been renamed *Leonid Brezhnev*. *Sibir* was completed in late 1977, and while basically a sister ship of the *Arktika* the internal design was refined. A third vessel, the *Rossiya* was completed recently, and a fourth vessel has been laid down.

In August 1977 the *Arktika* gave a spectacular demonstration of her capabilities when she became the first surface vessel to reach the North Pole. This involved a round trip of 2,500 km beyond the normal operating area of the Northern Sea Route. Ice was encountered up to four metres thick, and much of it was tough 'multi-year' ice. There was a serious purpose to this voyage, as the power and endurance of the new

nuclear icebreakers offered a considerable saving in time and distance between the ends of the Northern Sea Route if it was possible to use 'Great Circle' routings through the pack ice. A less spectacular, but equally significant voyage was undertaken early in 1978, when *Sibir* escorted a freighter through the entire length of the Northern Sea Route two months before the normal icebreaking season began.

The early onset of ice in October 1983 would probably have been a disaster but for the work of the *Leonid Brezhnev* (ex-*Arktika*) and the *Sibir*. The sheer number of vessels trapped was an interesting indication of the current scale of marine activity along the Soviet Arctic coast. It is apparent that the Soviets are capable of greatly extending the navigation season all along their Arctic shoreline, and far up the Siberian rivers. Year-round operations may not be entirely feasible all the time, but closures will be so reduced that they will not significantly effect the flow of materials along this remarkable transportation system.

The Coast Guards
Arctic icebreaking is the responsibility of non-military agencies in the three major nations with interests in this challenging ocean. The Soviets established a special agency in 1932, and the Canadians and Americans have assigned the responsibility to their respective Coast Guards. However while the differences between the Soviet and North American systems are obvious, it should be noted that the term 'Coast Guard' covers some sharp differences in character and policies as well. Suffice it to say that while the US Coast Guard is a 'para-military' organisation, Canada Coast Guard is civilian in all respects.

All three nations have icebreaking responsibilities outside of the Arctic. The Russians have developed a large (29 vessels), specialised fleet solely intended for Arctic operations. There are at least as many vessels

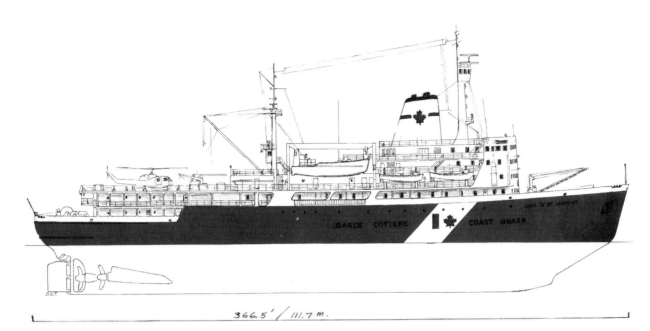

Above: The *Louis S. St Laurent* is Canada's most powerful icebreaker, and is the only one in the world with a conventionally fired turbo-electric powerplant. In restrospect this has proven to be an unfortunate choice, as the rise in fuel prices makes her a very costly vessel to operate.

Left: The Soviet nuclear-powered icebreaker *Sibir* led the freighter *Kapitan Myshevsky* through the Northern Sea Route two months before the 1978 navigation season was expected to begin. (*APN, courtesy of the Soviet Embassy*)

elsewhere (mainly in the Baltic) that could do useful work in the Arctic if the need arose. The US Coast Guard has 13 icebreakers, but it has responsibilities on the Great Lakes and the rivers, and it services the US base in Antarctica. Only five of its icebreakers are suitable for Arctic operations, and they are not deployed on a regular basis.

Canada, with its more severe climate and the important St. Lawrence Seaway has had a longer and more consistent commitment to icebreaking, and was prominent in early icebreaker development and operations. There are now 25 vessels in the Coast Guard fleet that are classified as icebreakers, but they vary greatly in design and capability. The seven 'light icebreakers' also serve as navigation tenders. There is a unique icebreaker/cable-ship, and the eight 'medium' and nine 'heavy' icebreakers are primarily intended to keep the St. Lawrence River open to navigation as long as possible, and for flood control near Montreal. Arctic operations have been secondary to other roles, and mainly developed in the 1950s to support DEW line radar outposts, scientific bases and native villages.

The Canadian vessels until recently could be described as a 'fleet of samples'. The largest and most powerful is the *Louis S. St. Laurent*, which was built in 1969. She is rated at 13,300 tons full load displace-

Above: Canadian Coast Guard icebreaker *John A. Macdonald.* (*Transport Canada*)

The *Sir John Franklin* entered service as *Franklin*. This photo, taken at Burrard Yarrows shipyard, North Vancouver in March 1978, reveals the hull form of a modern icebreaker. (*John Helcermanas*)

ment. As was noted earlier the machinery is a 24,000 shp turbo-electric plant, which with the rapid rise of fuel costs since she was built has left her a very costly unit to operate. She is a very capable vessel though, having reached a point 680 km from the North Pole in 1971. The *John A. Macdonald*, built in 1960, is in most respects a more useful vessel. Her displacement is 8,674 tons, and her machinery is diesel-electric rated at 15,000 shp.

Another icebreaker built in 1969, that has proven to be only a qualified success is the *Norman Macleod Rogers.* Her powerplant was a modest experiment in

Below: Polar Star is one of a pair of innovative US Coast Guard icebreakers that have powerful CODOG-electric machinery. After initial severe difficulties with the variable-pitch propellers the *Polars* have proven to be very capable and versatile vessels.

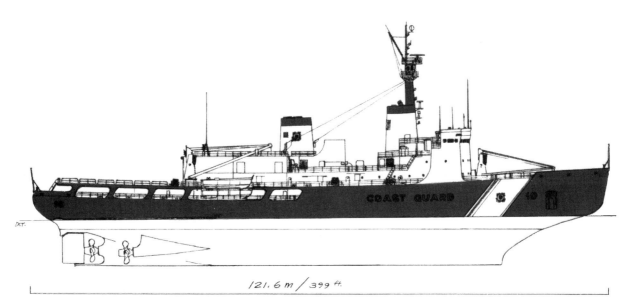

121.6 m / 399 ft.

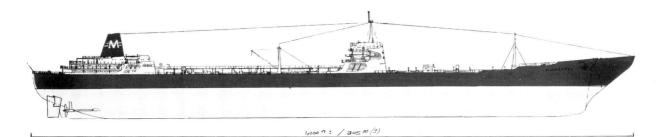

The US super-tanker *Manhattan* was extensively modified in the late 1960s as a trials ship for very large icebreaking merchant ships. The original bow is shown as a broken line. Although her pioneering voyages have not yet been followed up, she proved the concept of regular use of the North West Passage by such vessels.

CODAG machinery, with an output of only 13,200 shp. This has since been replaced by conventional diesel-electric machinery. The hull design however has served as the basis for the 'R' class vessels. This designation stands for 'river', and underlines the fact that Canada does not yet have a purpose-built Arctic vessel. The *Pierre Radisson* was the first of the new class, and she was commissioned in 1978. Displacement is 8,180 tons, and dimensions are 98.2 m × 19.5 m × 7.2 m. The diesel-electric machinery is rated at 13,600 shp. The *Sir John Franklin* was completed in 1979, and the *Des Groseillers* followed in 1982. One more vessel is under construction. As this class will be the mainstay of Canadian operations for some time to come, they will certainly have to undertake the majority of Canadian Arctic operations.

Canada Coast Guard has shown considerable interest in specialised Arctic vessels. Design studies have included a 40,000-ton nuclear-steam/gas turbine powered ship capable of steady progress through over three metres of ice. Nuclear propulsion has been ruled out, and attention turned to an only slightly less ambitious project. This was a 37,000-ton vessel, with CODOG machinery of 100,000 shp. It would have the capability of the Soviet 'Arktika' class, but not the endurance. The Coast Guard considered that year-round operations would be possible with two of these vessels, but they are not likely to be built in the near future.

During the Second World War the Americans built the seven icebreakers of the 'Wind' class. These proved to be excellent vessels, and two remain in Coast Guard service. Apart from the *Glacier* American icebreaker development lapsed until the late 1960s when a new class of six vessels was planned. In the event only two were built, and they have had more than their share of technical problems. The *Polar Star* was completed in 1976, and the *Polar Sea* followed in 1978. They have a 'split personality'! Most of the time they are quite similar to the 'Moskva' class in capability.

Displacement is only 10,863 tons (13,190 tons full load), and dimensions are 121.6 m × 25.5 m × 8.5 m. The diesel-electric powerplant is rated at 18,000 shp. However the engine room also contains three gas turbines capable of providing 60,000 shp when difficult conditions are encountered. With all engines operating these relatively modest vessels have a capability not far short of the 'Arktika' class. However because of the fuel consumption of the gas turbines endurance is limited. The *Polars* might be able to get to the North Pole, but they would run out of fuel on the way back!

This unique engine layout was not the cause of the vessels' technical problems. They were fitted with variable-pitch propellers that simply proved not to be strong enough for icebreaking operations. The ships propellers perform an important part of the process, chewing up the blocks of ice after the forepart of the ship has broken into the pack ice. If this were not done the ice would close-up behind the icebreaker much more quickly, and following ships would be damaged by the blocks of ice. The propellers function like the blades in a blender but under stresses similar to those of a steel rolling mill! Once the *Polars* propeller problems were solved they have become useful vessels with impressive capabilities.

Icebreaking merchant ships

In heavy ice conditions the icebreaker has usually been a specialised vessel that simply breaks a path for accompanying merchant ships. This is an over-simplification, but the icebreaker's primary purpose is to escort the merchant ships which carry the cargoes. The latter vessels will be ice-strengthened, but are not capable of independent operation in most of the Arctic for most of the year. However merchant ships with icebreaking capability have been in service elsewhere for many years. Ferries required for winter service in the Baltic, Atlantic Canada and the Great Lakes are quite capable icebreakers in their own right. Antarctic exploration requires vessels that are as much supply ships as they are icebreakers. As the demand for Arctic resources increased and shipping technology improved new breeds of icebreaking merchant ships were inevitable.

Oil was found on the North Slope of Alaska in great quantities in the late 1960s. However the primary market was in the Eastern United States, and none of the transportation alternatives were particularly attractive. It was decided to investigate a rather startling proposal – to ship it via icebreaking super-tankers through the North West Passage, and down the east coast to the refineries. The only way to test this bold concept was with a bold experiment. It was decided to convert the tanker *Manhattan* into an icebreaker, and send her through the North West Passage.

Manhattan was one of the first super-tankers, and was relatively over-built, of deep draught and had twin screws. The re-construction was quite extensive, and she emerged with a full load displacement of 155,000 tons, and with dimensions of 306.4 m × 47.2 m × 15.8 m. The steam turbine machinery was rated at 44,000 shp. Two voyages were made, one in the summer of 1969, and the other in the winter of 1970. Although she required the assistance of Coast Guard icebreakers (both American and Canadian) it was concluded that a purpose-built vessel could operate on a regular basis. In the event it was decided to build the Trans-Alaska Pipeline, and ship the oil in conventional tankers to US Pacific coast ports. However, an important lesson had been learned.

Two mines have been opened in the Canadian High Arctic in recent years. While these are operated all year round, ore is shipped only in the summer months. A consortium was formed to operate an icebreaking bulk carrier to serve the mines. The *Arctic* was completed in 1978, has a deadweight tonnage of 28,000, and dimensions of 209.5 m × 22.9 m × 10.9 m.

Canmar Kigoriak is an innovative and powerful OSV built for Canadian Marine Drilling (a subsidiary of Dome Petroleum). She serves as a support ship for Beaufort Sea oil exploration, and has pioneered a number of features that may be used in future icebreaking merchant ships. These include direct diesel drive, the 'spoon' bow, and a single shrouded propeller.

The direct-drive diesel machinery produces 14,770 bhp. Her icebreaking capability is limited, being able to steadily cut through less than a metre of ice. She has recently been reinforced, and there are plans to give her an improved bow in the near future.

The Alaskan oil discoveries encouraged extensive exploration in the Canadian High Arctic. Limited oil supplies have been found, but there are very large resources of natural gas. As these are too dispersed and of insufficient quantity to justify a pipeline there has been much interest in building icebreaking LNG tankers. Detailed designs had been prepared, but the recession suggests that we shall see such vessels later rather than sooner.

It is difficult enough in the High Arctic to reach on-shore resources, but off-shore resource potential is a real challenge! The Alaskan oil discoveries suggested that in addition to the possibility of oil in large quantities in the Sverdrup Peninsula and the Mackenzie Delta, the Beaufort Sea was worth investigating. The explorations of Dome Petroleum and Gulf Oil are fascinating stories in themselves that have involved the best and most ingenious efforts of civil engineering and marine architecture.

The most interesting of a wide variety of vessels specially built for work in the Beaufort Sea are a series of icebreaking off-shore support vessels. The *Canmar Kigoriak* was introduced by Dome in 1979. This relatively small vessel, for an icebreaker, (91.1 m × 17.3 m × 8.5 m) has a direct-drive diesel installation of 17,400 bhp. She is unusual in that there is only one propeller. Despite initial misgivings this has proven satisfactory. *Kigoriak* is capable of steady progress through ice a metre thick, and operates primarily as an anchor-handling tug. The *Robert LeMeur* is a similar vessel, intended as a supply ship. She was illustrated on p. 115 of the second edition of *Jane's Merchant Shipping Review*. This vessel is smaller than the

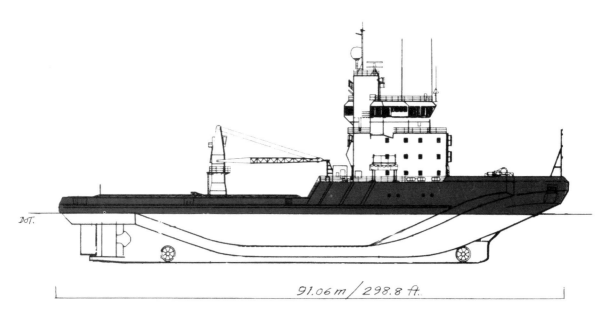

91.06 m / 298.8 ft.

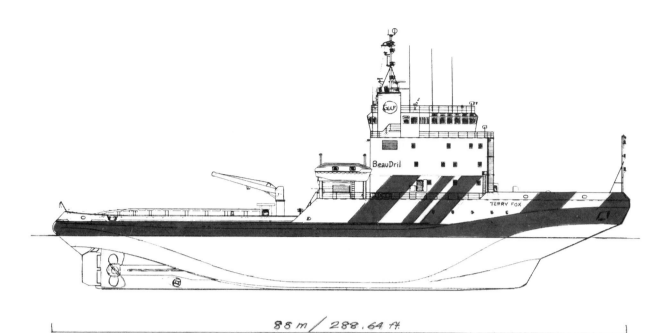

88 m / 288.64 ft

The *Terry Fox* and *Kalvik* are Canada's most capable ice-breakers. These anchor-handling tugs/supply ships support Gulf's Beaufort Sea oil exploration activities.

Kigoriak (82.5 m × 18 m × 5.7 m) and lower powered (9,800 bhp).

Gulf Oil is also very active in the Beaufort Sea, and its operations are supported by two pairs of multi-purpose icebreakers. The *Miscaroo* and *Ikaluk* have dimensions of 78.8 m × 17.2 m × 7.5 m, and the direct-drive diesel machinery is rated at 14,900 bhp. *Kalvik* and *Terry Fox* are slightly larger (88 m × 17.5 m × 8.0 m), and considerably more powerful (23,200 bhp). All four are used as anchor-handling tugs and supply ships, and can make steady progress through over a metre of ice.

All of the icebreaking OSVs have been designed in Canada, and are providing invaluable experience for large scale merchant ships that will be needed to exploit the resources of the High Arctic. They have proven the feasibility of direct-drive diesel machinery, and pioneered the use of a single shrouded propeller in the Arctic. A few months after entering service *Canmar Kigoriak* damaged her propeller, before a drydock had been moved north to support Dome's operations. The blades of this variable-pitch unit were designed for easy removal, and this was some consolation to the frogmen working below ice two metres thick. However, they were warmer than their colleagues on the surface, where temperatures ranged downwards from −40°C! These innovative vessels are Canadian-built, except the *Ikaluk* which was built by NKK of Japan. (It is interesting to note that Japan has icebreaker design experience, and that NKK recently completed the *Shirase* which is intended to support Japan's base in the Antarctic.)

When the Canadian government was reluctant to support the Coast Guard's proposal to build vessels capable of keeping the North West Passage open on a year-round basis, Dome appeared to be ready to build its own super-icebreaker. The proposed *Arctic Marine Locomotive* would have been a 45,000-ton, 150,000-shp vessel capable of ploughing through ice in excess of three metres in thickness. Near-fatal financial difficulties of the parent company ensured that this

Gulf Oil's icebreaking OSV *Terry Fox*, named after a young, one legged, cancer victim who became a hero because of his attempt to run across Canada in order to raise funds for cancer research. (*B C Jennings*)

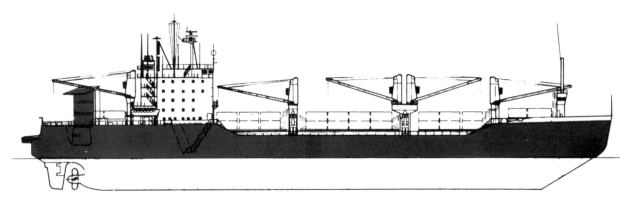

Norilsk was the first of 14 vessels of the SA-15 class, being built by Valmet and Wärtsilä for the Soviet Union. These multi-purpose cargo ships are capable of unassisted operation in ice one metre in thickness.

project would be shelved, but it is debatable as to how serious a proposal it was in the first place!

The Soviets have moved from reliance on ice-strengthened freighters escorted by specialised icebreakers in a rapid and comprehensive fashion. The route from Murmansk to Dudinka, at the mouth of the Yenisey River (1,600 km to the east) has become well established, and traffic has grown considerably. It was decided to acquire a series of multi-purpose cargo ships with the ability to operate independently to service this important route. Orders were placed for two designs of icebreaking merchant ships with Wärtsilä and Valmet of Finland. Initially six vessels were ordered from the former, and three from the latter. However, the contracts were soon adjusted to cover a single design – Wärtsilä's was selected. Subsequently three more vessels were ordered from Wärtsilä, and three more from Valmet, for a total of 14. The first, the *Norilsk* was completed in late 1982. This large class is rated at 16,500 grt, has dimensions of 174 m × 24.5 m × 10.5 m, and has direct-drive diesel machinery of 21,000 bhp. These vessels can operate in ice of one metre in thickness, and are now to be followed by a further five Mk II, SA-15 type, which were ordered this time from Valmet only, in August 1984.

As noted in the second edition of *Jane's Merchant Shipping Review* the latest Soviet development in ice-breaking merchant ships is nothing short of spectacular! The *Aleksey Kosygin* is a nuclear-powered barge carrier, with a displacement of 61,000 tons, a length of 260 m, and the ability to cut through ice a metre thick unassisted. If the 40,000 shp powerplant is not enough, a regular icebreaker can move in and give her a push!

Conclusion

In retrospect 1969 was a turning point in the development of Arctic shipping. Prior to that the navigation season was quite limited, icebreakers were modest in size and power, and techniques were simple and had changed little for decades. Pressure was growing to exploit the known on-shore resources, and to search for minerals and oil both on-shore and off-shore. It was time to apply new technology and old ingenuity.

Wärtsilä opened its research facility in 1969, and soon made dramatic changes to ship design. Other nations have followed this lead. The prototype nuclear icebreaker was receiving a new powerplant, and the first of a much larger and more powerful class of vessels had been laid down. Two classes of more conventional, but very powerful ships, the *Yermaks* and the *Polars* were being designed. The Alaskan oil discoveries led to the experimental voyages of the *Manhattan*, which confirmed that a large commercial vessel could use the North West Passage on a regular basis.

Since then there have been steady improvements in icebreaking technology and capability. The Soviets have developed a comprehensive Arctic marine transportation system, and the Canadians have successfully developed off-shore oil exploration techniques in one of the harshest environments on Earth. The recession diminished the demand for Arctic resources, and a number of impressive projects have been 'placed on the back-burner'. It is academic to wonder how serious and practical some of these studies were, but it is certain that the Arctic resources will be needed, and that the delay will mean that when the transportation systems are developed they will benefit from the improvements that are still taking place.

Apart from the mysterious naval activity under the ice, most shipping operations are conducted near the respective coasts. Therefore 'Super Power' tensions are minimal. However it is not hard to visualise the traditional icebreaker evolving into an armed naval escorts as indeed, Soviet icebreakers are an organic part of their Navy, commanded by ex-Navy officers in constant touch with naval authorities, and come under *direct* naval orders in emergency. It is more satisfying to conclude with a reminder that less than two decades ago only six vessels had made it through the North West Passage, often under conditions of extreme danger and hardship. Now, however, this formidable waterway is part of the regular cruising itinery of the luxury cruise ship *Lindblad Explorer*!

The Sailing of Statfjord 'C'

by A J Ambrose

The 'C' goes to sea. Five of the world's most capable ocean tugs haul the 775,000-tonne unit down Yrkes Fjord towards the open sea. (*Henk Honing/Wijsmuller*)

Wijsmuller's sophisticated anchor-handling tug *Typhoon*, and sister *Tempest*, were responsible for *pushing* the gravity-base structure to the mating site in Yrkes Fjord, then, for the final tow-out, took up wing positions outboard of the two Bugsier sisters. (*FotoFlite, Ashford*)

On 1 June 1984, one of the largest man-made structures ever to venture to sea proceeded under tow from Vats, in Yrkes Fjord just north of Stavanger, Norway, to its eventual destination in the Anglo-Norwegian Statfjord oil field, some 250 nautical miles to the north-west. This object was the massive 775,000 tonne oil and gas production platform *Statfjord 'C'*. Departing two months ahead of schedule and in the most advanced stage of construction of any such unit to date, she stood more than 250 metres high, measured over 114 metres long by 55 metres wide, and was valued at more than one thousand six hundred *million* US dollars.

Discovered in 1974 and situated stradling the boundary of the British and Norwegian economic zones in the northern half of the North Sea, the Statfjord oil field possesses recoverable reserves estimated to contain between 370 and 440 million

tonnes of oil and between 47 and 100 billion cubic metres of natural gas. When fully on stream in the late 1980s, its production will be approximately twice that of the next largest North Sea field (the UK's Forties field), and should provide as much as 30 million tonnes of oil per year using the three production platforms *Statfjord A*, *B* and *C* through to the year 2016. The Statfjord field, some 25 kilometres across and around 4,000 metres below the surface, is 84.09 per cent owned by Norway, 15.91 per cent by Britain, and is operated by the Mobil Oil group under the direction of Statoil, Norway's state oil corporation. Statfjord is the world's most prolific single offshore field proven and working to date.

Construction of the first Statfjord platform, the 648,000 tonne *Statfjord 'A'*, began soon after the field was proven in May 1974. *Statfjord 'A'* arrived on site in 1977 and commenced production in November 1979, achieving a daily production figure of around 300,000 barrels of oil, with a peak of 329,800 barrels per day.

In July 1981, the second platform departed for the Statfjord field, and by November 1982 had also commenced production. The *Statfjord 'B'* achieved

The platform being towed behind Wijsmuller's tug *Typhoon*. (*Courtesy Denzil Stuart Associates*)

thereafter an output of 180,000 barrels per day, and regularly exceeded this design requirement peaking up to 214,600 barrels per day, with only 16 of her 20 projected wells on stream.

The *Statfjord 'C'* scheme was launched in 1980 and is presently scheduled to commence production on 1 October 1985. It is expected however that production will actually start some time before this date, as the 'C' project has progressed particularly well.

The design of the *Statfjord 'C'* is similar in most respects to that of the earlier *Statfjord 'B'* platform. It follows the successful Norwegian *Condeep* principle of a two-piece structure, the bottom section or 'gravity-base unit' being constructed of concrete while the upper 'deck' section is of steel. Two main builders were used, these being Norwegian Contractors and Moss Rosenberg Verft respectively.

When these two sections were virtually complete, the 40,600 tonne steel deck section was floated out on two barges. Meanwhile, the 643,700 tonne gravity-base was floated out and ballasted right down until virtually submerged. The massive deck structure was then floated on, and when joined, the gravity-base was pumped out to lift the deck section to its normal operating height of 29 metres above sea level. The largest solid weight transfer accomplished to date was complete.

Better sea bed conditions on the site of the *Statfjord 'C'* platform had allowed the size of the platform's gravity base to be reduced a considerable amount from

The *Statfjord 'C'* at the inshore hook-up site north of Stavanger.

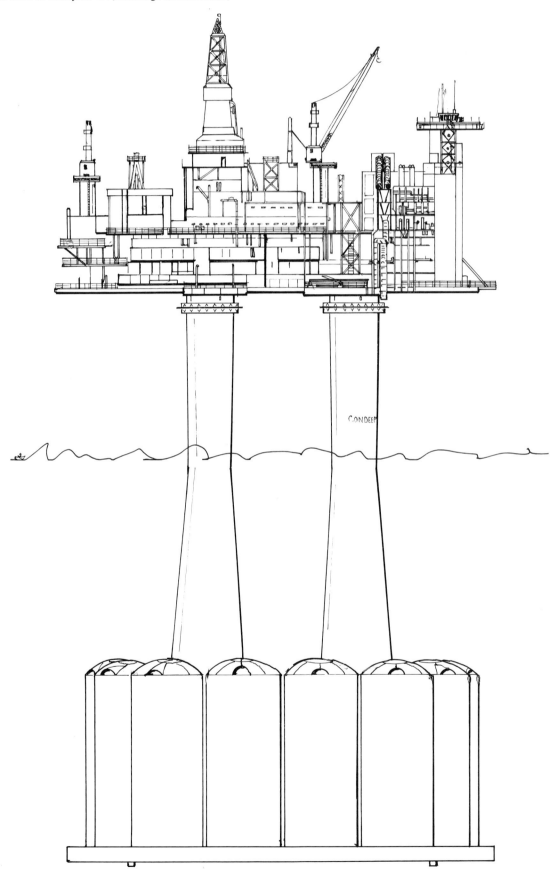

Statfjord 'C' in position. (*Courtesy Denzil Stuart Associates*)

that of the 'B' platform. Thus, the tow-out weight of *Statfjord 'C'* was less than the 824,000 tonnes of the 'B' platform, but at 775,000 tonnes all-up, the moving of *Statfjord 'C'* was still no easy task. Wijsmuller of the Netherlands and United Towing of the United Kingdom were to be the main towage contractors as was the case with the 'B' platform in 1981. Eight tugs were called up for the task, comprising a total bollard pull of 991 tonnes from a combined 77,160 brake horse-power. Five tugs were positioned forward: the West German *Artic* (2,046 grt, 12,800 bhp) and sister *Oceanic* (2,046 grt, 12,800 bhp), the Dutch 1984-built *Smit Singapore* (1,800 grt, 13,500 bhp) and Wijsmuller's *Typhoon* and sister *Tempest* (1,199 grt, 8,750 bhp). At the rear of the platform, three Anchor-Handling supply tugs were positioned, the *Frank Viking* (461 grt, 8,000 bhp), *Dag Viking* (929 grt, 8,040 bhp), and *Jon Viking* (929 grt, 7,040 bhp).

The Smit group's *Smit Singapore* took pole position for the tow, and was responsible for navigation over the 240 nautical mile journey. The *Oceanic* and *Arctic* positioned either side of *Smit Singapore* made up the other head positions, with *Typhoon* and *Tempest* outboard of them. The tows were connected to the platform 63 metres below the surface, with at the top of the caisons of the gravity-base Nylon Pennant wires connected to the deck of the platform.

Comprehensive detailed manuals were prepared for each tug covering every aspect of the tow. The state of the weather was vital. Wind speeds of more than 10–15 knots during the early stages of the tow would have forced a cancellation. A number of extra tugs and AH supply vessel tugs were on standby at this point, with a ninth tug connected during certain stages of the 38 mile tow down Yrkes Fjord to the open sea. This leg, which required a transit speed of no more than

one knot, was completed with the tugs on short wires to provide better control and manoeuvrability. When the open sea was reached nearly two days later, the five lead tugs lengthened their tows and increased towage speed to two knots for the next 150 miles. Meanwhile, the three Norwegian AH tugs had slipped their tows but remained on standby while the behemoth proceeded slowly North-north West, until the *Statfjord C* made its final approach to the field.

On arrival the tugs again changed position, with Wijsmuller's *Typhoon* and *Tempest* moving to the rear of the platform, while *Frank Viking* connected to the rig half way between the two to form a 'star' formation. Then began the delicate operation of ballasting the platform down to the seabed 149 metres below. Tolerances were minimal. The platform had to be positioned precisely, as already beneath the rig were pre-laid oil and gas flowlines which were to be connected to the platform through her leg caisons.

The operation was performed successfully. When in full service, *Statfjord 'C'* should be able to produce 210,000 barrels of oil per day. In addition, gas will be produced and pumped along the new 'Statpipe' gas line which will have a capacity for around four billion cubic metres and is anticipated to commence operation in January 1986. As for oil production, this will be shipped in tankers already operated by Statoil. Five tankers are presently in use, these serving both the Statfjord and Gullfaks field, but it is anticipated that this fleet will be increased in the immediate future as the *Statfjord 'C'* comes on line.

Statfjord 'C' is the last of the platforms for the Statfjord field, but is not the end of the story. Further north lies the *Troll* field, still south of the 62nd parallel and in *1,000 feet of water*. Development is due to start in 1989. To service wells more than 300 metres from the surface, which then extend down into the sub-strata some 5,000 feet will require some hefty platforms. Will the Troll field bring yet larger structures? It appears likely that it will.

The Reefer Trades in the mid-1980s

by Mats Enquist

To look into the future is not an easy task. Especially in the shipping business, and even more so in the refrigerated transport (or reefer) sector of the industry. This very specialised form of shipping possesses few, if any, easily readable trends on which to base long-term projections, as it is so often affected by sudden unforeseen and totally random events. Hurricanes, hailstorms, war situations, political decisions, oil price instability and drastic currency variations are all examples of factors which cause big and unexpected fluctuations in reefer shipping volumes. This forces the trade-flow of reefer goods to bend to new forms and directions, sometimes quite suddenly, and although some of these effects are only temporary, they can often cause long-lasting and even permanent changes in the nature of the business.

No doubt, such variations will continue to occur.

Building at Belfast's Harland and Wolff yard in 1984, are a quartet of reefers for Blue Star. Of 10,500 tonnes deadweight, they have a capacity of 13,110 cubic metres (463,000 cubic feet), a speed of 18 knots, and can maintain cargoes at temperatures as low as −23 degrees centigrade. (*Harland and Wolff*)

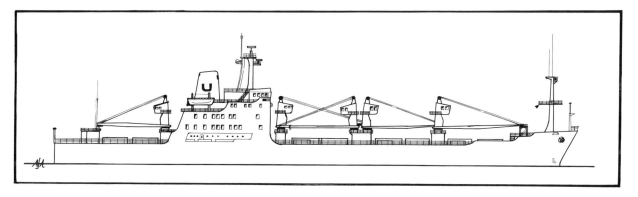

First installation of the new and extremely popular Sulzer 7 RTA 58 took place in the Bermuda-owned *Atlantic Universal* delivered early in 1984. This power plant gives the vessel a total output of 13,280 bhp at mcr. First of two sisters, they have a deadweight of 12,200 tonnes and a capacity of 17,070 cubic metres, consisting of 141 TEU and 5,381 1m × 1.2m pallets. (*Drawing: A J Ambrose*)

Nevertheless, despite this instability, reefer operators must attempt to look into the future, in order to provide the supply of the right tonnage to meet the demands of the market as they materialise.

Nutritious Food

Before looking into the future however, it is worthwhile to review the development of the trade over the last 25 years. People's desire to have a supply of fresh fruit, vegetables and other fresh produce all year round has existed for a long time, and during the 1960s and 1970s the rapid advances of technology created increased consumer spending power and dramatic economic development in the industrialised world. In the United States, for example, the banana consumption increased from 7.5 kilo/per capita to 9.9 kilo/per capita to provide a total requirement for 850,000 tons, and one could see an excellent growth potential for the future. Then, the pattern of consumption changed and focused on nutritious food; a pattern even more emphasised with the 'jogging' wave of the late 1970s/ early 1980s, with fresh fruit and vegetables having a more pronounced place within these new consumer habits.

Rationalisation

The general spiralling inflation and especially the increasing labour costs, followed by the oil price jump caused the transport costs to increase substantially. From the ship operator's side, these increasing costs had to be met by rationalisation. At first, during the 1960s this was mainly achieved by economies of scale, by increasing the size of vessels and consequently the size of cargoes. This development can be seen in the table below, which shows the corresponding fluctuations and increases in ship capacity over the period for one of the world's premier reefer fleets, namely, that of Sweden's Salen Reefer Services AB.

Type	Built	Size	Pallet Capacity	Speed (knots)
Arawak	1964	375,000	2,680	18.5
San	1967–68	408,000	2,850	19.0
Snow	1972–73	612,000	5,350	22.5
Winter	1979–80	605,000	5,800	22.0
Spring	1984	470,000	4,450	19.0

In addition to the rationalisations by size and unitisation, more fuel-efficient vessels were developed during the 1970s and early 1980s, and these aspects were to contribute much to the operators' abilities to remain profitable in a competitive market.

The great development of the reefer trades during this period did of course bring a lot of new countries and areas into the reefer world. After the oil price jump of 1979, the oil incomes in the Middle East countries created the base for a major food import market and today this is a significant and important facet of the reefer trade.

Radiated Fruit

One of the basic questions of the future of the trade is going to be the main method of preserving fresh produce during transit. Various different kinds of coating, controlled atmosphere radiation and other methods are under development. When talking with the food and fruit trade, it is, however, hard to find anyone who believes that these methods will have a large scale commercial use. Nevertheless, these new methods of preservation are not necessarily competing with refrigeration. They can, in fact, be a complement to refrigerated transportation, as many products presently impossible to transport over long distances due to limited shelf-lives can be brought into new markets by combining the new methods with refrigeration.

Salen Reefer Services *Spring Delight* has a capacity for 430,000 cubic feet and is one of a class of eight vessels built in South Korea and Japan. Fast handling of unitised cargoes are quickly loaded and discharged with a system of hatches which in only a few minutes can be opened on all four decks. (*Salen Reefer Services*)

New Products

Changing consumer tastes, new cultivation techniques and better transportation methods are destined to bring new products into new markets in the future. During the past five years avocados and pineapples are specimens of fruits which have changed from 'exotic' to 'volume' fruits for example.

The kiwi fruit is now entering the same development, with New Zealand the leading producer of this fruit, having massive, and realistic, production plans. By 1990 they plan to export as much kiwi as their apple export today. As the main markets for this fruit, Europe, Japan and the USA, are located far from New Zealand, the amount of tonnage that will be employed during the shipping period of May to August will be substantial.

With the exception of a few experimental shipments, the New Zealand kiwi has so far, only been

The 630,000 cubic foot *Anne B* is the first completion of a series of six reefers for Lauritzen Reefers. Two, including the *Anne B*, were built by Japan's Tsuneishi yard, the remaining four are being built by Hyundai Heavy Industries in South Korea, the final delivery scheduled in 1985. (*FotoFlite, Ashford*)

Blumenthal was the first vessel built with economy features from Germanischer Lloyd's 'Ship of the Future' research project. She has a cubic capacity of 475,000 feet and has a free fall lifeboat gantry on her stern. (*FotoFlite, Ashford*)

transported in containers. However, palletised shipping in modern reefer vessels will start on a large scale during 1985. Kiwi fruit is also developing in other areas, able to give a steady supply to markets outside New Zealand production season. This development is in many cases aided by the New Zealand growers as it is in their interests to maintain a year-round supply in order to change the consumer patterns for the fruit from 'exotic' to 'volume' demand. In addition, there are a range of other 'exotic' fruits and vegetables which are showing possibilities of following the same development in the future.

Unitisation

The trend favouring nutritious food and the 'keep your body in shape' attitude is likely to continue and consumers will tend to be very conscious and critical about the quality of fresh produce they are buying, and this will put handling and packing sharply into focus. Unitisation will continue and accelerate. The big issue in recent years was whether to palletise or containerise. Today, however, it is 'how and when' to use the container or the pallet respectively, with some traders even talking of pallets in containers as the optimum handling method. While this may be the optimum logistically, it will however, create costs too high to be justified on the existing levels of the market.

Container transport for refrigerated cargoes will in the main be provided by the liner companies within their regular routes. However, for trades requiring a more specialised and/or seasonal service, the pallet will be the best alternative.

In the beginning of the 1980s, we saw the development of dedicated reefer container services with bananas, on the short sea routes from Central America to the USA, and this was believed to be the start of a container explosion into the reefer markets. However,

this development seems to have terminated, and today the aim is to palletise. Among the reasons for this about-turn are the appearance of more pallet-friendly ships. Also, the container is not as economical on the longer routes, and inland distribution, especially in Europe, requires smaller unit loads than those of the container. Furthermore, the need for pallets is obvious in trades such as those of banana breakbulk where the cargo is often pallet-loaded after discharge from the ship, where today, for instance, this is the practice at Antwerp.

Obviously, the optimum benefit of palletisation logistics is not achieved until the pallet is used, unbroken, from the packaging plant in the producing country right through to its eventual destination. This practice is implemented today in almost every major fruit trade except for bananas.

When the present fleet of older banana vessels are phased out in the near future, they will be replaced by modern pallet-friendly tonnage. This will definitely be instrumental in creating more efficient unitisation when coupled with the advances of recent extensive research into ventilation, refrigeration and ripening of palletised bananas on board ship. Large scale tests have proven the practicability and improved economies of this form of handling over conventional breakbulk handling.

Shipowners' Role

The potential for a ship operator to rationalise and hold transport costs down is not only related to fuel economy today. Firstly, the largest potential savings in this respect have already been achieved with the range of fuel-efficient new tonnage presently coming into trade. Secondly, the incentive for this form of progress is lower now, as current predictions forecast a lowering oil price level rather than the opposite.

Therefore, the focus will have to turn to handling concepts and systems with the reefer ship forming the significant link in a fully unitised intermodal distribution system. This puts the requirement on the reefer operators' know-how and skills, and those of the ship designers and builders. The so-called 'pure' shipyard designs, which many of the more recent speculative orders for reefers have been, are not advisable in this respect, as the most suitable vessel design for a specific trade has to be developed jointly by the client and ship operator together. Thus, the success and survival of the reefer ship operator will be dictated by his ability to meet the future trade development and demand for a qualitive and reliable service, based on improved handling techniques as a factor of major importance.

The Gulf War: Economic War at Sea

by Anthony J Watts (Editor of *Navy international*)

During 1984 the Gulf War has seen some dramatic developments which yet again highlight the importance of sea trade to virtually *any* nation (excepting perhaps small landlocked countries) and how vulnerable that trade is to any threat – by sea or air.

Now well into its fourth year, and with no apparent lessening or ending of hostilities the Gulf War, like the First World War of 1914–18, has stagnated and generated into what, in modern day terms could, I suppose, be termed trench warfare. Certainly, following the gargantuan army assaults of the last three years, this year has seen very little really intensive fighting on land, and neither side has felt able to carry out one more 'last push' as major assaults in the 1914–18 war were termed. In fact it is probably true to say that, like the great powers in 1917, both Iraq and Iran are 'war-weary' – hardly surprising if one accepts even the conservative estimates of the cost in human life of just

One of the first casualties of the year was the Cypriot general cargo ship *Skaros* which was struck by an Exocet missile and was declared a total loss due to the subsequent fire. (*FotoFlite, Ashford*)

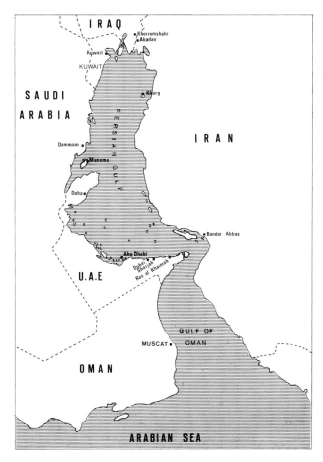

Map showing the Persian Gulf and surrounding countries. More than 100 vessels have been hit in this area since the commencement of hostilities. (*NAVY international*)

deploy French Exocet missiles and with the South Atlantic war still fresh in people's minds speculation was immediately rife that Iraq was going to deploy Exocet-armed Etendards against shipping in the Gulf. Further indications that Iraq would, in the long term, seek a different solution to the war was the contract signed with Italy for the construction in Italian shipyards of four 'Lupo' class frigates and six 'Assad' class corvettes, together with a large replenishment tanker similar to the Italian 'Stromboli' type. Like Germany in the First World War, Iraq was preparing to seek a solution to her war at sea.

From a purely strategic point of view such a solution makes a great deal of sense. Iran is almost completely dependant on her oil exports from the rich fields around Kharg Island in the North of the Gulf for foreign exchange – and foreign exchange is absolutely vital if Iran is to maintain her war machine and replace losses from whoever is prepared to supply her.

The 10,292 grt Indian-registered general cargo ship *Apj Ambika* was struck by a missile causing her to sink in the Khor Musa Channel. (*FotoFlite, Ashford*)

The 1963-built Greek bulk carrier *Iapetos* was struck by an Exocet missile at the end of March 1984. She was severely damaged by fire and her owners Kelina Inc of Panama sold her to breakers in Pakistan. (*FotoFlite, Ashford*)

fighting soldiers. Already some sources are quoting losses as high as half a million men, not counting civilian casualties, nor the tens of thousands thought to have been slaughtered by the Khomeini regime for what they view as anti-nationalist, or counter-revolutionary attitudes.

With such enormous manpower losses, which have a severe effect on Iraq's capability to prosecute war with a relatively small population, and Iran's inability to replace or repair war damaged or destroyed equipment, it was inevitable that one of the participants should seek a solution to the war by some means other than by land warfare.

With much wider support from other Arab states and Western and Soviet countries and her much greater reliance on technological resources than on manpower it was not surprising that such moves should be made first by Iraq.

The first intimation that alternative methods of waging war would be sought was the rumour and final confirmation that Iraq was to receive five French Dassault Super Etendard strike aircraft in the autumn of 1983. It was already well known that Iraq could

Oil is Iran's life-blood. Iranian oil also happens to be the life-blood of many industrialised nations and that oil has to be transported by sea down the length of the Gulf and out through the narrow Straits of Hormuz.

The scene was thus well set for a major threat to international shipping in international waters. However, the expected heavy attacks did not materialise quite as soon as expected. There are two possible reasons for this. Firstly, with only five Etendards, Iraq doubtless wished to conserve her meagre resources and to use them only when she could be sure of achieving a major victory. Also it would take time to train the Iraqi aircrews to be proficient in handling and maintaining the aircraft to ensure achieving the optimum operational capability from them.

Secondly, it may well have been hoped that the mere threat of attack against her oil exports would cause Iran to moderate her attitude and perhaps

eventually to lead to peace. It was not to be, however.

The despatch of the Etendards to Iraq caused considerable concern to international bodies. The first to voice its opinions was no less than the UN Security Council who, on 31 October 1983, intervened in the war with a statement that it affirmed the right of free navigation and commerce in international waters in the Gulf, and called upon Iran and Iraq to end the war, before it eventually forced shipping lines to refuse to enter the area for fear of sustaining unacceptable losses.

The arrival of the Etendards in Iraq prompted Iran to reiterate that if they were used to deploy Exocet missiles, then Iran would retaliate by sealing off the Straits of Hormuz. This reply was, however, regarded by many as a merely hollow retaliatory gesture. Firstly, to block the Straits would be far more disadvantageous to Iran than it would be to Iraq, simply because of Iran's reliance on the use of the Straits for the passage

Four views of the 357,100 dwt tanker *Safina Al Arab* after she was hit by an Exocet missile. The Swedish tanker *Sea Saga* (178,808 grt) transhipped some of her cargo in an operation which took place approximately 30 miles east of Bahrain. (*International Transport Contractors*)

of shipping exporting her oil. Secondly, there was the problem of actually achieving a blockage of the Straits. There is only one narrow channel suitable for the passage of VLCC, but it is so deep that it is unsuitable for mining, and to sink ships in the area would achieve nothing.

Following delivery of the Etendards, Iraq decided promptly to test the Iranian response and on 3 November carried out an air attack against the Greek cargo vessel *Avra* in convoy with 12 other ships off the port of Bandar Khomeini. The attack is thought to have been carried out by a Puma helicopter with an Exocet missile which caused only superficial damage to the *Avra* with only three crew members slightly wounded.

Another attack, again thought to have been carried out by a helicopter, resulted in the sinking of the Greek cargo ship *Antigoni* on 21 November, fortunately without loss of life.

By the end of 1983 events in the Gulf had reached an extremely delicate stage and stability throughout the whole Gulf region was seen to be resting on a very thin knife edge. Iran had still not carried out her threat to block the Straits of Hormuz, but such was the general threat throughout the area that various countries began intensive behind the scenes efforts to get the two sides to reach some sort of peace agreement. Britain for one was conducting a slow, covert consultation, and even Syria became involved. The United States, for once, did not seem to have a major role to play, for many local nations were extremely wary of her motives for being interested in the area, and did not really relish the prospect of the small American task force stationed in the South of the Gulf to ensure safe passage for international shipping in international waters in the area.

For a while events in the Lebanon completely overshadowed the Gulf War, and a lull ensued in the fighting in the area. However, at the start of February 1984, events suddenly took a turn for the worse, and the long expected attacks against merchant shipping in the Gulf began.

The first of a series of major attacks against Iranian-organised convoys in the north of the Gulf took place on 31 January. In the first of a long series of disputed claims, in which there was usually some substance of truth, although the real facts often took months to emerge, Iraq claimed in an hour-long attack to have sunk five Iranian naval vessels in the area of the Khor Musa creek, followed by the sinking of another three ships in air raids the following day. Naturally the Iranians denied the Iraqi claims and there was much confusion for a time as to what had actually happened. Eventually it became clear that the Iraqi reference to naval targets meant, in fact, merchant ships. It eventually emerged that a bulk carrier, the Cypriot *City of Rio*, was mined on 1 February, while the Greek cargo vessel *Skaros* was set on fire by an Exocet missile and severely damaged the same day, as was the Cypriot vessel *Neptune* shortly after. All three vessels were sailing in the same convoy.

With this major attack on a convoy Britain agreed to participate in a convoy scheme in the area while the United States drew up contingency plans to sweep the Hormuz Straits for mines, both countries despatching naval forces to the area.

It seemed as if the long awaited 'final push' was underway. Iran opened a land offensive and Iraq threatened to launch missile and air attacks against major Iranian cities and ports. But as had so often happened in the past it all petered out, the stalemate continued, both sides baring their teeth at each other, but doing little else.

Fearing that eventually she might be unwillingly drawn into the conflict should air attacks against merchant shipping spread, Saudi Arabia began searching the tanker broker market for spare hulls. Eventually 25 tankers were chartered and used as floating oil depots in which some 50 million barrels of Saudi oil were stockpiled (some 10 per cent of current Saudi production).

In a further air attack on 16 February a Liberian bulk carrier was set on fire by an Exocet missile and badly damaged. Events appeared to be reaching a climax and on 18 February Iran put all her air and naval forces on maximum alert in order to prevent any Western naval forces from passing through the Straits of Hormuz. On 20 February at a meeting of the Gulf Co-operation Council (Saudi Arabia, Kuwait, UAE, Bahrain, Qatar and Oman) Ministers expressed grave concern over the deteriorating state of affairs in the Gulf and voiced fears over the eventual outcome of any foreign intervention in the area, particularly by the major powers.

Then, early on 1 March, Iraq carried out its most devastating attack to date. In a major air raid against a seven-ship convoy near the port of Bandar Khomeini helicopter-fired Exocet missiles sank an Indian cargo vessel and set two others on fire which were ultimately declared to be constructive total losses. One of these was the largest and first British ship to be attacked, the 29,486 dwt bulk carrier *Charming*. Various eye-witness reports emerging since this raid indicate that the *Charming* was hit by a heat-seeking missile rather than an Exocet, but details cannot be confirmed.

A number of governments put a ban on their merchant ships entering the war zone, but as no further raids developed, restrictions were relaxed, and tankers and bulk carriers continued to sail up to the northern Iranian ports.

However, a further series of raids took place at the end of March beginning of April in which a number of merchant vessels were struck. It was also reported that some of the Iraqi Etendard strike aircraft armed with Exocet had been involved in these raids.

The first of these attacks involving the Etendards turned out to be somewhat of an embarassment to the Iraqis. The attack on 27 March resulted in the Greek tanker *Filikon L* loaded with Saudi crude oil and bound for Sicily being struck. Even more unfortunate was the fact that the ship was subsequently found to have been struck outside the Iraqi declared exclusion zone, some 65 km SW of Kharg Island.

As it happened, the Exocet did not detonate and was later disarmed and removed by a team of explosive experts from the American destroyer USS *O'Brien*. Fortunately only minor damage was suffered by the tanker which was able to proceed on her journey

Map showing approximate positions of significant ship attacks in the Gulf in the first eight months of 1984. (*NAVY international*)

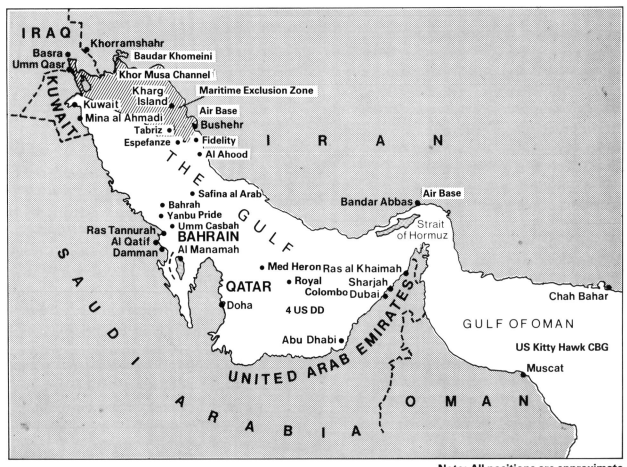

Note: All positions are approximate

The 214,992 dwt tanker *Yanbu Pride* owned by Arabian International Maritime Co of Jeddah was struck by Iranian rockets on 16 May 1984 but was able to sail for the Fujairah Anchorage on 25 May 1984 despite fire damage. (*FotoFlite, Ashford*)

having been first towed to Dubai where essential repairs were carried out.

On 25 April the Iraqis again found themselves in a highly embarassing situation. That day the 357,100 dwt tanker *Safina al-Arab*, a Swedish-chartered Saudi-owned vessel suffered an explosion and severe fire some 120 nm south of Kharg Island. For some days the cause of the explosion remained unknown. Finally, after an incredible salvage feat, the fire was put out and it was established the ship had been struck by a missile. Iraq noticeably failed to claim responsibility for the attack while the Saudis refused to comment on the fact that one of their ships had loaded a cargo of Iranian crude oil at Kharg Island. Finally on 2 May, President Saddam Hussein of Iraq claimed in an interview with Kuwaiti journalists that Iraqi Super Etendard aircraft had attacked a number of ships in the Gulf including a Saudi vessel chartered to a foreign concern which rented her to Iran.

During May attacks on merchant shipping in the Gulf intensified. With Iraqi air raids beginning to have a considerable effect on Iranian trade it was not surprising that Iran should seek some retaliation. It later transpired that three vessels were struck by rockets and in one case possibly a Maverick missile fired from Iranian F4 Phantom aircraft, two of the vessels being Kuwaiti tankers.

However, it was the third attack on the 214,992 dwt Saudi tanker *Yanbu Pride* which resulted in the calling of a further emergency meeting of the Gulf Co-operation Council. This led to a decision to take the question of

air attacks on tankers to the UN Security Council.

The rise in the number of attacks and the scale of damage and loss being suffered led to a sharp increase in insurance rates, together with speculative buying of oil in anticipation of a possible blockade of the Gulf, or the decision by a number of countries to cease sending their ships to the area.

In spite of the seriousness of the situation, a meeting of members of the Arab League failed to agree on a Kuwaiti call for a joint defence pact to be invoked in the event of a member suffering aggression. In spite of their reluctance to call on the major powers for support, both Kuwait and Saudi Arabia, determined to defend their air space, were finally forced to seek outside aid. Saudi Arabia received a large number of American Stinger shoulder-launched heat seeking missiles for putting on her vessels while Kuwait, refused permission to purchase Stinger missiles by the Americans, concluded an agreement with the Soviet Union for the supply of considerable quantities of armaments, including air defence systems.

Following an Iranian attack on a Kuwaiti tanker on 10 June off the coast of Qatar, British Shipowners extended the Gulf War Zone to an area covering some 3,500 m². Fears over the withdrawal of foreign shipping in the face of attacks spreading further down the Gulf led to members of the Gulf Co-operation Council proposing a plan to create a safe route for shipping using the Gulf.

For a time diplomatic moves and a cease fire at sea seemed to have an effect, but on 24 June the peace was broken by an Iraqi air raid directed against shipping at Kharg Island, the first time Iraqi pilots had carried out a direct attack on the heavily defended island.

Part of the terminal at Kharg was subsequently closed and a limit of 300,000 tons imposed on the size of tankers using the terminal.

The Kuwait Oil Tanker Co's 1982-built tanker *Kazimah* only received minor damage after being hit by Iranian rockets in June 1984. (*FotoFlite, Ashford*)

Following a meeting of the Gulf Co-operation Council it was decided that the most satisfactory way of protecting shipping in the Gulf would be to provide air cover as opposed to convoy escort, and routing the shipping close to shore where it could be within protective range of shore defences.

An intermission followed these major attacks and emphasis seemed to shift to events in the Red Sea. However, the uneasy lull was broken on 7 August when Iraqi aircraft attacked a Liberian tanker. This was followed up on 9 August by an Iraqi air attack on an oil terminal near Kharg Island. Iranian fighter aircraft were now observed to be providing air cover over convoys and in the fierce fighting on 9–10 August, Iraq claimed to have downed three Iranian F4 Phantoms and five merchant vessels destroyed.

A further attack on 23 August led to speculation that the Iranians had at last developed a counter to the Iraqi attacks. On 23 August Iraq claimed to have attacked a 'large naval target', ie a tanker. Salvage tugs which went to the scene of the action from Bahrain however, found only a small Iranian supply boat which they said was quickly towed away before they could approach it. Shortly afterwards, an Iranian official stated that his country had at last developed a counter to the Iraqi Exocet attacks, the threat was claimed to have been neutralised. It has been surmised that the small supply boat struck on 23 August was, in fact, a small unmanned decoy carrying some form of reflector creating an image large enough to confuse the Exocet homing system.

Doubtless many more such attacks carried out by both Iraq and Iran will occur before the war is ended. To date however, they seem to have had very little effect on either side, nor on shipping companies willing to run the risk to carry cargo, but inevitably insurance rates must rise if losses continue to be sustained. If Iraq seeks to achieve a solution to the war at sea by using attacks against economic trade, then her best chance of success will probably lie in trying to destroy the Iranian oil terminals and offshore oil rigs.

MERCHANT SHIPS ATTACKED IN THE GULF BETWEEN 1/1/84–27/8/84

Name	Type	Tonnage (dwt)	Flag	Cargo	Date attacked	Remarks
Iran Salam (ex-Arya Zar)	Cargo	16,247	Iran		2/1/84	Struck by rockets; badly damaged
Neptune	Cargo	8,364 grt	Cypriot		1/2/84	Set on fire by mine or missile; badly damaged
City of Rio	Bulk carrier	16,300	Cypriot	Ballast	1/2/84	Mined; badly damaged
Skaros	Cargo	10,617	Cypriot	Ballast	1/2/84	Exocet struck engine room; declared CTL
Al Tariq	Bulk carrier	16,819	Liberian	Ballast	16/2/84	Exocet; set on fire, badly damaged
APJ Ambika	Cargo	10,929 grt	Indian	General	1/3/84	Struck by missile, sank
Sema-G	Cargo	9,675	Turkish	Iron	1/3/84	Struck by missile, set on fire – badly damaged; declared CTL
Charming	Bulk carrier	29,486	British	Alumina	1/3/84	Struck by missile, badly damaged; declared CTL
Filikon L	Tanker	85,123	Greek	Crude oil	27/3/84	Super Etendard Exocet; minor damage
Heyang Ilho	Offshore supply vessel		South Korean		27/3/84	Sunk
Iapetos (ex-Turicum, ex-Ivory Star, ex-Jarosa)	Bulk carrier	26,214	Greek	Ballast	29/3/84	Exocet – set on fire, severely damaged; declared CTL
?Iran Dahr	Bulk carrier	19,833	Iranian?	?	29/3/84	Struck by missile, damaged
Varuna Yau			Indian		3/4/84	Trapped in Shatt al Arab. Set on fire by Iranian Army shelling
Rover Star	Tanker	50,975	Panamanian	Ballast	22/4/84	Exocet – minor damage
Safina al Arab	Tanker	357,100	Saudi	Crude oil	25/4/84	Exocet – set on fire, badly damaged; declared CTL
Sea Eagle	Cargo	8,206 grt	Liberian	Fertiliser	2/5/84	Exocet – minor damage
Al Ahood (ex-Venture Britannia, ex-Conoco Britannia)	Tanker	117,710	Saudi	Crude oil	7/5/84	Exocet – set on fire; declared CTL
Tabriz	Tanker	69,498	Iranian	Crude oil	12/5/84	Super Etendard Exocet – slight damage
Umm Casbah	Tanker	79,999	Kuwaiti	Crude oil	13/5/84	Struck by Iranian rockets; slight damage
Esperanza II	Tanker	61,928	Panamanian	Ballast	13/5/84	Super Etendard Exocet – set on fire, badly damaged; declared CTL
Bahrah	Tanker	30,509	Kuwaiti	Ballast	14/5/84	Struck by two Iranian missiles, set on fire; badly damaged
Yanbu Pride (ex-Mobil Pride)	Tanker	214,992	Saudi	Crude oil	16/5/84	Struck by Iranian rockets; set on fire
Fidelity	Bulk carrier	28,410	Panamanian	Steel	19/5/84	Super Etendard Exocet – sunk
Chemical Venture	Tanker	29,427	Liberian	Ballast	24/5/84	Struck by Iranian rockets/heat seeking missile, set on fire; badly damaged
Savoy Dean	Bulk carrier	38,259	Liberian	Grain	26–27/5/84	Exocet – minor damage
Buyuk Hun	Tanker	153,274	Turkish	Ballast	3/6/84	Struck by two Iraqi Super Etendard Exocet – set on fire, badly damaged; declared CTL
Giant Kim	Bulk carrier	32,107 grt	Panamanian		3/6/84	Struck by Iraqi missile, set on fire; badly damaged

Kazimah	Tanker	294,739	Kuwaiti	Ballast	10/6/84	Struck by Iranian rockets; slight damage
Alexander the Great	Tanker	325,645	Greek	Crude oil	24/6/84	Exocet – set on fire; badly damaged
Tiburon	Tanker	260,150	Liberian	Crude oil	27/6/84	Exocet – set on fire; severely damaged
Won Jin	Cargo	10,205	South Korean	Iron	1/7/84	Struck by two Exocet – set on fire; severely damaged
Alexander Dyo	Bulk carrier	13,316	Cypriot	Iron ore	1/7/84	Set on fire; badly damaged
Erne (ex-*Yeral*)	Bulk carrier	15,178 grt	Panamanian	?	1/7/84	Grounded during air attack; minor damage
Sitia Venture	Bulk carrier	15,991 grt	Panamanian		1/7/84	Collided with *Al Kabeer*. Grounded during air attack; minor damage
Al Kabeer	Bulk carrier	16,575 grt	Panamanian		1/7/84	Collided with *Sitia Venture* – grounded during air attack; minor damage
Primrose	Tanker	276,424	Liberian	Crude oil	5/7/84	Struck by Iranian rockets, set on fire; minor damage
British Renown	Tanker	261,011	British	Ballast	10/7/84	On way to pump oil from *Tiburon* – struck by two Iranian rockets, set on fire; slight damage
Friendship L	Tanker	267,589	Liberian	Crude oil	7/8/84	Exocet – set on fire; minor damage
Cebu (ex-*Care*, ex-*Carola*, ex-*Carola Reith*)	Bulk carrier	38,250	Singapore		12/8/84	Explosion alongside at Bandar Khomeini, cause unknown. Set on fire, badly damaged
Endeavour (ex-*Nigma*)	Tanker	47,310	Panamanian	Crude oil	18/8/84	Struck by Iranian missiles – set on fire; slightly damaged
Amethyst	Tanker	53,425	Cypriot	Crude oil	24/8/84	Exocet – set on fire; seriously damaged
Cleo I	Tanker	35,730	Panamanian	Ballast	27/8/84	Struck by Iranian rocket; minor damage
St Tobias	Tanker	254,520	Liberian	Crude oil	11/9/84	Struck in ballast tank by an Iraqi missile – declared CTL
Adib	Bulk carrier	34,997	Iranian		12/9/84	Struck in hold space – slightly damaged
Seetrans 21	Utility/Supply	99 grt	West German		13/9/84	Sunk by an Iraqi gunboat – six killed
Royal Colombo	Tanker	126,998	South Korean	Crude oil	16/9/84	Struck by missile – moderate damage
Med Heron	Tanker	123,597	Liberian	Ballast	16/9/84	Struck by missile – considerable damage
World Knight	Tanker	258,437	Liberian	Crude oil	8/10/84	Struck by Iraqi bomb – set on fire, considerable damage, six crew killed
Sivand (ex-*British Navigator*)	Tanker	218,587	Iranian	Crude oil	12/10/84	Struck by missile. On fire
Gaz Fountain (ex-*Gay Lussac*)	LPG tanker	29,451	Panamanian	Propane/Butane	12/10/84	Struck by three rockets
Jag Pari	Tanker	29,139	Indian	Crude oil	12/10/84	Struck by four missiles
Sivand (ex-*British Navigator*)	Tanker	218,587	Iranian	Crude oil	15/10/84	Struck *again* by Iraqi aircraft
Pacific Protector (ex-*Northern Protector*, ex-*Sea Driller*)	Diving support vessel	1,530 grt	Panamanian		19/10/84	Attacked by Iranian F-4 Phantom II aircraft with four rockets – three killed

The German Coastal Ferry Scene

by Gert Uwe Detlefsen

All of the East Frisian Islands off the coast of Lower Saxony can only be reached by ship. Off the coast of Schleswig-Holstein the islands of Föhr, Amrum and Pellworm, the 'Halligen' and numerous very small islands are connected by ferries which are considered vital to the local communities. In the Baltic, there lies the island of Fehmarn, Germany's largest island (which has only been reached since 1962 by the Fehmarnsund bridge of the 'Vogelfluglinie'), and the fjords of Flensburg, Schlei, Eckernförde and Kiel as well as the Lübeck Bay; all are natural locations for excursion and liner/ferry services. The red-rocked island of Helgoland, in the middle of the German Bight, is the operating region of about a dozen or more predominately larger passenger vessels, most built specially for this service, while around the other coastal and island

regions more than 250 West German ferries operate. The majority are fitted for day passengers, but increasingly now carrying vehicles too.

The first vessel which called regularly at the island of Helgoland 38 miles away from Cuxhaven at the

Idyllic scenes like these are now a thing of the past. No steamer is now in service for German coastal passenger lines. The last of them, the Flensburg-owned *Alexandra*, built 1908, was withdrawn from service in 1976.

This picture shows the steamer *Föhr-Amrum* of Wyker Dampfschiffs-Reederei laying at the middle-bridge of Wyk on the island of Föhr in the North Sea. The 211-grt vessel was built in 1908 at Howaldtswerke Kiel and served her owners faithfully for exactly 50 years. After another six years of service as *Hansa-Linie* she was broken up in 1964. (*Gert Uwe Detlefsen*)

mouth of the river Elbe was the Dutch steamer *De Beurs van Amsterdam* in 1829. At about the middle of the last century a regular trade from German North Sea ports was established – for many years in summer only. The Hamburg-Amerika-Line, the North German Lloyd and since the Second World War the state-owned HADAG of Hamburg have all served Helgoland. All now history.

The HADAG, who managed, with their sister company HADAG Cruise-Line, Hamburg's last large luxury cruising ship *Astor*, faced criticism due to heavy losses and use of state subventions and were forced to withdraw from the Helgoland service due to losses experienced there as well. The ships, the *Wappen von Hamburg*, 4,437 grt and fitted for 1,800 passengers, and the *Alte Liebe*, 3,819 grt and fitted for 1,980 passengers, were sold. The Flensburger Seetouristik KG, a shipping company which originated from the so-called 'butter-excursions', decided to continue the service with their motor vessel *Poseidon*. However, in the spring of 1984 they bought the *Wappen von Hamburg* and left her on her traditional Helgoland run, but the voyage now starts at Cuxhaven instead of Hamburg, and the company were able to announce after a few weeks service that they were now operating at a profit. Next year Seetouristik will again offer departures from Hamburg on certain days during the season. In appearance the ship is more or less unchanged, the green bands of HADAG are now the

blue ones of her new owners and the small green-red-white bands of HADAG's Helgoland service have also disappeared. The twin funnel uptakes now sport the new owners characteristic 'S'.

HADAG's other vessel the *Alte Liebe*, built in 1962 by Blohm & Voss, will return to the Helgoland service, but again for new owners. Sold in 1964 to Swedish buyers, bought back two years later and employed as an additional vessel for the service between Cuxhaven and Helgoland, she spent the end of the 1982 season laid up waiting new orders and a buyer. The Bremer Seebäderdienst D. Oltmann then purchased the ship and moved her, still under her old name, to Bremen where she will be completely modernised and rebuilt. She will commence next year's season from Bremerhaven to Helgoland replacing the ugly-looking *Roland von Bremen*, a former reefer which was converted into a passenger liner in 1966. Built in 1939 as the *Indian Reefer*, this veteran was to be disposed of at the end of the 1984 season. The *Alte Liebe* will trade under the new name *Helgoland*.

Besides these 'prominent' and large vessels about a

Although it would be possible, no passenger vessel is allowed to berth at Helgoland. All passengers have to use the so-called 'boerte-boats' (seen left of the bridge) for disembarking. These boats give employment to about four dozen Helgoland seaman. Illustrated here is the 433-grt *Klaar Kiming* of Wyker Dampfschiffs-Reederei anchored off the silhouette of Helgoland in summer 1984. (*Gert Uwe Detlefsen*)

Following the tragic death of Capt Visser in 1958, Cassen Eils continued operating the company under his own name. Today he operates eight modern ships from Cuxhaven, Norderney and Büsum to Helgoland and from Eckernförde, Kiel and Kappeln on services on the Baltic.

Another regular visitor to Helgoland is the Wyker Dampfschiffs-Reederei Föhr-Amrum GmbH, a company which has now celebrated their 100th anniversary. Founded as a fourth company to connect Wyk, the capital of Föhr, with the mainland by steamship, the WDR is now the only company left serving Föhr and the neighbouring islands of Amrum and the small unsheltered islands of Hooge and Langeness. The three combined car/passenger ferries *Utblande* (built in 1980), *Nordfriesland* (1978) and *Schleswig-Holstein* (1972) trade between the mainland port of Dagebüll and Wyk on Föhr and Wittdün on Amrum. The first two vessels carry 975 passengers and 45 cars, the latter 875 passengers and 45 cars. The WDR also own the *Amrum* (480 passengers and 20 cars) and the car ferry *Insel Amrum* (45 cars). The *Pidder Lyng* 999 grt with accommodation for 800 passengers and the smaller *Klaar Kiming*, 434 grt and 655 passengers, serve Helgoland from Hörnum on the island of Sylt, and from Dagebüll, Wyk, Wittdün, Tönning and Husum.

For excursions in shallow waters between the islands

dozen smaller, but more modern ships carry hundreds of tourists every year to the Red Rock. One of the owners engaged in this trade is Cassen Eils of Cuxhaven. Born in 1923 on the East Frisian island of Norderney he was a seafarer before starting the service to Helgoland in 1951 in partnership with Captain Ludwig Visser using the 57-year old vessel *Rudolf*.

One of the smallest passenger ships trading to Helgoland is shown here: the *Flipper*, 412 grt and built by the Mützelfeldtwerft at Cuxhaven in 1977. The ship is licenced for 581 passengers and her owner, Cassen Eils, has registered her on the island of Norderney, from where she trades to Helgoland. (*Gert Uwe Detlefsen*)

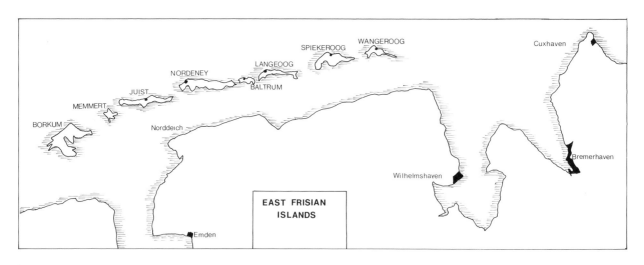

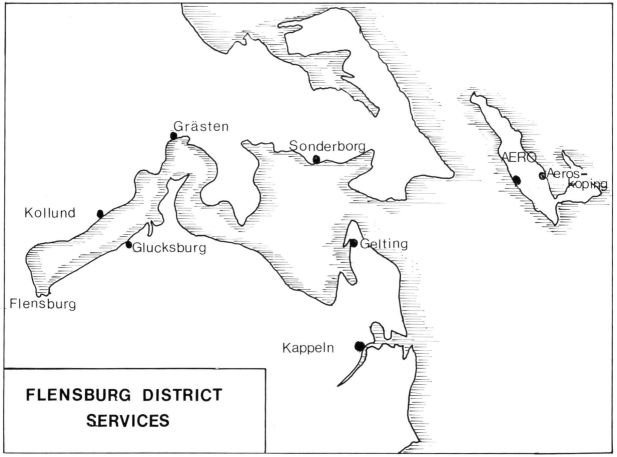

the WDR has the two smaller ships *Störtebeker* and *Rüm Hart*. With the exception of the *Rüm Hart* and *Pidder Lyng* all the newbuildings since the end of the war have come from the Husumer Shipyard and they are among the best-looking ships to be found in the German coastal waters today.

The yard also constructed the combined car/passenger ferries *Pellworm* and *Pellworm II* which connect the islands of Nordstrand and Pellworm. Nordstrand is also linked by a dam.

The waters of the German coastal and inter-island ferry system. (*Drawings: Michael J Ambrose*)

The companies domiciled in Lower Saxony and serving the East Frisian islands are also relatively old established companies, founded for the sole purpose of serving a certain island with 'steamers'. Before the age of steam, fishers and owners of sailing ships were offering sailings to and from the islands from time to time. When the tourist era started at the end of the last

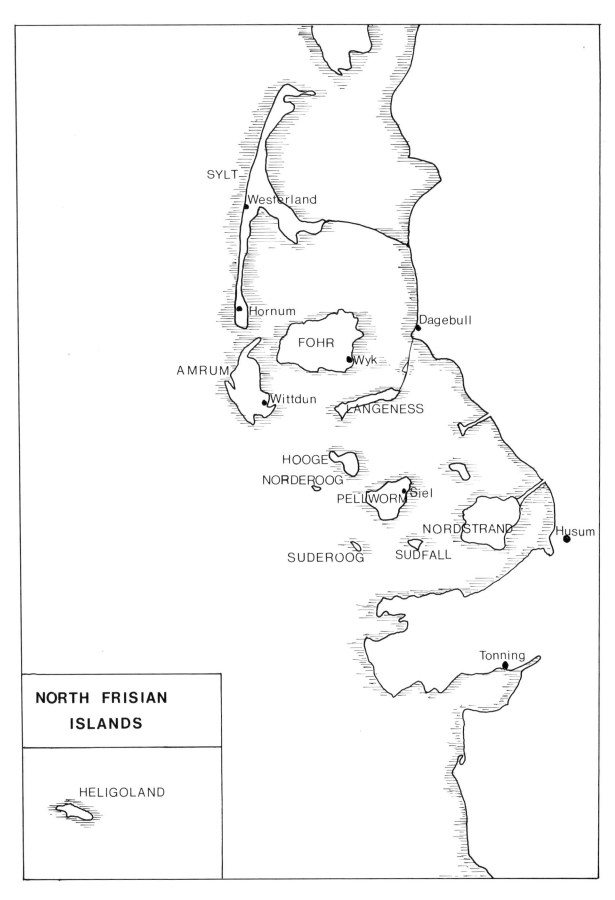

SYLT

Westerland

Hornum

FOHR

Dagebull

AMRUM

Wyk

Wittdun

LANGENESS

HOOGE

NORDEROOG

PELLWORM

Siel

NORDSTRAND

Husum

SUDEROOG

SUDFALL

Tonning

NORTH FRISIAN

ISLANDS

HELIGOLAND

Islands like Föhr in the north of Germany can only be reached by ferry. Since these islands (like nearly all German North Sea islands) are popular tourist areas, the ferries have larger capacities than the pure island traffic would support. The *Schleswig-Holstein* of Wyker Dampfschiffs-Reederei was built in 1972 at Husumer Sciffswerft and is the first of three similar ships of the latest generation for the trade between Dagebüll and Wyk. The 918-grt ship can carry 800 passengers and 45 cars. (*Gert Uwe Detlefsen*)

century the operators were compelled to offer more regular services which could only be provided by steamers. To finance same, new companies were founded. After a time of concurrence and arrangements, those companies which are still in existence today were left to build up their fleets. Up and until the Second World War the majority of ships were relatively old steamers or rebuilt motorships. In the 1950s the first generation of modern motorships were put into service. When the private car became the preferred means of transport, the owners had to follow with new ships, as the first combined car and passenger ferries were offering only a limited amount of car space.

The new generation of ships can take between 20 and 80 cars or an equivalent volume in trucks. With the rising use of road transport the island trading pattern changed to include more road vehicles. Vehicles are not permitted on all the islands however, and on Baltrum and Wangerooge only a few public vehicles are registered. In spite of this the ferries trading to these islands are more or less combined

car/passenger ferries since they also transport the supply vehicles.

The longest voyages, of over three hours sailing time, are between Emden and Borkum, the most westerly of the German islands. The AG 'Ems' serves

The Amrumer Schiffahrts-AG lasted only 11 years. Founded in 1960, it was amalgamated with the WDR in 1971. The ugly-looking car/passenger ferry *Amrum* was built for the ASAG by the Husumer Shipyard in 1968. Now owned by the WDR, the 212-grt ferry for 480 passengers and 20 cars serves the route between Schlüttsiel-Island of Langeness-Island of Hooge and Wittdün (island of Armrum). (*Gert Uwe Detlefsen*)

this route with three ferries, *Rheinland*, (942 grt), *Westfalen* (940 grt) and the Japanese-built *Emsland* of 1,599 grt. In 1984 they sold *Nordlicht* to Bernhard Warrings at Carolinensiel who will keep the ship in the island trade, while AG 'Ems' took over a new-building from the Martin Jansen yard as a replacement.

The AG Reederei Norden-Frisia is domiciled on the island of Norderney and operates the largest East Frisian fleet. All their ships are named *Frisia* with a number to differentiate. From the mainland port of

The longest voyage from the mainland to a North Sea island is that between Emden and the East Frisian island of Borkum, the trip taking about three hours. The *Rheinland* was built at the shipyard of C. Cassens at Emden in 1974 for the AG 'Ems' Emden. The 999-grt ferry can take 1,600 passengers and 60 cars. (*Gert Uwe Detlefsen*)

Norddeich (where the well-known German telephone station is situated) the *Frisia* ships serve Juist and Norderney. The ships are a combination of car/passenger ferries and pure passenger ships.

The islands of Baltrum and Langeoog have their own shipping companies and both own three ships each at the present time. Their modern vessels are named after the respective island, eg. *Baltrum* with a number. This also applies for the island of Spiekeroog, but here there are only two ships at the present time. The last of the East Frisian islands is Wangerooge. This island is served by the German state railways, through their shipping department.

At the other German North Sea ports, namely Wilhelmshaven, Dangast, Fedderwardersiel, Bremerhaven, Cuxhaven, Büsum, Strucklahnungshörn, Hörnum, Wittdun and List are many, mainly small, passenger ships for the so called 'butter tours'. On these excursions lasting about one hour the passengers can buy cigarettes, sweets, perfume, butter and other foodstuff duty-free. The fares for such shopping tours are very low – in winter time many ships carry tourists free of charge, profits being made on the sale of duty-free goods.

This trade is the sole existence for these ships. While the majority of the 'ferries' are all newbuildings, the 'butter-steamers' are a mixed collection, old and new ships being run on the services. Of course, the

The *Frisia* series of ferries connected the mainland port of Norddeich with the islands of Juist and Norderney. Here is the *Frisia I*, looking similar to an aircraft-carrier, leaving Norddeich for Juist. Like all the other six car ferries of the AG Norden-Frisia this ship was built in 1970 by the Jos. L. Meyer Shipyard. She can take 1,500 passengers and 50 cars and has a gross-tonnage of 840 tons. (*Gert Uwe Detlefsen*)

The *Langeoog III* (*right*) and the identical sister *Langeoog IV* were built by the Julius Diedrich Shipyard at Oldersum in 1979 for the shipping trade to the island of Langeoog. The 495-grt ships can take 800 passengers and a limited number of trailers for the island supply. No public traffic is allowed at Langeoog, so cars are not carried on board. (*Gert Uwe Detlefsen*)

The *Lady of Büsum* offers so-called 'shopping-tours' from the North Sea port of Büsum. On these trips of one hour duration a limited number of duty-free articles can be purchased. The ship was built as *Danica* by the Husumer Schiffswerft in 1980 for shopping-tours in the Baltic sea and was sold to Rahder & Mordhorst at Büsum in 1983. the 338-grt ship can accommodate 316 passengers. (*Gert Uwe Detlefsen*)

older ships have all been modernised and can only be identified at a second glance as being veteran. Some owners, like Kurt Paulsen of Strucklahnungshörn near Husum have eight attractive vessels, all newbuildings from the Husumer Shipyard. Others like Werner Schaal of Cuxhaven, have just one. His vessel, the 267 grt *Nige Ooge* was built as the island ferry *Pellworm* for that island in 1930 by the Kremer-Yard and sold in 1966 to Mr Schaal when the line changed over to a car ferry.

Many ports offer 'butter tours' to as many as five or more ports, the passengers being brought to the piers by bus from the inland towns since the large centres of population are essential for the success of these 'butter trips'. The shopping trade is important to almost all Baltic passenger ships, and also on board the ferries trading to Scandinavia and Poland from Gelting, Kiel, Travemünde and Puttergarden. That apart, their main business is, of course, the transport of tourists, their cars, lorries and trailers.

The story of the ferry scene in the Baltic is a different one. The 'butter trips' within the lower Baltic have a second variant, the 'big ration' tours. When a vessel leaves the three mile zone and calls at a foreign port, the customs allow the sale of a 'large ration', ie 200 cigarettes, one litre of alcohol, ten pounds of butter and other things up to 200 DM. Danish ports such as Graasten, Sonderborg, Aero, Bagenkop and Roedby are not too far away from German ports and can be reached in two to four hours, depending on where the ship starts from.

Nearly every German Baltic port, from Flensburg through Langballigau, Neukirchen, Maasholm, Kappeln, Eckernförde, Kiel and the small villages at the Kiel Fjord, Burgstaaken, Heiligenhafen, Neustadt, Niendorf and Travemünde has its own fleet. Flensburg, the Fjord of Schlei, Kiel and Travemünde had liner and excursion traffic before the shopping tours started in the 'fifties. In the 1960s this grew into big business. About 3,000 people are now employed in Schleswig-Holstein alone, on board or directly connected with these excursion ships, and as the Common Market has now declared that at least the small tours are to be illegal, many people are naturally

Kurt Paulsen of Nordstrand now owns eight smaller vessels all named *Alder* and followed by a number. He offers excursions in the North Frisian islands and shopping tours from various ports. The *Adler III* was built by the Husumer Shipyard in 1975 and can carry 191 passengers. (*Gert Uwe Detlefsen*)

Originally built as the *Münsterland* for the AG 'Ems' for the Emden–Borkum trade, the *Fehmarn* is sailing on the Baltic following her sale to Flensburg owners in 1976. She offers shopping tours to Danish ports (where larger quantities of duty-free goods may be purchased). This ship of 735 grt can accommodate 1,000 passengers. (*Gert Uwe Detlefsen*)

Actually the company is much older, being the successor of the legendary 'Flensburg-Ekensunder DG', which before the First World War owned 50 ships. In 1897 the company was amalgamated with the Sonderburger DG to become 'United Flensburg and Sonderburger DG'. In 1935 Förde-Reederei took over the remainder of the fleet and built it up again. Today 20 ships are serving many routes on the Baltic and the North Sea. Among a number of smaller ships the company operates five ships of just below 1,000 grt. Many of their ships have been taken over as new-buildings, half a dozen have been purchased in this way. Förde-Reederei have also taken over, with their daughter company Bäder-Reederei, the services of Willy Freter of Heiligenhafen who built up a large fleet and went bankrupt a few years ago when he

Below: One of the few pure ferries on the Baltic, and also the newest, is the *Strande* of Kieler Verkehrs AG. She was delivered in Spring 1984 by Paul Lindenau and can take 300 passengers. The 295-grt ship connects Kiel with the villages around the Kiel Fjord. (*Gert Uwe Detlefsen*)

Above: A typical ship of the first post-war generation of passenger ships of Flensburg Fjord is the 152-grt *Kollund*, built by the Husumer Schiffswerft in 1967. The ship is managed by Förde-Reederei Flensburg and is employed on the 20-minute run between the German port of Flensburg and the Danish port of Kollund. (*Gert Uwe Detlefsen*)

afraid of losing their employment. Without these shopping tours there would be very little demand for excursion ships. Due to high running costs the fares would then have to be considerably higher, so that only a very small number of people would continue to make use of the ships. For those 'fans' one ship at each port will be sufficient. Regarding the big tours the future is quite rosy because there is no way that Brussels and its bureaucrats can forbid them since they would then have to stop sales on every ferry and on all planes as well. The majority of the people concerned simply do not understand why, when duty free shops at airports are being allowed, their tours are not. The majority of the day trippers, especially outside the tourist season, are pensioners who enjoy these trips as a means of cheap shopping and as a method of spending their time with people of their own age. Should such trips really have to be stopped then many people with lose their jobs and many of the owners will go bankrupt since there would be little need otherwise for such ships. No one in Germany will buy a 'butter steamer' then.

For many years now, owners have learnt to live with the danger of the 'butter tours' being stopped and they are still investing in new ships and modernisation. In the past, new ships were constructed but now, due to the ever rising costs and limited expections of amortisation, owners prefer to purchase ships second-hand. In this way, established owners disposing of their older tonnage give new owners the chance to obtain ships at reasonable cost for their trade.

The largest owner on the Baltic as regards the number of vessels is the Förde-Reederei GmbH of Flensburg, who celebrated 50 years of trading in 1984.

became involved in real estate speculation. He was a fisherman who made a fortune with the building of the Fehmarnsund Bridge, which he then invested in the passenger trade from his hometown Heiligenhafen. In his best times he was known as the 'King of Heiligenhafen'.

Another important 'butter company' is the KG Seetouristik of Flensburg who, however, operate their ships not from Flensburg but from Burgstaaken at Fehmarn island and from Travemünde. They also own the Helgoland trader *Wappen von Hamburg* as mentioned earlier. The Seetouristik ships are all larger than the others. Their *Baltic Star*, better known as the German Vietnam hospital ship *Helgoland* and built in 1963 at Howaldtswerke Hamburg, is 2,855 grt and registered to carry 1,300 passengers. *Käpt'n Brass* and *Dania* are newbuildings fitted for 830 and 600 passengers respectively, while their *Poseidon* and *Fehmarn* (900 and 630 passengers respectively) were purchased from other German owners.

The Kieler Verkehrs AG of Kiel is the only company really serving in regular trade at the Kieler Fjord, with its ships connecting Kiel with the suburbs on the

A former ferry of the Wyker Dampfschiffs-Reederei on their service from Dagebüll–Wyk–Wittdün, is the *Baltica* of Seetouristik Kappeln. As one of the last vessels of the first post-war generation of newbuildings she changed hands in 1982, going from WDR to Rolf Böttcher at Neustadt, who sold the 373-grt ship in 1983 to her present owners. She has accommodation for 660 passengers. (*Gert Uwe Detlefsen*)

water front. The company has just started renewing its fleet with less attractive 'waterbuses', all built at the Lindenau-Schiffswerft at Kiel.

The small passenger ferry scene around Germany is very colourful, and anyone interested in seeing this fascinating armada of attractive white ships shouldn't hesitate too long to see them trading. If Brussels carries out its decisions, the majority of them – except the 'real' ferries – will probably be laid up somewhere to rot away before they are towed off to be scrapped, so ending one of the most popular, fascinating and socially-rewarding aspects in the long line of German nautical history.

The Survival of Scottish Shipbuilding

by Jim Prentice

Shipbuilding has always been one of those heavy industries held firmly in the grip of cyclical economic pressures, producing periods of feverish activity followed by hard times when orders are either hard to come by or non-existent. The Scottish shipbuilder, in common with his European brethren, could just about cope with such conditions, certainly they have done so successfully for many years, but since the 1960s, higher living standards and changing attitudes to work have affected costs of production to such an extent that Far Eastern shipbuilders have established themselves as the dominant force in world shipbuilding. As far as Scotland is concerned, the industry is in decline

The *Loftnes* was delivered to Jebsen (UK) Ltd in July 1984. She is seen returning to Govan from trials on 6 July 1984.

to the extent that only six shipbuilding yards remain in production today where once there were dozens. In this review it is my intention to look at these yards, their past, present time, and perhaps attempt to make an inspired guess about their future.

Glasgow is no longer dependent on heavy industry as it once was, but it still retains shipyards at Govan (merchant ships), Scotstoun (warships) and Clydebank (mobile oilrigs), directly employing 5,000 to 6,000 people. Govan Shipbuilders had its origin as Fairfields but, in the late sixties, it became part of the ill-fated Upper Clyde Shipbuilders. The yard somehow managed to survive the wreck, albeit with support from the public purse, so that when British Shipbuilders became a reality on 1 July 1977, Govan formed an important part of the new organisation. During the first three years after nationalisation Govan's three building berths completed six of the versatile 'Kuwait' class

cargo vessels, which were suitable for most dry cargoes and ideal for fast cargo handling. The accent then shifted to bulk carriers when four vessels of 16,500 deadweight and three of 4,400 deadweight were built as part of the infamous Polish order which was no doubt taken by British Shipbuilders just to keep the yards working. 1981 saw the revival of the previously successful 'Cardiff' class bulk carriers of which 29 were built, with two further ships each of 26,100 tons deadweight. The next three years saw the completion of a further nine bulkers in the tonnage range 35,000 to 67,000 deadweight. The last two vessels, *Lakenes* and *Loftnes* were delivered during the first half of 1984 and the current order book includes three 20,000 deadweight colliers for delivery to the Central Electricity Generating Board during 1985 plus a tanker of 60,000 tons deadweight for Hong Kong owners. The latter vessel will be the first tanker to be built at the yard since the *British Commodore* of 1966.

A couple of miles downstream from Govan lies the warship building yard of Yarrow (Shipbuilders) Ltd. The yard was nationalised in 1977 and even in 1984

Built by Fergusons of Port Glasgow, the *Isle of Arran* operates on the Cal-Mac service from Ardrossan to Brodick. In the photograph she is leaving Ardrossan. The Arran hills are in the background.

Bay Driller is the latest jack-up rig to be delivered by UIE of Clydebank. She is seen on her way to the Tail of the Bank for 'fitting out' to be completed.

litigation was still ongoing between the former private owners and the Government regarding compensation for the assets taken over. It now looks as if the yard will be returned to private ownership in the not too

distant future. Unlike Govan, the building ways are covered and this ensures efficient production, as work may proceed irrespective of weather conditions. Yarrow built some of the Vosper-designed 'Amazon' class frigates (Type 21) and currently work is progressing on the frigates HMS *Brave* and HMS *London* of the 'Broadsword' class (Type 22). Diversification into glass-reinforced plastic hulls brought forth the 'Brecon' class. Mine Counter-

Mwokozi was built by Fergusons for Kenya Ports Authority and delivered during July 1984. In the photograph she is returning to the fitting-out quay in James Watt dock, Greenock. The BP mobile production platform *Sea Explorer* can be seen above the stern of *Mwokozi*.

British Spirit was the last conventional ship built by Lithgow. It is hoped that the new management may once again build conventional ships at the Lithgow yards.

measures ships (MCMV) *Cottesmore* and *Middleton*, while *Hurworth* is still under construction, the latter vessel being commissioned into the Royal Navy on 15 August 1984. Export orders have been scarce over recent years and amount to only *Tonb* and *Lavan*, landing ships for the Iranian Navy. It is hoped that the order for HMS *Norfolk*, first of the Type 23 frigates, will be followed by up to seven more and that export orders will be forthcoming.

At Clydebank, the once famous and proud yard of John Browns no longer build ships but since the collapse of Upper Clyde Shipbuilders the yard has produced mobile oil drilling rigs. Ownership went initially to Marathon Ltd of the United States then passed to the French concern Union Industrielle et d'Entreprise (UIE).

Twenty miles or so downriver from the Glasgow yards lie the yards of Ferguson Brothers and Scott Lithgow, taking up as they do, virtually all of the waterfront from Port Glasgow to Greenock. Ferguson Brothers (Port Glasgow) Ltd was established in 1902 by three members of the Ferguson family, formerly managers with Fleming & Ferguson of Paisley. The firm was taken over by the Scott Lithgow Group in

One of four tugs built by Ailsa of Troon, the *Nguvu II* poses in the sunshine on her return from trials on 30 March 1984.

the late 1960s and along with the latter became part of British Shipbuilders on 1 July 1977. During 1980 British Shipbuilders amalgamated Fergusons and Ailsa of Troon under a common management company. The Ferguson yard is really quite small, only two berths capable of building vessels up to 330 feet in length. Both are open to the elements. Since 1977 it has produced 18 vessels including three mini-bulk carriers, two passenger ferries, three barges, two fishery protection vessels, one dredger, the forepart of a liquid gas tanker, an OSV and five tugs. Of these, the 1984 deliveries include the *Isle of Arran* for the Caledonian MacBrayne Ardrossan to Brodick service, plus two tugs for the Kenya Ports Authority of Mombasa. An ash carrier for the Central Electricity Generating Board plus two oil rig supply vessels will keep the yard working throughout 1985.

Close by to Fergusons is the sprawling complex of Scott Lithgow. The company history goes back to 1874 when the firm of Russell & Company was established to build standard design sailing ships and latterly steam tramp ships. 1891 saw the company reconstructed when William T Lithgow took over. In 1918 the yards of Robert Duncan & Co, William Hamilton and Dunlop Bremner were taken over under the name of Lithgow. A merger with Scotts Shipbuilding &

Engineering Company of Greenock took place in 1967 hence the name, Scott Lithgow. The Group then became part of British Shipbuilders on 1 July 1977. Vessels continue to be listed by Lloyd's Register as having been built either by Scotts or Lithgow. So far as Scotts are concerned, production from 1977 to the present included a mini-bulker of 3,500 deadweight, a self-propelled dynamically positioned drill ship called *Pac Norse I*, and three multi-purpose cargo vessels of

St Helen was the last ship to be built by Henry Robb Ltd of Leith. She is seen on the stocks on 7 August 1983.

The relatively sophisticated liquid gas tanker *Tarihiko* was delivered to New Zealand owners early in 1984 once problems concerning her modern steering system were overcome.

21,000 tons deadweight. Over the years Scotts have carried out warship building and repair work, including submarines. The Royal Fleet Auxiliary's *Fort Grange* and *Fort Austin* were built by Scotts during 1978–79 while the seabed operations vessel HMS *Challenger* was delivered to the Royal Navy during 1984. Lithgow, over the same period, scaled down actual shipbuilding preferring to concentrate instead on structures for the off-shore oil industry. Ships built from 1977–79 included two multi-purpose cargo vessels of 18,000 tons deadweight plus two 268,000 deadweight tankers. The final ship to be handed over during 1983 was the *British Spirit* of 198,000 deadweight for British Petroleum. As regards work for the off-shore oil industry, only the support vessel *Iolair* for British Petroleum has been delivered. With losses of £73 million in 1983 and the delivery of the mobile drilling rig *Sea Explorer* to BP extending further and further into the future, the Group was finally sold by British Shipbuilders on 28 March 1984 to Trafalgar House PLC after that company had come up with an acceptable offer. The rig contract has been renegotiated and work proceeds on it and another similar contract, albeit with a much reduced workforce.

The remaining Clyde yard is located well down Firth at Troon, Ayrshire, where building of steel-hulled vessels began in 1887 and has continued to the present day. Due to the yard not having a large enough building capacity, it was not nationalised in 1977 but a year later was included when it became known that the private owners wished to cease trading. A modernised yard, it has a building hall covering two slipways capable of taking vessels up to 380 feet in length. From 1978 until the present, 11 vessels have been completed. These include a buoy tender for the Middle East, the passenger ferry *Loch Mor* for Cal-Mac, a liquid gas tanker for New Zealand owners, a 4,400 deadweight bulker from the Polish order, a sand dredger for the Thames company Civil & Marine, the stern section of the liquid gas tanker *Traquair* and an OSV, *Star Vega*. During 1984 four tugs, *Simba II, Nguvu II, Chui* and *Duma* have been delivered to the Kenya Ports Authority of Mombasa while a passenger ferry for the Shetland Isles Council is completing. Like the Ferguson Yard at Port Glasgow, Ailsa have two oil rig supply vessels on order and this will keep the yard working throughout 1985.

Apart from the yard at Methil in Fife where structures are built for the off-shore oil industry there is now no shipbuilding on the River Forth. Closure of the Henry Robb shipyard took place shortly after its last vessel, the vehicle/passenger ferry *St Helen* was completed for Sealink during November 1983. The closure brought to an end a long connection with shipbuilding on the site which is located within the enclosed docks at Leith. When nationalised in July 1977 the Company was known as Robb Caledon Ship-

builders Ltd, the partner being the Caledon yard at Dundee. Lack of orders compelled British Shipbuilders to close the Caledon yard during 1980 whereupon the yard at Leith reverted to its former name of Henry Robb Ltd. A notable vessel, completed for the Corporation of Trinity House, London, was the extremely well appointed buoy and lighthouse tender *Patricia*. Other completions during the period of nationalisation included a liquid gas tanker, a coaster, a dredger, the passenger/vehicle ferry *Claymore* for Cal-Mac, crane barges for Poland, two OSVs and two tugs for Nigeria.

The remaining Scottish yard is that of Hall Russell in Aberdeen. Since nationalisation the main customer has been the Ministry of Defence, the vessels being either patrol or torpedo recovery vessels. The only exceptions were three tugs for Shetland Towage Ltd in 1978 and an OSV for Seaforth Maritime (Aberdeen) Ltd in 1982. Delivery of the five 'Peacock' class patrol vessels for the Royal Navy should be completed by early 1985 while work on the £28 million Ministry of Defence order for three mooring and salvage vessels will have commenced. The yard is modern with covered berths capable of building vessels up to 470 feet in length and steps are already being taken to privatise its ownership.

What then of the future? In the face of continued world overcapacity in shipbuilding, the Scottish industry has become leaner and more competitive, to the extent that it should be able to hold its own in world markets without further contraction. Warship orders remain at a reasonable level, consequently Yarrows are in the enviable position of having a secure future in the 1990s. The other yards have sufficient work to take them through most of 1985 so there is still time to secure further orders. Additionally there is a distinct possibility that new submarines/repair work will go to Scotts and just an outside chance that the new management may once again build conventional ships at the Lithgow yards.

The Privatisation of Sealink

by Russell Plummer

After a build-up that seemed to last an eternity, the final passage of Sealink UK's harbour interests and fleet of more than 30 vessels into the private sector was swift and almost serene with the £66m July purchase by the Sea Containers Group causing only a brief and rather half-hearted chorus of protest. It quickly became clear that while other potential bidders had been hogging the headlines, the Bermuda-based container leasing enterprise had done its homework sufficiently well to be in a position to outline long-term plans within hours of House of Commons confirmation of the cash sale.

If anything, the pace of developments accelerated as the year progressed with Sea Containers' American-born president James Sherwood regularly emerging to fill in background detail. The overall objective, he insists, is to increase profits by producing a larger but more slickly organised ferry operation in which the maximum emphasis will be placed on improving the level and quality of shipboard service.

Car ferry services between Portsmouth and the Isle of Wight have been revolutionised since the introduction of the sisters *St Catherine* and *St Helen* which were among half a dozen passenger and vehicle vessels to sail in 1984 in the altered Sealink livery. Sealink British Ferries hope to order a third ship of the same design for the Lyminton–Yarmouth route during the present year and longer term plans include replacement of the veteran Portsmouth–Ryde passenger ferries with smaller fast ferries. (*Sealink British Ferries*)

Vortigern, aground at Ostend during Sealink's problem period in 1981–82. Today, a totally different atmosphere prevails around the operator, and the early 80s apathy seems to have disappeared. Sealink has been revitalised. Even the BR-style sandwiches and plastic cups are going overboard. Future prospects look good! (*Courtesy Ray Wilson*)

Privatisation of British Rail's ferries and harbours subsidiary had been in the air for a long time and when the battle finally hotted up in the opening months of 1984 only three serious contenders lined up following the Government decision to rule out bids from European Ferries and P&O under monopoly considerations. Then, at the eleventh hour, Trafalgar House dropped out and this left as front runners Sea Containers and a mix embracing City financial interests, the National Freight Corporation, Sealink's existing management and the James Fisher Shipping Group which had become known as the Sealink consortium.

Sea Containers' bid was ultimately accepted and although they received assets with a book value of £108m, some existing debts to British Rail also had to be taken on. Even so, the deal was described as 'the ferry sale of the century' by Ken Siddle, managing director of a still disgruntled European Ferries which, he claimed, would have paid up to £75m had they been allowed to take part in the bidding.

Sea Containers, formed in 1965 by Sherwood and two associates, has built-up assets in excess of £600m including 250,000 containers, four factories manufacturing containers and seven ships. Other activities included ship chartering but it was a downturn in this sector which prompted the move into the ferry business and it quickly became apparent that there was a certain amount of common ground. Sea Containers at once selected Parkeston Quay, Harwich – one of the major port facilities acquired with Sealink – as their main United Kingdom container base and repair/refurbishing centre as well as outlining plans for the development of the adjoining Bathside Bay site as an extensive container terminal.

The actual purchase of Sealink by Sea Containers' newly-formed, wholly-owned UK subsidiary British Ferries was completed on 27 July with the new company's board, headed by Mr Sherwood, adopting a mainly planning and monitoring role, leaving day to day management in the hands of the existing Sealink board which remains largely unaltered in composition. For operational purposes the fleet has come to be known as Sealink British Ferries and the only changes

Summer excursion services on Lake Windermere were part of the Sealink package acquired by British Ferries and the three ship operation had a record 1984 season with 615,000 passengers carried between Lakeside, Bowness and Ambleside. However, SBF feel the tourist potential can best be exploited by sale of the fleet to its associate company SeaCo Inc which has interests including hotels and the Venice-Simplon-Orient Express. Pictured at Lakeside are the veteran *Tern*, dating from 1891 and originally steam powered, and the *Swan*, built in the 1930s along with sister *Teal*. A fourth Unit, *Swift*, dating from 1900, has been laid-up for the last couple of years. (*Russell Plummer*)

to the striking new white and two-tone blue livery unveiled in the spring of 1984 is the addition of the words 'British Ferries' after the new italicised style of lettering for the name 'Sealink' on the ships' hulls.

The first priority for Sealink British Ferries was to completely reorganise the loss making Channel Islands services from Portsmouth and Weymouth with a £5m investment launching a high quality 'Starliner' overnight link in and out of Portsmouth as well as re-equipping vessels for a new 'Sunliner' daylight Channel Islands service from Weymouth.

The ferries allocated to the 'Starliner' service, *Earl Granville* and *Earl William* – originally acquired second-hand after initial construction for Scandinavian owners – are being completely rebuilt internally to provide luxury cabin accommodation for just 400 passengers who will pay fares inclusive of berth, dinner and breakfast. The cabins are designed for conversion into en-suite day rooms when the two ships are used additionally for a Portsmouth–Channel Islands service via Cherbourg, through which SBF are hopeful of obtaining a foothold in passenger and vehicle traffic

The Folkestone-based sisters *Hengist* and *Horsa* had the distinction of bringing the new Sealink colours to English Channel services. During 1984 the majority of ferries continued in the old Sealink livery with monastral blue hulls but the British Rail symbol was removed from funnels which were plain red with black tops. (*Russell Plummer*)

Sealink British Ferries are upgrading services between Weymouth and the Channel Islands and a new pattern of daylight sailings under the 'Sunliner' banner will be worked by *Earl Godwin* and *Ailsa Princess*. Internal facilities have been improved on both ships and *Ailsa Princess*, built in Italy in 1971 for the Stranraer–Larne route, is likely to be renamed during 1985. *Earl Godwin* first served the Channel Islands on charter in 1974 and was purchased the following year. The vessel started life as *Svea Drott* and ran between Helsingborg, Sweden, and Travemünde in Germany. (*Russell Plummer*)

Sealink's new colours were introduced to the Irish Sea by the Fishguard–Rosslare vessel *Stena Normandica* which is on long-term charter from Stena Line AB of Sweden. *Stena Normandica* is one of four similar vessels built in 1974–75 for the charter market. Two of them have been bought by CN Marine of Canada and now operate as *Marine Nautica* and *Marine Atlantica* while the other member of the quartet is now *Reine Astrid* in the Belgian RTM fleet and is used between Ostend and Dover. (*Sealink British Ferries*)

between mainland France and the Channel Islands.

Taking the place of *Earl William* in runs between Weymouth and both Jersey and Guernsey will be the *Ailsa Princess* which has been based at the Dorset port for the seasonal sailings to Cherbourg in the past three years. Both *Ailsa Princess* and the existing vessel *Earl Godwin* receive improved on-board facilities and a fifth ship, *Manx Viking*, is being allocated to the South

Sealink unveiled a striking new white and blue livery in the spring of 1984 when fleet flagship *St Nicholas* made a special visit to Dover fresh from overhaul and repainting at Dunkirk. The new colours were progressively applied to all major vessels during 1984–85 winter refits and the words 'British Ferries' are being added to the Sealink hull logo.

St Nicholas continues to work the prestige Harwich–Hook of Holland service and the present two vessels employed by SBF's Dutch partners will be replaced by a 30,000-ton super-ferry ordered in the summer of 1984 for delivery in 1986. (*Russell Plummer*)

Western Division to take over the Weymouth–Cherbourg route. The *Manx Viking* was bought from Spain's Aznar Line in 1978 and used to start the Manx Line service between Heysham and Douglas in the Isle of Man, entering the Sealink fleet when the route was fully absorbed in 1981. A larger vessel, *Antrim Princess*, is being moved from the Stranraer–Larne route to take the place of *Manx Viking* at Heysham and other Irish Sea tonnage is involved in significant switches for 1985 schedules.

SBF continue the traditional pooling arrangements with the French, Belgian and Dutch state fleets with the exception of the Newhaven–Dieppe route which has been given exclusively to French SNCF. And this year, for the first time, there is a major British presence in Belgian services with *St David* transferred from Holyhead–Dun Laoghaire crossings to run exclusively between Dover and Ostend alongside vessels of the Belgian Government shipping agency Regie des Transports Maritimes (RTM). Meanwhile, a Belgian ferry is to fill in for *St David* at Holyhead.

Services to French ports from Dover and Folkestone continue in the pattern established in 1984 with Boulogne served from Folkstone by a trio of British vessels while there is British/French collaboration on the Dover—Calais 'Flagship' service. One variation for 1985 is the revival of Dover–Boulogne sailings at the insistence of the French, and SBF's own long term objective is to concentrate passenger operations at Dover where the complex will be improved, Folkestone becoming principally a freight port.

To some extent SBF are forced to mark time in 1985 but by next year a building programme of a major

Earl William is one of two ferries converted into a 400-berth configuration to operate the new luxury 'Starliner' Portsmouth–Channel Islands service. Originally the Thoresen Car Ferries vessel *Viking 2* she later operated for Townsend Thoresen but retained Norwegian registry until purchased by Sealink in 1977. *Earl William* opened the Portsmouth–Channel Islands route but has worked mainly from Weymouth in recent years. The 'Starliner' service will be shared by *Earl Granville*, another former Scandinavian flag ferry which started life as *Viking 4* in the fleet of Viking Line consortium members Rederi AB Sally of Finland. (*Russell Plummer – Sealink*)

vessel every 12 months is envisaged. It is also planned to start totally new passenger routes between Harwich and Denmark as well as a Mediterranean circuit from Venice to Istanbul and Kusadasi, which is a logical maritime extension of the Venice–Simplon–Orient Express operated by Sea Containers' associate company SeaCo Inc which also has hotel interests bought from British Rail in 1983.

SeaCo are also expected to buy the Lake Windermere excursion operation that was acquired as part of the overall Sealink package. During the 1984 season from Easter to October the three Windermere vessels in commission, one of them over 90 years old, carried a record 615,000 passengers and it is felt that the full tourist potential of the fleet can be best developed through SeaCo's expertise in the leisure field. To allow SBF to concentrate on major passenger/vehicle and freight services, another minor off-shoot, the Tilbury–Gravesend passenger ferry is being sold.

SBF are eager to increase freight business in parallel with passenger expansion and new container services are planned from Harwich across the North Sea and up the River Rhine to Duisburg in Germany as well as from Portsmouth to Cherbourg and the Channel Islands. The existing Harwich–Zeebrugge service will also offer calls at Rotterdam and, on the Irish Sea, two of Sea Containers' own 'Tackler' class ships are to be phased in for the Holyhead–Dublin/Belfast Freight-liner services.

It is planned to float British Ferries on the London Stock Exchange within three to five years when earnings can justify a satisfactory share price. Sealink's turnover in 1983 was £260m with all but six of the 24 routes said to be profitable. Yet the £6.6m operating surplus from the ferry operation was only marginally ahead of the £6.2m earnings from facilities controlled by Sealink Harbours Ltd.

Well over half the revenue from the seven main harbour operations at Folkestone, Newhaven, Fishguard, Holyhead, Heysham, Stranraer and Harwich Parkeston Quay comes from Sealink ships and the rest is split almost equally between Continental partner fleets and other companies. At present, no services using the seven ports are in direct competition with SBF, although this will change when the Harwich–Denmark link is introduced in opposition to the long established sailings to Esbjerg by DFDS Danish Seaways.

Satellites and Ships

by Dag Pike

The role of satellites in merchant shipping is growing. Today satellites provide essential communication links for shipping on a worldwide basis and navigation systems which give worldwide coverage with a good degree of accuracy. Satellite information also improves the accuracy of weather forecasts and satellites also provide a link in developing emergency reporting systems.

The role of satellites is growing and today's facilities are only the tip of an iceberg which within a few years will encompass almost every aspect of merchant shipping and make satellites and shipping inseparable partners. One of the most advanced areas of satellite use in connection with merchant shipping is in communications. The first Marisat satellites were launched in 1976 by the United States and provide a communications system for merchant shipping. This was designed to replace the existing short-wave radio communication links which were suffering increasingly from congestion, interference and unpredictability. Conventional communication systems were also labour intensive requiring specialist skills to operate them, whereas satellite communications links offered the prospects of telephone and telex systems which could be operated in a similar manner to those located ashore without skilled help.

As the Marisat satellites were being launched the development of an international organisation to operate global maritime communications was also being developed and in July 1979 INMARSAT came into being and began operations in February 1982.

A typical Transit receiver for merchant ship use.

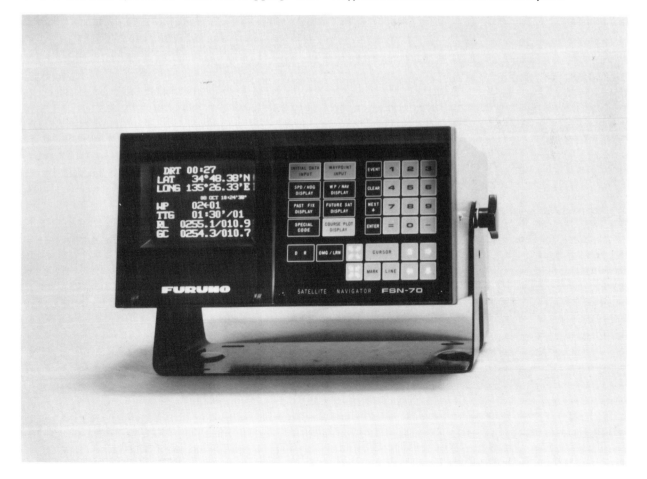

One of the early Navstar GPS receivers with antenna designed for survey positioning. Navigation receivers will be much more compact.

INMARSAT is a unique organisation established as a result of a conference held by IMO. Although IMO is a United Nations agency INMARSAT is not, nor is it funded by governments, but it is supported by both private and public organisations which are the national telephone authorities of the countries which are signatories of the INMARSAT agreement.

The Marisat satellites were transferred to INMARSAT and new satellites have been added to the system to provide a back-up service. Further satellites are planned in the near future to expand the capabilities of the INMARSAT communications links.

Over 3,000 ships are currently fitted with satellite communication terminals but this number is expected to grow rapidly for two reasons. At present satellite communications equipment has to be carried in addition to conventional radio equipment so that the satellite equipment is an additional expense for the ship owner. Many ship owners recognise the benefits of the excellent communication links provided by satellite equipment and are prepared to pay the difference, but a big expansion is expected when the satellite equipment can replace the standard equipment so that the ship owner need only carry one type. The other reason for the expansion of the satellite equipment is the reduction in both the cost and the size of the equipment and here great strides are being made. Compact above deck equipment will allow satellite communications terminals to be fitted to small vessels such as fishing and offshore support ships while the reduction in costs will make these installations more viable from the ship owners' point of view.

With the expansion in the fitting of satellite terminals will come the expansion in the range of facilities available through these terminals. Currently under development is a worldwide distress alerting system operating through satellite links which will give an immediate response to distress situations. Automatic transmissions will indicate both the position of the distress vessel and its name either through the main transmission equipment if this is operational or through EPIRBs which will maintain the distress transmission even if the vessel sinks rapidly. In this way satellite links should do a great deal to improve safety at sea but their role does not stop there.

The satellite communications link gives the prospect of vessels being monitored from the shore and this is likely to be an increasing role for satellite communications. Already many satellite communication systems are linked directly with position finding equipment so that the position of a vessel can be determined from the shore, but in the case of vessels carrying dangerous cargoes more sophisticated links are envisaged which will give early warning of any interference with sensitive cargoes.

Such systems are already in use with vessels carrying radio-active materials and could be quickly adapted to other classes of vessel which might be sensitive to terrorist attack.

On a more mundane level, automatic interrogation is being expanded to the monitoring of vessels' machinery and the introduction of high speed data transmission via satellite enables ship owners to have complete records of a vessel's operation so that maintenance can be planned in advance to ensure the minimum of delay. As shipping automation increases the role of the satellite communications link will become even more vital and it is envisaged that shipborne computers will link directly with computers on shore to provide the integrated links essential for safe automated ship operation.

Considerably older than the use of satellites for communications for merchant shipping is the use of satellites for position fixing. The development of the

The tell-tale SATCOM antenna which is now becoming a common feature on merchant ships.

The SATCOM antenna on Cunard's *Sea Princess*.

Transit satellite navigation system began as far back as 1958 and was operational in 1964. This system was released for commercial use in 1967 and at that time provided the first worldwide electronic position finding system for merchant shipping. Five Transit satellites circle the earth on comparatively low polar orbits and these orbits are accurately monitored by ground control stations.

Positions are determined by Doppler measurements from the satellite transmissions and can give position accuracies of a fairly high order providing accurate speed and course information is given to the shipborne receiver.

The only snag with the Transit satellite navigation system is that positions can only be determined when a satellite is above the observer's horizon which occurs at periods between 35 and 100 minutes. This is quite adequate for ocean navigation but not frequent enough for reliable coastal navigation. This means that the Transit system, while providing worldwide coverage, is not a fully worldwide system in the sense of meeting every user requirement. A similar system developed by the USSR called the *Tsikada* (Cicada) has similar limitations.

It was these limitations which led to the development of the Navstar GPS satellite navigation system.

Due to become operational in 1988, some sections of this system are already in use and commercial receivers have already been developed. The Navstar GPS system will employ 18 satellites uniformly spaced in six orbital planes inclined at 55 degrees. When fully operational this system will provide three-dimensional position finding on a worldwide basis. It is being developed by the US Department of Defence which was also responsible for the Transit system and, unlike Transit, Navstar GPS will be available for commercial users as soon as it is fully operational. However, commercial users will have to accept a degraded level of accuracy compared with that potentially available from the system.

The proposed accuracy level for Navstar GPS for commercial users is currently set at 100 metres. This will be available continuously and compares favourably with the accuracies of the Decca Navigator and Loran C systems and will generally be adequate for coastal as well as ocean navigation.

Such accuracy levels are unlikely to be sufficient for port approach navigation in many cases but the development of differential navigation systems for selected areas could upgrade the accuracy to between 10 and 20 metres which will be more than adequate for all merchant shipping navigation requirements.

Although Navstar GPS is well advanced in its development programme it is by no means the only

Typical of the capabilities of the INMARSAT system is the ability to transmit TV pictures to the shore with special equipment.

worldwide satellite navigation system being proposed or developed. In the USSR the *Glonass* system will have similar capabilities to that of Navstar and will operate in a similar way, but its availability for commercial shipping has not been released at this time.

Both of these satellite systems are primarily designed for military purposes and there have been proposals from several quarters for a purely commercial system to be developed to meet the specific requirements of commercial shipping and aircraft. One of these is Navsat which is being developed by the European Space Agency and it is claimed that such a system would be both cheaper and give greater accuracy levels than the military systems. These improvements could be obtained largely because there is no need to build security into the system.

Granas is another satellite based navigation system developed in West Germany, again for a purely commercial system but like Navstar, Granas is purely a paper exercise at this point in time and there appears to be little prospect of development on either of these systems once Navstar becomes fully operational.

One glimmer of hope on this front in development of a purely commercial system is that part of the INMARSAT mandate is the operation of satellite navigation systems as well as communications systems. Because of its international nature there is considerable logic in INMARSAT developing and operating a purely commercial navigation system. Concern has been expressed in many quarters about merchant shipping relying for their navigational requirements on a system under the control of either American or Soviet military organisations, and it is possible that this concern will develop to a level which will provide the necessary funding for INMARSAT to develop a new commercial satellite navigation system. In this event it looks as though the European Space Agency system could be a front runner.

Combining navigation and communication systems is considerable logic and a system which meets both these requirements is being developed on a commercial basis in the USA. The Geostar Corporation is developing the Geostar system which it is claimed will provide both highly accurate position information as well as limited communications capability. The system also offers the prospect of collision avoidance information and with these features could be all-embracing in terms of marine requirements.

As initially conceived the Geostar system is not worldwide but is capable of expansion. The initial system is proposed to cover the USA and adjacent waters and would employ two satellites in geostationary orbit. These satellites are purely communications links between very powerful ground computers and the user's receiver/transmitter. Positions are determined by measuring the time difference of the signals received via each satellite and accuracies down to five metres are claimed. Communications will be limited to simple

coded messages and distress indication would be a logical part of this communication system. The powerful ground computers would be able to identify potential collision situations and this would only be practical if all vessels are fitted with the equipment. The system is aimed at land, sea and air users and would be available on the payment of user fees to cover the costs.

The Geostar system is planned to be in operation by 1987 and the significance of this date is obvious when compared with the 1988 start-up date for Navstar GPS. By pre-empting the Navstar system it is hoped to attract many commercial shipping users operating solely in US coastal waters.

User fees are an essential part of the Geostar system and have been proposed also for the Navstar GPS system. However it appears that the Navstar user charges will be waived because of difficulties of collection and enforcement. This will add to the appeal of the Navstar system and for most shipping users its worldwide coverage will be its great attraction. Receiver costs in the initial introductory stage are likely to be around the 10,000 dollars mark but this figure is expected to drop rapidly as receiver develop-

Marconi's *Oceanray* SATCOM installation for use on the INMARSAT system, possesses one of the smallest and lightest antennas on the market. The miniaturisation of SATCOM is necessary before it can become viable on the smaller vessels thus creating the increased market potential that is required. (*Marconi Company*)

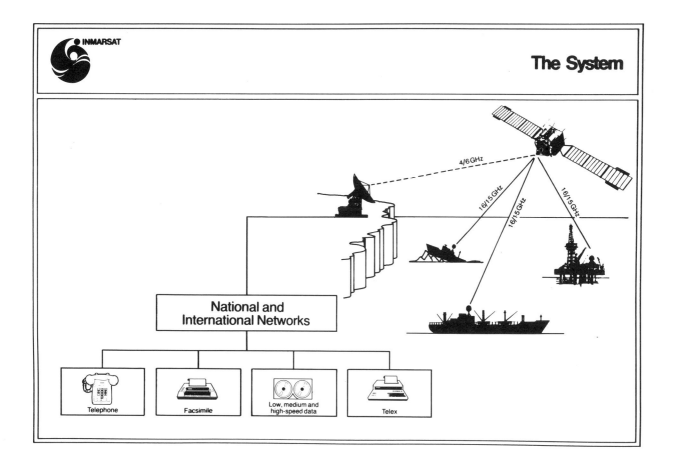

National and
International Networks

Telephone | Facsimile | Low, medium and high-speed data | Telex

ment progresses and, if the Transit experience is anything to go by, receivers costing around 1,000 dollars will eventually become available. The eventual cost of receivers is likely to be directly related to the extent of the market but the low cost will attract fishing and yacht users to create a very extensive market from which merchant shipping will benefit.

Meteorology is also benefitting greatly from the use of satellite observations. Five geostationary and four orbiting satellites are used for meteorological observations. These transmit pictures of cloud coverage and other information directly to earth and systems are becoming available whereby these pictures can be received directly onboard ship. Satellite coverage of weather features greatly improves the accuracy of weather forecasts and the ability to receive direct pictures from satellites will combine with the weather forecasts to give shipping a comprehensive picture of weather patterns. Similarly satellite observations can also measure wave heights and directions so that shipping will be provided with a much more accurate picture of its environment and, perhaps equally important, of the environment along its proposed track.

While satellites can produce an overview of the weather and sea conditions they can also be used for surveillance of shipping and this is also likely to become an increasing feature of maritime operations. Ships can be identified from satellites and their course and speed monitored on a worldwide basis, and while much of this information is currently used for military purposes there is an obvious role here for satellites in regulation and control of merchant shipping.

From a safety aspect this monitoring could have considerable benefits and could be used to direct nearby ships to a vessel in distress as well as providing possibilities for collision avoidance and vessel routing. For vessels carrying sensitive cargoes satellite monitoring could reduce the possibilities of interference with the cargo and such satellite monitoring could be an essential tool in the fight against terrorist activities if these start to extend to shipping operations.

Satellite monitoring has sinister overtones when considered in relation to the freedom of shipping but as shipping moves towards partial and then complete automation such monitoring will become essential if the right degree of safety is to be assured. Satellites will play an essential role in the move towards shipping automation and their influence on shipping operations over the next decade is likely to revolutionise many aspects of ship operations and provide the key to greater efficiency and greater safety.

New Lines to South America — Converting Conventional Cargoes to Containers

The European-South Americas trades have been served for many years by a multitude of conventional steamships from such famous stables as Royal Mail Lines, Pacific Steam Navigation, Nedlloyd, and various others, operating, in the main, conventional cargo vessels. Recently however, more and more goods have become part of the container revolution and 'the box' has been seen more and more on the decks of these vessels. Thus, almost inevitably, there dawned the day when the level of containerised cargo was such that justification existed for the establishment of a cellular container liner service, not in the form of a radical new concept, but simply in the natural process of development.

Transnave's *Isla de la Plata*, completed by Samsung as *Cordillera Express*, sister to *Humboldt Express*. Each has 34,000 dwt and is powered by a Hyundai-B&W developing a total power output of 23,800 bhp giving 18.5 knots. (*FotoFlite, Ashford*)

It came as no surprise therefore, when in the early 1980s the EUROSAL consortium was formed, to provide the Republics of the west coast of South America – Colombia, Ecuador, Peru, Chile and Bolivia – with a transition from conventional to container services.

The EUROSAL (EUROpe South America Line) consists of nine companies. There are the Pacific Steam Navigation Company (PSNC), Armement Deppe, Hapag-Lloyd, Johnson Line, Nedlloyd, Marasia, CSAV, Linabol and Transnave, of Britain, Belgium, West Germany, Sweden, Holland, Spain, Chile, Bolivia and Ecuador respectively.

The services include calls at Antofagasta (north Chile), Callao (Peru), Guayaquil (Ecuador) and Buenaventura (Colombia). The liners then transit the Panama Canal en-route to the United Kingdom, Spain and northern Europe, offering sailings every 12 days to and from the northern continental ports, and every 24 days to and from the United Kingdom, Sweden and northern Spain. Other ports in South America are served by feeder vessels operated by the individual consortium members.

Normally, one of the pre-requisites of switching a trade from conventional cargo shipping to container ships is port facilities matched to the fast handling and moving of boxes. This was one of the major stumbling blocks encountered by the Lines at the South American end of the routes, as while European ports had the infrastructure, many of the South American ports did not. After lengthy consultations with all concerned, it was therefore decided that special vessels would need to be provided, each equipped with some level of intrinsic container-handling gantry facilities.

Consequently, in 1982, the individual lines of the consortium placed orders for their new ships which were to subsequently commence operations in 1984. Five of these new vessels were to enter service this year, the *Andes, Humboldt Express, Bo Johnson, Isla de la Plata,* and *Maipo,* and another two may join the service later.

Each member of EUROSAL is allocated a proportion of the slots on the new ships, and through separate marketing the individual companies can maintain their own identities, while enjoying all the advantages of the more frequent and comprehensive services and facilities that their membership of the consortium provides.

The mv *Andes*

by John B Hill

John B Hill is the Chief Superintendant of Furness Withy (Shipping) Ltd.

On 27 August 1982, a contract was signed between Furness Withy (Shipping) Ltd of London, and Hyundai Heavy Industries of Ulsan South Korea, for the construction of one of a fleet of new container ships to work the EUROSAL container line sailings between Europe and the west coast of South America. Of 1,900 TEU capacity and due for delivery in April 1984, the *Andes*, as she later became known, represented a significant milestone in the evolution of not only the EUROSAL service, but also in the development of Furness Withy's South America trades previously served by fairly conventional tonnage in the shape of vessels such as the Pacific Steam Navigation Company's *Oropesa* and *Oroya*.

Described as a multi-purpose container vessel, the *Andes* was constructed in one of the large Hyundai

---

Andes at sea, on her first line-sailing to South America. (*FotoFlite, Ashford*)

Andes' bows start to take shape in the building dock at Ulsan in October 1983. (*John B Hill*)

building docks, together with three other vessels. First sections were laid down in August 1983, floating-out took place four months later, and delivery was in April 1984. The principal particulars of the ship are shown in Table 1.

Built with raised forecastle, transom stern and a high accommodation block towards the after end, the *Andes* conforms closely in outward appearance to other container ships of similar size, with the exception of the large gantry crane on the foredeck. The vessel is divided into six holds, five forward of the engine room and one aft. All holds, with the exception of No. 6, are fitted with cellular guides.

No. 1 hold is designed for the carriage of dangerous cargoes meeting the IMCO Dangerous Goods Code Class 3 for inflammable liquids, while No. 5 is specially constructed to carry 40-foot insulated containers of the 'port hole' type – refrigerated by means of ducted cold air.

Designed primarily for the transport of bananas from Guayaquil, Ecuador, the refrigerated container system was supplied by A P V Hall International Ltd, Dartford. The refrigerating machinery comprises three Hallscrew compressor package units and a complete brine system, which can maintain containers at temperatures ranging from −23°C to 15°C.

No. 5 hold is fitted with 20 Halltherm 'Searod' vertical ducts, each duct supplying air at the required temperature to a stack of six or seven containers, thus enabling a total of 132 40 ft I S O Standard refrigerated containers to be transported. The refrigeration system is fully automatic, temperature control monitoring

Container guides in main holds. Apart from the provision for carrying refrigerated containers in No 5 hold, the ship has electrical sockets for supplying power to 99 integral refrigerated containers carried on deck. (*Hyundai*)

Andes in the building dock in Ulsan in late '83. Three other ships were building in the dock simultaneously. (*Hyundai*)

TABLE 1
PRINCIPAL PARTICULARS OF THE MV *ANDES*

Dimensions	202 (oa) × 32.2 (bm) × 9.5 metres design (moulded) draught.
	Summer loaded draught: 12.02 m
Capacities	37,020 dwt; 11,600 tonnes water ballast in peak double-bottom and deep tanks; 3,500 tonnes fuel oil in No. 2, 3 & 4 double-bottom tanks, and 500 tonnes diesel oil in deep tanks
Container capacity	Number of TEU below deck 836
	plus 40 ft reefer containers 132
	Number of TEU above deck 802
	In addition, a further 228 *empty* TEU can be carried in a fourth tier on deck
Service speed	18.5 knots
Complement	11 officers, 12 ratings

being accomplished by a Sentralink System which incorporates a Seawatch Console with print-out facilities and visual display units.

To cater for the shipment of large quantities of copper ingots or cathodes in bulk, No. 2, 3 and 4 holds are designed to carry copper on the tank tops to a height corresponding to two containers. This facility involved strengthening the tank tops, providing access for fork-lift trucks and improving lighting and ventilation in the areas concerned. Care has been taken to ensure adequate air circulation in anticipation of carrying coffee in ventilated containers in the same holds.

Thirty main deck hatch covers of the Macgregor pontoon type are fitted and to allow for carrying loaded containers, three-high on deck, special attention was paid to the strength of the covers.

The largest of the hatch covers weighs about 30 tons and for lifting these, and containers in South American ports which do not have container cranes, a 40-ton capacity travelling crane has been installed to serve Nos. 1, 2, 3, 4 & 5 holds. Manufactured by Messrs Orenstein & Kopple, Lübeck, the crane weighs 250 tons, is electro-hydraulic in operation, and positioning of the hoist above specific container bays is controlled by computer.

The only other lifting appliance fitted on deck comprises a 6-ton monorail hoist which is installed behind the accommodation. By means of extending telescopic arms, this crane has a 6-metre outreach from the ship's side and serves hatches which enable stores and spare parts to be transported directly to the provision rooms and the lower regions of the engine room.

Deck machinery is electric/hydraulic in operation and was manufactured by Hyundai to Fukushima/Brattvaag design. Apart from two separate 15-ton pull

137

windlasses, used solely for anchor handling, there are eight mooring winches, four situated on the forecastle and four on the after deck. Each winch is self-contained with hydraulic motor and auto tensioning device and can be controlled remotely from the ship's side. To cope with swell conditions which prevail in certain South American ports extra strong mooring bollards have been fitted and additional deck stiffening provided in way of the bollards.

Including the wheelhouse, there are seven decks altogether, the lower deck housing changing rooms, offices, hospital, air conditioning machinery, ballast control room, etc.

The next deck accommodates store rooms, the galley and dining saloons for officers and ratings. The galley is equipped with a conventional electric range and numerous labour saving devices; the lay-out of the equipment and the location of the saloons has been carefully arranged to facilitate self-service catering.

A small duty messroom is situated near to the galley and has the necessary equipment to supply hot drinks and snacks at any time.

'B' deck, above the galley and saloons, is devoted to recreational facilities. Identical smoke rooms with bars are provided for officers and ratings, the rooms having large low windows and both bars being connected to a central bulk-beer dispensing system.

Also on this deck, are spacious TV and Games Rooms, designed for use by both officers and ratings, a sauna room and a small outside swimming pool.

Andes' crane and foredeck hatch-tops. A Bromma-Smides remotely controlled telescopic spreader is attached to the crane for handling 20 and 40-foot containers. To minimise corrosion and salt water damage to crane controls and machinery, such machinery has been located almost entirely in dry spaces within the travelling gantry and the crane operating arms. (*Hyundai and John B Hill*)

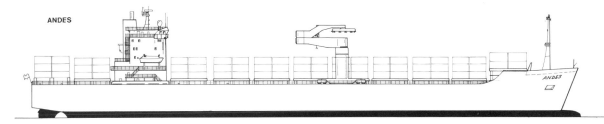

Profile view of the *Andes*. (Drawing: *Michael J Ambrose*)

'C' deck is devoted to crew accommodation, while the two upper decks contain quarters for officers and cadets.

Officers and crew members all have private bathrooms, and identical suites are provided for the Master and Chief Engineer on 'E' deck.

Throughout the accommodation extensive use has been made of plastic laminated bulkheads and special attention was given to sound insulation of living spaces. All cabins have fitted carpets, while passage-ways and working space have vinyl deck covering.

The galley and toilet spaces are floored with terrazo and extensive use is made of stainless steel fittings to minimise maintenance.

Apart from a particularly spacious wheelhouse, the Navigating Bridge Deck provides for only the pilot's cabin, the radio room and a toilet.

The wheelhouse arrangement is conventional insofar as it contains the usual steering column, chart-table, an engine control console, plus an impressive array of navigation aids and communications equipment.

A Racal Decca automatic adaptive pilot system, with dual electric control is fitted, together with an Arma Brouwn gyro-compass and a S G Brown course recorder.

The main superstructure block, constructed in the bottom of the building dock and lifted aboard prior to fitting out in an almost complete form. (*Hyundai*)

The foredeck during fitting out showing the hatch openings with two of the outboard forward hatch tops in position. (*John B Hill*)

As is usual in container ships, the accommodation and navigating bridge takes the form of a high, narrow erection, with the funnel, fan intakes, etc, partially built into the structure. *Andes* is seen here during fitting out in February 1984. (*John B Hill*)

The echo-sounder is of Simrod manufacture and a Hokushin speed log is installed. There are two Racal-Decca radar sets, one with ARPA and the other being type RM1629C.

A Mark 21 Decca Navigator is provided, and there is a Decca DS4 satellite navigator, with input from the electro-magnetic log and gyro-compass.

In addition to the I M R main radio installation, a IMRC Mascott 2000 satellite communication system with telex facilities is provided. Communication is further supplemented by means of H F radio-telephone.

To cover unmanned operation of the propelling machinery at night, and bridge control of the main engine when manoeuvring, there is an Tersaki control console incorporating engine room alarm repeaters, gauges, engine movement recorder and a call system for engine room staff. A separate crew call system is located elsewhere in the wheelhouse.

Above: Starboard quarter view of *Andes* during fitting out in February 1984. An elevator is installed to serve all decks below the wheelhouse, and there is an extension down to engine control room level. (*John B Hill*)

Left: The Fuji shaft-alternator. This supplies current to the main switchboard through a synchronous compensator, converter and inverter. On trials the unit was able to provide full output at 75 rpm, and during further tests a stable load of 500 kW was carried down to 42 crankshaft revolutions. (*John B Hill*)

Below: Andes' main engine under construction. A unique feature of this is the provision of a Fuji 1,000 kW alternator attached directly to the forward-end of the crankshaft. (*Hyundai*)

Andes' at the fitting-out berth in Ulsan harbour. (*John B Hill*)

The naming ceremony, Ulsan, 27 March 1984. (*John B Hill*)

The *Andes* is fitted with a 1,200 kW Nakashima/ Stone-Vickers bow thrust unit; propeller starting and pitch controls are situated in the wheelhouse and on the bridge wings.

The main propelling machinery comprises a direct-coupled Hyundai-built, Burmeister and Wain 5-cylinder L90 GBE diesel engine, with a maximum output of 19,390 bhp, and a service rating of 17,450 bhp at 93 rpm. This is designed to operate on heavy fuel oil of viscosity up to 6,000 seconds Redwood No. 1 at 100°F. At full load, fuel consumption is about 53 tons per day.

In addition to the shaft alternator, three Wärtsilä 6R32 diesel generators are fitted. These machines are coupled to Fuji alternators, each having an output of 1,700 kW at 720 rpm. Although a fuel blender has been installed, the generators are able to run on the same grade of fuel as the main engine and to date both main engine and auxiliaries have been operating successfully, utilising fuel of about 3,600 second Redwood viscosity.

For emergency use, a 6-cylinder Yanmar diesel generator is installed, capable of producing 350 kW.

The engine room is equipped with the usual electric drive auxiliary pumps, and compressors, all centrifugal pumps being of Teikoku/Hamworthy manufacture.

Three air compressors were supplied from Japan by Suction Gas Equipment Co, and there is an Atlas-Copco unit which supplies low pressure air for deck maintenance services.

A total of five Alfa-laval oil purifiers are provided – two for heavy fuel oil, one for diesel oil, and two for lubricating oil.

Other engine room equipment includes an Aalborg auxiliary boiler, a Greens exhaust gas economiser, and a 30 cubic metre per day Nagase-Nirex evaporator.

In the air-conditioned control room are the main switchboard, the machinery control console and the cargo refrigeration monitoring and print-out equip-

Andes on sea trials off Koje Island in March 1984. (*John B Hill*)

ment. The Teraski switchboard is equipped with automatic synchronising and load-sharing facilities for the alternators. The same manufacturer is responsible for engine room monitoring and alarm systems, comprising facilities for the automatic print-out of main engine and auxiliary operating temperatures and pressures. A fully equipped air-conditioned workshop is situated adjacent to the Engine Control Room.

The ship in its entirety was constructed under survey of Lloyds Register of Shipping and is classed and registered as + 100Al, containership + LMS, UMS and RMC.

At time of writing *Andes* had concluded two round voyages between Europe and South America and has demonstrated its versatility and fully justified the special design features which were incorporated into the specification.

Andes sails from Ulsan on 18 April 1984 at the commencement of her maiden voyage to Antofagasta and thence to Europe. (*John B Hill*)

Three Island Freighters — A Pictorial Sample of a fast-disappearing Type

by Jim Prentice

The general cargo vessel of 'three island' profile has been a prominent feature of the shipping scene for over a century. The 1950s and 1960s saw the production of designs of which naval architects could be justly proud since the vessels had graceful hulls, nicely proportioned superstructures and above all, splendidly shaped funnels. Curves were 'in' while straight lines were conspicuous by their absence. Not so the new container and ro-ro vessels which, as their nickname suggests, are box ships to carry boxes.

The 'three island' vessels are fast disappearing from revenue earning service, those illustrated being photographed in German, Dutch and Belgium waters during 1983–84. As one might expect with such elderly tonnage, ownership of the vessels illustrated is in the hands of either the USSR and its occupied territories, or Third world countries and territories of the so-called convenience flags. They have all but disappeared from the flags of nations with high operating overheads nowadays, and continue service only where low wages and/or subsidies continue to keep them in business.

Above: *Ludza* (USSR): Surprisingly this vessel is almost identical to *Kolpino*, having been built one year later by the same shipyard. The squat funnel, aerodynamic super-structure and masts are more in keeping with design of the late 1950s. Two 8-cyl Gorlitzer Masch oil engines of 2,500 bhp gives a speed of 12½ knots. Photograph: outbound from Rotterdam, 29 June 1984. (*Jim Prentice*)

Left: *Kolpino* (USSR): Built by Schiffswerft Neptun of Rostock, East Germany in 1958 she has a funnel reminiscent of pre-war design. Of 2,997 grt, her dimensions are 102.42 × 14.41 m. A compound 4-cyl and LP turbine by Karl Liebknecht (2,450 ihp) gives a speed of 12½ knots. Photograph: outbound from Rotterdam, 20 July 1983. (*Jim Prentice*)

Below: *Komiles* (USSR): Built in Poland by Stocznia Gdansk in 1960 and designated the B514 series. Of 4,533 grt, her dimensions are 123.88 × 16.74 m. A 5-cyl Sulzer 5,450 bhp engine gives a speed of 14¼ knots. Photograph: inbound to Grangemouth, 14 July 1984. (*Jim Prentice*)

Above: Slupsk (Poland): Built by Aalborg Vaerft of Denmark in 1965. Of 2,965 grt, her dimensions are 99.52 × 14.03 m. A 5-cyl B & W oil engine of 2,500 bhp gives a speed of 14¼ knots. Owner – Polish Ocean Lines. Photograph: westbound in Kiel Canal, 8 May 1984. (*Jim Prentice*)

Top right: John Brinckman (East Germany): Swedish-built by Oresundsvarvet A/B, Landskrona as *Belnippon* in 1964. Sold 1973 to VEB Deutfracht/Seereederei of Rostock. Of 6,313 grt, her dimensions are 138.82 × 18.45 m. An 8-cyl Gotaverken oil engine of 9,700 bhp gives a speed of 19 knots. Being designed for speedy transportation of refrigerated cargo she has particularly fine lines. Photograph: westbound in Kiel Canal, 5 May 1984. (*Jim Prentice*)

Right: Odysseus (Liberia): German-built by Kieler Howaldtswerke AG Kiel in 1967 as *Asseburg*. Sold 1979 to Caribbean Reefer Co Inc. Of 5,284 grt, her dimensions are 148.04 × 19.23 m. A 10-cyl Kieler Howaldtswerke MAN oil engine of 14,000 bhp gives a speed of 23 knots. Like *John Brinckman* she is a reefer but with a more impressive funnel. Photograph: Kiel Canal – westbound, 7 May 1984. (*Jim Prentice*)

Below: Staszic (Poland): Polish-built by Stocznia Szczecinska in 1963. Of 5,702 grt, her dimensions are 145.68 × 18.55 m. A 6-cyl Sulzer oil engine of 7,800 bhp gives a speed of 16¾ knots. Can carry 12 passengers. Owners – Polish Ocean Lines. Photograph: westbound in Kiel Canal, 8 May 1984. (*Jim Prentice*)

Above: Capetan Leonidas (Greece): British-built by Bartram & Sons Ltd, Sunderland in 1967 as *Tongariro* for New Zealand Shipping Co Ltd, London. Sold 1979 to Seaspeed Maritime Inc, Greece and renamed *Reefer Princess*. Sold again 1981 to Platana Maritime Co SA of Greece taking present name. Of 8,233 grt, her dimensions are 160.81 × 21.72 m. An 8-cyl Clark-Sulzer oil engine of 17,600 bhp gives a speed of 19½ knots. Classified as a reefer. Note the funnel colours of the Argentinean ELMA Shipping Co. Photograph: inbound Rotterdam, 20 June 1984. (*Jim Prentice*)

Kronos (Greece): Built 1967 by Ishikawajima-Harimi HI of Aioi for Japan Line, Tokyo as *Japan Totara*. Sold 1977 to Miaoulis Shipping Co Ltd of Piraeus, taking present name. Of 7,009 grt, her dimensions are 139.71 × 19.23 m. A 6-cyl I.H.I. oil engine of 7,200 bhp gives a speed of 16¼ knots. Has reefer capacity. Photograph: sailing from Antwerp, 19 June 1984.

Quelimane (Portugal): Built 1963 by Oskarshamns Varv, Sweden as *Evina*. Sold 1968 to Companhia Nacional de Navegacao of Lisbon, taking present name. Of 8,719 grt, her dimensions are 147.83 × 18.80 m. An 8-cyl Gotaverken oil engine of 6,500 bhp gives a speed of 15 knots. Has reefer capacity. Photograph: outbound Rotterdam, 14 July 1983. (*Jim Prentice*)

Jalakendra (India): Built 1965 by Hindustan Shipyard Ltd of Visakhapatnam for Scindia Steam Navigation of Bombay. Of 9,379 grt, her dimensions 152.91 × 20.10 m. A 6-cyl Masch Augsburg-Nürnberg oil engine of 8,000 bhp gives a speed of 16½ knots. Has reefer capacity. Photograph: inbound Rotterdam, 27 June 1984. (*Jim Prentice*)

Santo Amaro (Brasil): Built 1958 by Stocznia Gdansk, Poland. Present owners are Frota Amazonica SA of Santos, Brazil. Of 3,557 grt, her dimensions are 103.89 × 14.61 m. A 16-cyl Holeby oil engine of 2,640 bhp gives a speed of 12 knots. Photograph: outbound Rotterdam, 21 June 1984. (*Jim Prentice*)

Mithat Pasa (Turkey): Built 1961 by Mitsubishi S.B. & E Co Ltd, Shimonoseki for Denizcilik Bankasi of Istanbul. Of 3,652 grt, her dimensions are 106.61 × 15.07 m. A 5-cyl Uraga oil engine of 3,200 bhp gives a speed of 16 knots. Has accommodation for six passengers. Photograph: outbound Rotterdam, 29 May 1979. (*Jim Prentice*)

Hai Ning (China): Built 1969 by Stocznia Komuny Paryskiey, Poland for Peoples Republic of China. Of 8,727 grt, her dimensions are 152.61 × 19.49 m. A 6-cyl Cegielski-Sulzer oil engine of 7,200 bhp gives a speed of 16½ knots. Photograph: outbound Rotterdam, 25 June 1984. (*Jim Prentice*)

Above: Ferial (Ghana): Built 1959 by Lübecker Flender-Werke, Lübeck for Holland Amerika Lijn of Rotterdam as *Korendyk*. Subsequent changes of name were – *Volta Wisdom* (1972), *Odupon* (1977), *Ferial* (1980). Present owners are Remco Shipping Lines Ltd of Accra. Of 5,366 grt, her dimensions are 140.16 × 18.95 m. A 6-cyl Kon Maats De Schelde-Sulzer oil engine of 7,200 bhp gives a speed of 16 knots. Has reefer capacity. Photograph: outbound Rotterdam, 25 June 1984. (*Jim Prentice*)

Below: Ohio (Lebanon): Built 1960 by Wärtsilä of Abo, Finland for Svenska Atlant Linien of Gothenburg as *Svaneholm*. Subsequent changes of name were *Sameland* (1973), *Dafnos* (1978), *Ohio* (1980). Present owners are Ganmar Shipping of Beirut. Of 5,749 grt, her dimensions are 147.05 × 18.95 m. A 6-cyl Gotaverken oil engine of 7,300 bhp gives a speed of 17 knots. Has reefer capacity. Photograph: outbound Rotterdam, 21 June 1984. (*Jim Prentice*)

South Korean Shipbuilding – A Change in Approach?

by Dennis H Mann

Dennis L Mann is Lloyds Register of Shipping South Korea agent and representative. He is one of the world's foremost authorities on the South Korean maritime industries.

Fifteen years ago, South Korea did not really *possess* a shipbuilding industry. There were a few small yards, which managed to turn out fishing vessels and a variety of smaller units, but there were no builders even remotely comparable to those of the massive Korean shipbuilding industry of today. Now, South Korea boasts the second largest shipbuilding industry in the world, and is unlikely to be toppled from that position in the immediate future. But, can this massive expan-

Hyundai Heavy Industries took over three docks from its sister ship repair company at the beginning of 1984. Two of these docks, of 400,000 dwt and 250,000 dwt, are being used for newbuildings, while the third of 150,000 dwt is used for redocking. Five new cranes have been built and erected to service the building docks, and five new ships were scheduled to be floated out of these two docks in the year.

sion continue? It appears not. Already, South Korean builders have felt twinges of instability ripple through the industry, and the emergence of China as a shipbuilding nation, the fierce entrenchment of the challenged Japanese, and the general exacerbations of world overcapacity in almost all areas of shipping and shipbuilding, are beginning to take their toll. Even on South Korea.

Nevertheless, South Korean expansion has not finished. More increases in shipbuilding capacity are in hand. Yet, the wind of change is blowing, and the future development of South Korean shipbuilding over the next ten years will not mirror that of the past decade. Changes in strategy are becoming increasingly apparent in a number of areas. Consolidation, improved productivity, more flexible financing, more emphasis on design and development skills, and qualitive rather than quantitive progress, seem to be the projected aims for the forseeable future. Profitability enhancements also seem to figure more than they appear to have done in the past, and the 'dumping' criticism, although not always justified, is likely to

become less of a major topic as South Korea settles into her position as a world leader in merchant shipbuilding, maintaining her projected share, of around 25 per cent of the world market.

Although South Korea's big two, Dae Woo and Hyundai, have been increasing their building capacity with the other yards holding their own too, there has been a particularly significant, conscious effort to

Right and below: Hyundai's new test facility is aimed primarily at improving hull and propeller design to provide greater economical advantages to the ship owner.

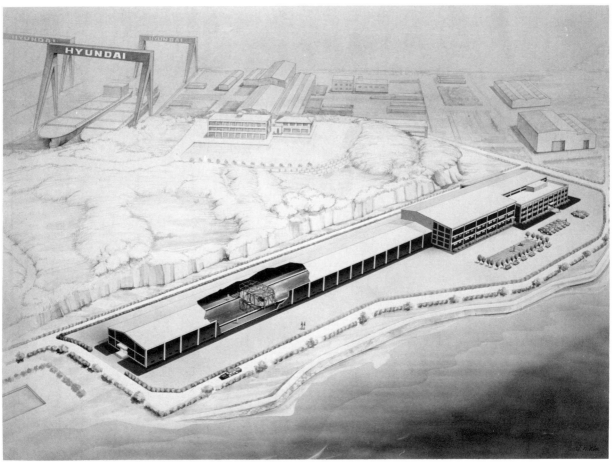

The launching of the crude oil carriers *Major Somnath PVC* and *Lance Naik Karam Singh PVC* on 14 June and 31 June 1984 respectively. Hyundai's Ulsan yard will have completed eight of these 67,000-dwt vessels for the Shipping Corporation of India by 1985.

The 630,000 cubic foot *Australian Reefer* undergoing outfitting work at No 1 Outfitting Quay of Hyundai's Ulsan shipyard. She will be delivered to her Danish owner J. Lauritzen A/S in November 1984.

improve quality rather than just quantity of late. This has resulted in the awarding of Quality Assurance Certificates from some of the major Classification Societies to Dae Woo, Hyundai and Korea Shipbuilding. These certificates are important accolades to the yards concerned, as they require the establishment of stringent and comprehensive control procedures, and have been awarded previously to only a limited number of the world's top builders. Basically, the award of these certificates, which can only cover certain defined stages in a ship's construction, permit the yard's own quality control personnel to pass work without the attendance of a surveyor, thus preventing

some of the stoppages previously necessary in the production programme. The surveyors, meanwhile, monitor the agreed procedures and spot check that the work still maintains the necessary standards and requirements.

Hyundai progress

Apart from an increase in new building activity brought about by the addition of two newbuilding docks, taken over from their sister ship-repair company, Hyundai Heavy Industries (HHI) have progressed well with the addition of two further research facilities during the year. The first of these is a model ship test basin, believed to be the first owned by a private company. The facilities include a deep water towing tank, a cavitation tunnel and circulating water channel, covering an area of 11,000 square metres, and are intended to help improve hull and propeller design. The second facility, a welding institute, will carry out research into various types of welding techniques and associated technology, and will help the yard to improve its welding efficiency.

Among the vessels completed by Hyundai this year, are a series of 67,000 dwt crude carriers, a series of 40,000 dwt product tankers, various bulk carriers (including combination vessels designed to carry containers), three sophisticated ro-ro vessels for Barber Blue Sea (detailed elsewhere in this edition), a series of refrigerated vessels, and the container ship *Andes* (also detailed elsewhere in this edition). Hyundai's completions for the year (shown in Table 1) are thus substantial, and with work having started during 1984 on another 33 vessels for delivery in 1985, added to the new orders from Greece and the Far East which were received in the latter part of the year, Hyundai's future therefore looks well.

Recently, the Hyundai group has gone through a phase of reorganisation in which the Hyundai Off-

View of mv *Archon's* upper deck area. She was delivered to her owner Aeron Marine Shipping Co of the USA on 19 June 1984.

TABLE 1
HYUNDAI HEAVY INDUSTRIES' SHIP COMPLETIONS DURING 1984

Ship	Type	Deadweight	Owner/Operator
Major Somnath Sharma PVC	Crude carrier	67,000	Shipping Corporation of India
Lance Naik Karam Singh PVC	Crude carrier	67,000	Shipping Corporation of India
Lieutenant Rama Raghoba Rane PVC	Crude carrier	67,000	Shipping Corporation of India
Naik Jadunath Singh PVC	Crude carrier	67,000	Shipping Corporation of India
Company Havildar Major Piru Singh PVC	Crude carrier	67,000	Shipping Corporation of India
Captain Gurbachan Singh Salaria PVC	Crude carrier	67,000	Shipping Corporation of India
Major Dhan Singh Thapa PVC	Crude carrier	67,000	Shipping Corporation of India
Subedar Joginder Singh PVC	Crude carrier	67,000	Shipping Corporation of India
(First eight in a series of 11)			
Flying Officer Nirmal Jit Singh Sekhon PVC	Products carrier	40,000	Shipping Corporation of India
(First in a series of four)			
Barber Tampa	Ro-Ro/Container	30,400	Barber Blue Sea
Barber Texas	Ro-Ro/Container	30,400	Barber Blue Sea
Barber Hector	Ro-Ro/Container	30,400	Barber Blue Sea
Chelsfield	Bulk carrier	39,000	Dreyfus Group
Harefield	Bulk carrier	39,000	Dreyfus Group
(First two of a series of six)			
Wadi al Nakheel	Bulk carrier	45,000	National Line of Egypt
(First of a series of four)			
Australian Reefer	Refrigerated cargo	600,000 m³	Lauritzen Group
African Reefer	Refrigerated cargo	600,000 m³	Lauritzen Group
(First two of a series of four reefers)			
Esmeralda	Bulk carrier	36,500	Comninos Group
Esperenza	Bulk carrier	36,500	Comninos Group
Al Amir	Bulk carrier	65,000	Gulf East
(Second of a series of two)			
Aurora	Bulk carrier	63,800	Aeron Marine
Archon	Bulk carrier	63,800	Aeron Marine
Ulla	Bulk carrier	18,000	MOC Group
Trudy	Bulk carrier	18,000	MOC Group
Andes	Container	37,020	Furness Withy Group
Kowulka	Gypsum carrier	23,000	Australian owners
C A Margaronis	Bulk carrier	23,500	Diana Shipping
Spring Dream	Reefer	470,000 m³	Salen

and five bulk/container ships for a Panamanian subsidiary of Hyundai's own shipping company, to be named *Pacific Prosperity, Pacific Pride, World Champion, World Peace* and *World Success.*

shore and Engineering Company Ltd was created in order to centralise the group's off-shore activities. The new company can offer the design, engineering, fabrication, transportation and installation of all kinds of off-shore and certain types of on-shore structures. With a workforce of 6,500, it has two building yards capable of producing 150,000 tonnes per year of both jackets and modules.

Work presently in hand is substantial, and includes:

The *Win* process-platform project (off Bombay) for the Oil and Natural Gas Commission of India – a turnkey project which includes both the construction and erection of a jacket and all topsides modules for the platform, plus modifications and additions to the surrounding structures.

GOSP 2 + 3 for the Saudi *Marjan* offshore facilities for ARAMCO – another complete turnkey project consisting of the fabrication and erection of 11 jackets, eight modules, and connecting bridges.

The fabrication and hook-up of six modules and four bridges for the Union Oil Company's *Satun* and *Platong* Field facilities in the Gulf of Thailand.

The fabrication and transportation of seven decks, modules, and the flare boom for Texaco's *Harvest* platform off California, and about five other major off-shore projects destined to keep the Company busy for quite some time.

As for Hyundai's re-fitting and ship repair company, Hyundai Mipo Dockyard, contraction and rationalisation have been the major features for 1984. Having lost nearly 50 per cent of its total area when it passed the three of its seven dockyards to HHI, the company now has only one site adjacent to the No. 2 off-shore yard in Ulsan Harbour, and has supplemented

Hyundai Offshore's Yard No 1, where the company's main offices are situated. The yard covers an area of 500,000 square metres and is situated on the coast next to the HHI shipbuilding yard near Ulsan.

Hyundai Offshore's Yard No 2 of 320,000 square metres. It fronts onto Ulsan harbour and is only a few miles from the main Hyundai complex.

its repair business by obtaining six conversion jobs, and even completing newbuildings in the shape of three 3,700 dwt asphalt carriers for Indonesian owners.

The conversion jobs consisted of:

Lengthening the four Scandutch container ships *Selandia*, *Jutlandia*, *Nihon*, and *Toyama*;

removing a 62 metre section from the cargo tanks of *Chevron London*, reducing its deadweight from 250,000 to 150,000 tonnes;

converting the *Mawashi Tabuk*, a 22,000 dwt general cargo ship into a livestock carrier. A job started in late 1984 and estimated to take 11½ months to complete – involving the addition of 4,000 tons of steelwork – converting the cargo holds into five decks and adding a further four decks above the existing maindeck, and moving the wheelhouse to the forward end of the new structure. The end result will be a capacity for 79,000 SEU (sheep equivalent units).

Hyundai Precision and Industry Co covers the demolition end of the business in the Ulsan area and is located next to the No. 2 Offshore yard in Ulsan

Harbour. The most notable ship to be scrapped during the year was the *Ulsan Master*. This vessel started its life as the *Pierre Guillaumat* and is in fact the largest ship to have been built at 555,000 dwt. (The *Seawise Giant* holds the record for the largest ship at 565,000 dwt, but she was jumboised to reach this size.) Before succumbing to the breaker's torch, the ship lay alongside for several months in 1983, and rumours of possible conversion into a floating crane or botel were being passed around. It seems a sad reflection on the state of the shipping business that no further use could be found for this vessel, as she was only seven years old when she arrived at Ulsan.

Finally, within the Hyundai group, are Hyundai Engine and Machinery Co (HEMCo) and Hyundai

The *Nord Atlantic*, a 150,000-dwt shallow draught bulk carrier. In addition to the newbuildings completed during 1984, two bulk carriers were delivered by Hyundai. These were the 150,000 dwt Nord Atlantic and the 63,700 dwt *Westin Won*. Both were originally completed in 1983 as the *Cast Orca* and the *West Dallori*, but were not previously delivered due to the problems of the potential owners/operators. (Drawing: *Michael J Ambrose*)

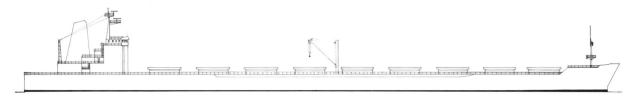

An aerial view of the Hyundai Mipo Dockyard. Approximately 280 vessels were handled by the complex in 1984 even though 50 per cent of capacity had been passed to HHI. These repairs included collision and grounding rectification, as well as normal steel renewal, painting and overhauling of machinery. The largest vessel handled to date has been the 285,000 dwt *Berge King*.

Selandia, the first of four Scandutch container ships being extended by the Mipo Dockyard. New 15-metre sections will be inserted to increase the capacity of each vessel by 220 TEU.

Electrical Engineering Co (HEECo), both located in the HHI yard, and supplying major items of equipment to the builders. At present HEMCo is the only Korean builder of large slow-speed marine diesel engines. HEMCo produces most of the major items of electrical equipment for marine purposes as well as a considerable amount of industrial equipment. Its switchgear division produces a variety of switchboards, control consoles, distribution panels and starters. Circuit

breakers are also assembled and used in the switchboards. The Transformer division can manufacture transformers up to 750 MVA at 545 KV as well as the much smaller ones for marine use. The machines division produces both AC and DC motors and generators. Major marine equipment supplied in 1984 consisted of 53 main switchboards, 49 control consoles, 195 transformers and 140 generators. Of these some 80 per cent were for HHI ships, while the remainder were despatched to other builders.

Dae Woo – Korea's other giant

Located at Okpo on Koje Island off the south coast of Korea, is Dae Woo Shipbuilding and Heavy Machinery Ltd, the second largest of the South Korean yards. The shipbuilding division started 1984 by completing the last one of a series of seven semi-submersible drilling rigs for domestic owners, but has since returned to more conventional types of vessels.

The bulk of the work undertaken in the year has

The last of the seven rigs completed by Dae Woo. The yard took on these difficult structures when newly opened some four years ago, representing a tremendous show of confidence in their own abilities. The *Doo Sung*, a semi-submersible rig, was for the Korea Drilling Co.

Dae Woo's floating dock, bought in to alleviate the repair divisions capacity shortage.

TABLE 2
DAE WOO SHIPBUILDING'S COMPLETIONS DURING 1984

Ship	Type	Deadweight	Owner/Operator
American New York	Container	57,800	United States Lines
American New Jersey	Container	57,800	United States Lines
American Maine	Container	57,800	United States Lines
American Alabama	Container	57,800	United States Lines
American Virginia	Container	57,800	United States Lines
(First five in a series of 12)			
Iran Dastgheib	Bulk carrier	40,000	Iran Shipping Lines Ltd
Iran Kashani	Bulk carrier	40,000	Iran Shipping Lines Ltd
Iran Chamran	Bulk carrier	40,000	Iran Shipping Lines Ltd
Iran Ghafari	Bulk carrier	40,000	Iran Shipping Lines Ltd
(First four of a series of 20)			
Global Fortune	Bulk carrier	60,000	Global Shipping Co of Korea
Ocean Korea	Bulk carrier	60,000	Pan Ocean Bulk Carriers
Nand Krishna	OSV/Tug	1,450	Essar Bulk Carriers of India
Nand Heera	OSV/Tug	1,450	Essar Bulk Carriers of India
Nand Panna	OSV/Tug	1,450	Essar Bulk Carriers of India
Nand Godavari	OSV/Tug	1,450	Essar Bulk Carriers of India
Nosac Tasco	Ro-Ro		Wilhelmsens
(First of two)			

A further 25 ships are due to be delivered during 1985.

revolved around two massive orders for United States Lines and the Iranian National Line. The former order was of course the much publicised 4,380 TEU container ships, 12 of which having been ordered for US Lines new east-about Round-The-World service. The latter order was for twenty 40,000 dwt bulk carriers for worldwide service. In order to complete these massive orders within the contract dates, both existing dry docks are being used exclusively for newbuilding work, and as such, the Dae Woo Repair division found it necessary to acquire a 52,000-ton lifting capacity floating dock to augment its small existing unit. Around 30 vessels were overhauled by the Repair division during 1984.

Dae Woo's Offshore division had a successful year, with expansion being the order of the day. The existing 150,000 square metre yard is in the process of increasing to 500,000 square metres; the length of quay is moving up from 400 metres to 2,318 metres; a new Tabular manufacturing shop has been set up to fabricate the full range of pipes and tubes for off-shore structures, and the work output for 1984 included seven major projects for jackets, modules, barges, etc, for off-shore fields as far away as Libya and California.

The associated company of Dae Woo, Shin A Shipbuilding Co Ltd located on Miruk Island in Choong

Nand Panna, one of the four supply vessels for Essar Bulk Carriers of India, built by Dae Woo Shipbuilding.

Dae Woo's No 2 dock, used exclusively for new construction work this year, was augmented with the construction of a new 450-ton gantry crane.

Moo on the south coast of Korea, has turned much of its facilities in 1984 to helping its parent company. All the hatch covers, totalling some 1,200, will be fabricated for all the United States Lines container ships, the Iranian bulk carriers and the Dae Yang bulk carrier presently on order. Bow blocks are also being assembled for the US and Iranian ships. In addition to the above, the yard has delivered a 2,700 dwt heavy-lift ro-ro vessel named the *Haewoo Frontier* to the Haewoo Shipping Co. Work will be started on a further four vessels, a 3,000 dwt multi-purpose ship for Nam Sung Shipping Co, two 350 dwt general cargo coasters for Korea Express Co, and a 3,000 dwt flat barge for the Dong Bang forwarding Co.

Other yards continue to develop

One of Korea's older companies is Korea Shipbuilding and Engineering Corporation (KSEC) located in the southern city of Busan. The company has an associated company The Busan Drydock Co located next to the main yard. Vessels completed by KSEC in the year are as follows:

Al Dhibyaniyyah, the last in a series of 57,000 dwt

In July 1984 the jacket for the Texaco Harvest Field was lifted at Dae Woo's Offshore division.

tankers for the Abu Dhabi National Tanker Co;
Spring Delight and *Spring Desire*, reefer vessels for Salen;
Yanbu 22 and *Gizan 22*, tugs for the Saudi Arabian Port Authorities;
Pacific Bridge, a 1,244 TEU container vessel for the Korea Marine Transport Co;
Maria Gorthon and *Ada Gorthon*, two 9,900 dwt ro-ro vessels for Gorthons, and two as yet unnamed bulk carriers of 37,000 dwt for Pan Ocean.

In addition work has started on a further four vessels due for delivery in 1985.

The supply of ancillary equipment for ship and offshore structure building is another area of South Korean industry which has expanded considerably in recent years, fuelled by the boom in shipbuilding. They have increased their business not only because of the number of vessels being constructed but also because of the increased percentage of equipment they can now supply. Yet another area of South Korean expansion is the ship demolition spectrum too. Here, in a peripheral area of the shipping industry which runs counter to the norm (ie: it is a *growth* area), South Korea's scrapyards have been busy. This not only provides another market area, but is also extremely useful to the Korean economy in helping to offset the country's lack of exploitable raw materials.

Certainly, South Korea can be proud of its shipbuilding, repairing and breaking industries in 1984, especially so considering the general worldwide climate. It remains to be seen however, whether the present expansion rate can be continued. It would appear to be most unlikely, and already fears of considerable additional competition are looming on the horizon. Not, however, from neighbouring Japan, the world's largest shipbuilding nation, but from a newly emerging, rapidly developing society not too far to the north. It is from the People's Republic of China, where, in the not too distant future, one could well see an expansion of the shipbuilding industry, which could not only *mirror* South Korea's rapid expansion, but possibly *stunt* it too.

The harbour tug *Dong Bang* completed by Dae Dong Shipbuilding Co Ltd for Dong Bang Forwarding Co.

The 6,500 dwt log carrier *Ocean Rainbow* completed by Dae Dong Shipbuilding for Panamanian owners.

The Traumas of the TEU Transporters

by A J Ambrose

Following the lean years of the recession-troubled early 1980s, it seems that once again the volume of the world's container traffic is set to grow. But while containerisation is a growth industry sure enough, can the growth factors predicted possibly be sufficient to sustain the enormous amount of new tonnage which has entered the trade in 1984, and that which is under-construction for appearance over the next few years? The answer to these questions do not seem to be optimistic.

Growth, for the period 1985–86, is currently predicted to net an overall increase in actual 'boxed' cargo of around 17 per cent for the two year period. Meanwhile, the available ship capacity, for the same two year period, is set to rise by around 26 per cent. Coupled to the existing level of overcapacity in the box trades, it does not therefore need the services of a

mathematician to establish that the presently saturated market can only become worse, and that the economic supply and demand curve will fall so low that the business of container shipping will become totally profitless for most operators.

During 1984 many new cellular and part ro-ro container ships have entered the 'box' trades, making the year something of a significant milestone in this aspect of nautical and trading history. But it is not only the new ships which make the year significant, it is also their nature of operations and trading – best

The first of two sister ships for Empresa de Navegacao Allianca, the 26,850 dwt/20,995 grt 1,402 TEU container ship *Copacabana*, on her maiden voyage down the English Channel en-route for South America in the summer of 1984. (*FotoFlite, Ashford*)

Following the collapse of Cockerill in 1982 – Belgium's largest shipbuilder – the Cockerill Hoboken yards were taken over by Boelwerf. Since the takeover in 1983, Boelwerf have completed several vessels proving that the yard is fully operational again, and still capable of producing quality tonnage. A prime example of one of the yard's specialities is evidenced in the 1984-built *Maeterlinck*, the first of two sister 38,000 dwt/2,257 TEU container ships. *Maerterlinck* is for the Belgian Compagnie Maritime Belge (CMB) Europe-SE Asia services. The sister ship *Rhine Express* was delivered in late 1984. (*FotoFlite, Ashford*)

exemplified by the inauguration of United States Lines and Taiwan's Evergreen Line's new Round-The-World services, utilizing between them a fleet of no less than 36 large new ships!

The size of these vessels is increasing too, and already plans are in hand for the construction of a series of massive barge and container carriers of a quarter of a million tons each, destined to enter service on the already highly competitive North Atlantic liner market.

Since Malcolm McLean (former head of Sea Land and now behind the wheel of US Lines) really pushed the container ship into being in the early 1960s, the trade has expanded massively. Can this expansion possibly continue, or will the box trades follow the path and history of the large tanker market? Will the very large container carrier and the very large crude oil carrier follow a similar pattern of development? Shall the future hold nothing but lay-up in store for the present generation of container ships? Effectively, the answer to this last question can only be yes. And if the present spate of new ordering continues, it will be sooner rather than later that these patterns begin to emerge.

There are three obvious solutions to the overcapacity problem: early scrapping of the older steam-turbine vessels with their massive fuel bills such as OCL's *Jervis Bay*, a freeze on new-constructions, and a general rate increase across the board for container shipping. All three options are problematic.

Firstly, few owners will scrap ships if they can obtain a better price on the secondhand market, selling to the

less developed countries where such items as low crew wages means that these vessels can continue operation economically. Secondly, the developed countries *need* to build new more economic larger vessels just to retain their competitiveness in the present harsh trading environment, as otherwise they would simply be driven out of the box trades altogether. And thirdly, there is no body which could enforce rate rises, and there

Yet another large new container ship to enter service in 1984 is the Van Der Giessen De Noord-built *Nedlloyd van Dieman*. Powered by a Schelde-Sulzer of 14,875 bhp, this 29,730 dwt vessel has a service speed of 15 knots, and possesses a healthy economy of operation. Ship speeds are increasingly less vital than they were in previous years. (*FotoFlite, Ashford*)

The multi-purpose container ship *Savannah*, a 12,500 dwt/700 TEU vessel for Claus-Petter Offen. She was completed in 1984 by West German builders Seebeckwerft, and is a development of their 12,440 dwt/616 TEU 'Key 12' design. This yard, and indeed many West German yards, are prolific builders of container tonnage in this range. (*FotoFlite, Ashford*)

would always be undercutting to attract cargoes, the more so if cargoes are hard to obtain in the first place. Furthermore, there is the problematic fact that rate rises could well mean that less cargo would actually be containerised, as the economies of intermodal carriage could well be outweighed by competitive rates offered in the break/bulk and general cargo shipping sector. Thus, even an annual growth rate of 8½ per cent could

The 1984-built *Veronique Delmas* is one of builder Chantiers de l'Atlantique's new range of 'Chantel' designs which offer 1,000, 1,500, 2,000 and 2,500 TEU option standard design vessels aimed at developed and Third world country trades. *Veronique Delmas* is one of four sister 1,500-type vessels completing this year from this yard which has every intention of fuelling the overcapacity problems with their 'off the shelf' designs. As indeed are many others. (*FotoFlite, Ashford*)

Heyo Jansen's *Heicon* on her maiden voyage in 1984. Built by Bremer Vulkan, she is the first of three of these 'CMPC 1150' type multi-purpose container carriers for this owner. (*FotoFlite, Ashford*)

be over-optimistic. Such are the trials and tribulations of a container ship owner!

Short of adopting policies of subsidy, a very retrograde step in any circumstance, there seems little that can be done until the market actually collapses, thus removing excess capacity into lay-up and eventual scrapping. How then can the developed nations hope to continue? The answer is all too simple: by building larger and larger vessels, using reduced crews, and incorporating the very latest in technological advances to provide highly efficient cargo-handling systems, coupled to advanced hull forms with economic fuel efficient machinery, which will combine to provide very low operating overheads per TEU. And this is precisely the trend which can be observed at the present moment with the appearance of such vessels as the 12 massive United States Lines ships. The vicious circle continues.

Currently, to achieve profitability, the average container ship needs to obtain a load factor approaching 60 per cent of total available shipboard slots. As new vessels emerge, such as the new US Lines and Evergreen Line ships, more economic operations allow this figure to be reduced to about 50 per cent. Based on current predictions therefore, a projection of trade developed, coupled to the continued appearance of new tonnage, will mean that these new vessels should, relatively easily, be able to work economically in the near to forseeable future. Thus, it will be the older and less cost-effective vessels that will really feel the pinch.

As of 1 January 1984, there were just under 900,000 TEU shipboard slots deployed. Based on the prediction

Completed by Swan Hunter in the first half of 1984 was the *Hoegh Duke*, one of four sister ships for Lief Hoegh. She has a deadweight of 42,000 tonnes and is powered by a Kincaid B&W 5L80GA developing 14,500 bhp/10,664 kW which provides a service speed of 16.5 knots. She is a true multi-role vessel, able to carry most forms of general cargo, bulk cargoes, timber, even cars and, of course, 1,666 TEU containers. (*FotoFlite, Ashford*)

of 25 per cent growth rate between that date and the end of 1986, there *should*, therefore, be no more than 1,125,000 shipboard slots by the end of 1986. Within this period, US Lines 12 new ships alone will bring 52,560 slots into service, while Evergreen's new 24 'G' class ships will add a further 65,472 TEU slots. Thus, of the 225,000 new slots which can safely be accepted into the market place, just two operators alone will have accounted for more than 118,000 of them! Ignoring the possibility of the materialisation of the 250,000 ton monsters, Sea Land, Maersk Lines, Lykes Lines, Hapag-Lloyd, Trans-Freight Lines, The Shipping Corporation of India, C.Y. Tung, the Japanese 'Big 6' consortium, the China Ocean Shipping Company and many others are *all* bringing new large tonnage into service during this period. In total, no less than 400,000 new slots are, so far, booked to appear before the end of 1986. This figure, it must be remembered, *does not* include a vast number of new slots which are additionally appearing from the non-cellular sector in their new ships and conversions, where greater levels of container stowage are appearing aboard general cargo combination ro-ro and bulk/container carriers.

Obviously, some reductions to capacity will be made as ships are lost to natural and man-made hazards, while others will undoubtedly go to the breakers yards. Yet another capacity reducing aspect will be the ships which are taken up for military

OCL's *Jervis Bay* was one vessel removed from trade this year. She broke away from tugs while en-route to the ship-breakers yards, and ran aground on the French coast. Not too many reductions of this nature are likely to aid the over-capacity problems though, but there are one or two due for the breakers.(*FotoFlite, Ashford*)

Louis Maersk, one of a class of 43,431 grt container ships built during 1984 for Denmark's Maersk Lines. She has 3,390 TEU shipboard slots and represents the typical third generation 3,000 TEU plus vessels now gaining in popularity among owners. (*Odense Steel Shipyard Ltd*)

service, such as those which are being recruited into the United States FMA Reserve Fleet. But this demand has tailed-off somewhat during 1984, and unless other countries such as the United Kingdom and European nations embark upon a similar scheme, the container trades can anticipate no respite from this quarter, and mass lay-ups will be the inevitable result.

The most frightening aspect of all however, must surely be the prospect of the appearance of the 250,000-tonners. Generally, the size of container ships has been limited due to operators' desires to build ships that will transit the Suez and Panama canals, where the latter's maximum 33 metre beam and 11.4 metre draught has dictated design criteria somewhat. But with operators now becoming prepared to sacrifice operational flexibility and ignore secondhand sale prices in order to attain a ship where high-economy operation over predefined route networks can provide a realistic return on outlay, while holding off much of the competition too, one can expect, even predict quite realistically, that a substantial number of these giant vessels will make their presence felt by the early 1990s.

Whereas port restrictions have also held back on the emergence of these superships, even this factor is now receding into the background as more and more ports turn their attention to providing facilities for the ships of the future. Scrutiny of the latest edition of *Jane's Freight Containers* for example, will show that port development is proceeding apace with new and improving container-handling facilities being provided throughout the world, including Bahrain, Hamburg, Rotterdam, Hong Kong, Keelung, New York, Osaka, Port Kelang, Seattle and Southampton where expansion is the order of the day. At the same time Bombay, Calcutta, Cochin, Colombo, Curacao, Karachi, Madras, Rangoon, Rio Haina, and ports in China, Egypt, Libya and Thailand are all benefitting from completely new container-handling facilities which come on-stream either during 1984 or during the 1984–86 period. Perhaps the most significant of these however, is the Europe Container Terminal's (ECT) Maasvlakte trans-shipment centre in Rotterdam's Europoort, where five new cranes are being installed. Three of these new cranes are able to handle up to 50 units per hour while all five can accept containers of up to 50 feet in length. Their significance? They have an outreach from the quay wall of 40 metres. Or, put another way, they can handle a container ship that is wide enough to accommodate no less than 16 rows of boxes across its beam!

The Expansion of Evergreen

by James Weatherley

The phenomenal growth of Taiwan's Evergreen Line has reached yet another new dimension in 1984, with the commencement of their fully-containerised, both-way, Round-The-World service. This ambitious new undertaking, requiring an investment in excess of $1,000 million at a time when trade is tight and competition is fierce, has naturally ensconsed Evergreen in their position in the limelight of the international container transportation trades. From its inception just 15 years ago with the 6,913 grt steam turbine general cargo vessel *Central Trust*, purchased for just $600,000 from Japan, Evergreen has expanded to become one of the world's largest and most modern

fleets, possessing in excess of 50 ships which, with the exception of one training vessel, are *all* less than ten years old.

But success breeds jealousy and conflicts. Many commentators have attacked the go-it-alone expansionism of Far Eastern concerns like Evergreen, and the activities of 1984 have unfortunately brought Evergreen into direct confrontation with other established operators. The entry into the highly competitive North Atlantic trades, the collapse of the Far Eastern Freight Conference agreement, the commencement of the RTW service, and other areas of competition, will undoubtedly bring Evergreen to battle during forthcoming months. Certainly, Evergreen Line/the Evergreen Marine Corporation, is an interesting Company to study.

Conceived by Mr Chang Yuang-fa, a former banana-boat mate, the Evergreen success story has

Evergreen was initially formed as Central Marine and began trading with the 6,913 grt *Central Trust*. The first actual 'Ever' vessel, however, was the 1948-built 2,144 grt *Ever Lite* (ex-*Takaosan Maru*). (*Courtesy Dunelm Public Relations Ltd*)

The inauguration of Evergreen's Round-the-World service took place on 19 July 1984, when the 36,500 grt *Ever Garden* sailed from Hong Kong at the commencement of the world's first fully containerised RTW service. *Ever Garden* sailed for the USA on the east-bound route, while a week later, her sister-ship *Ever Genius* sailed from Tokyo bound for Europe before continuing onto New York and thus beginning the west-bound leg.

Seen here at Felixstowe on her maiden voyage is *Ever Grade*, one of the 16 'G' class ships which operate Evergreen Line's Round-the-World service with sailings every ten days both east-bound and west-bound. In 1985, another eight identical ships will enable sailings to become weekly in both directions. (*Evergreen Marine Corporation*)

been spectacular by most conservative business standards, and possesses its share of intrigue too. For one thing, Mr Chang Yuang-fa's lack of strong business background, coupled to his Company's massive expansion, has often fired speculation that he is backed by some elusive major financier or business concern. Commonly, the giant Marubeni trading corporation has been cited in this role, and it is certainly true that Evergreen and Marubeni do share particularly strong business bonds. However, these have always been

denied by Evergreen, who say that no outsider has ever invested in them and that they have always financed their own expansion. According to Evergreen, their expansion is based upon their commercial strength, efficiency, and inherant flexibility which has allowed them to recognise and cater to expanding markets largely ignored by other shipping majors.

In 1968 when trading commenced with the *Central Trust*, the economies of the Far East and South East

The rapid escalation in the size of Evergreen is evident from this Table showing the increase in fleet tonnage compared to the cargo tonnage figures achieved by Evergreen Line. It well illustrates the ratio of expansion, and indeed, the efficiency of planning which characterises the whole Evergreen operation.

Number of ships and their tonnage (deadweight) K/T			Cargo handled (unit: 1,000 tonnes)
1968	1 vsl of	10,095	25
1969	4 of	56,837	49
1970	7 of	97,329	143
1971	8 of	97,713	285
1972	13 of	147,641	429
1973	15 of	155,171	533
1974	12 of	133,342	566
1975	15 of	216,734	565
1976	22 of	299,432	1,039
1977	22 of	320,572	1,641
1978	23 of	375,399	2,593
1979	29 of	500,375	3,996
1980	28 of	519,647	5,145
1981	26 of	485,026	5,524
1982	28 of	570,741	6,172

The 12,413 grt *Ever Spring* after jumboisation. When she entered service in 1976 she became the first fully cellular vessel to join the Evergreen fleet, and inaugurated the Line's Far East-US East Coast service. (*Courtesy Dunelm Public Relations Ltd*)

Asia were beginning to expand in a large way. Evergreen saw this and identified trades in which little competition had then developed. They adopted aggressive marketing policies which gave them some virtual monopolies in certain relatively small-bore trading areas, and while the big concerns were battling it out on the high traffic-density routes, Evergreen were enjoying permanent growth with few of the

The 9,079 grt *Ever Trust*, one of Evergreen's two training ships. An unusual staff system operates at Evergreen, whereby shore-based and sea-based staff are rotated to give each the opportunity to understand the problems faced throughout the operation. Evergreen gives considerable priority to effective training, and operates a shore-based college in addition to the training ships.

Ever Trust in her former guise as the 10,442 grt *Ever Safety*. (*Courtesy Dunelm Public Relations Ltd*)

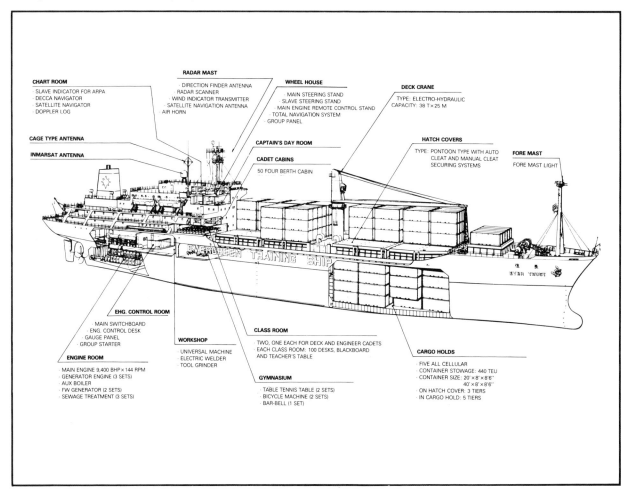

CHART ROOM
· SLAVE INDICATOR FOR ARPA
· DECCA NAVIGATOR
· SATELLITE NAVIGATOR
· DOPPLER LOG

RADAR MAST
· DIRECTION FINDER ANTENNA
· RADAR SCANNER
· WIND INDICATOR TRANSMITTER
· SATELLITE NAVIGATION ANTENNA
· AIR HORN

WHEEL HOUSE
· MAIN STEERING STAND
· SLAVE STEERING STAND
· MAIN ENGINE REMOTE CONTROL STAND
· TOTAL NAVIGATION SYSTEM
· GROUP PANEL

DECK CRANE
TYPE: ELECTRO-HYDRAULIC
CAPACITY: 38 T × 25 M

CAGE TYPE ANTENNA

INMARSAT ANTENNA

CAPTAIN'S DAY ROOM

CADET CABINS
50 FOUR BERTH CABIN

HATCH COVERS
TYPE: PONTOON TYPE WITH AUTO
CLEAT AND MANUAL CLEAT
SECURING SYSTEMS

FORE MAST
FORE MAST LIGHT

EHG. CONTROL ROOM
· MAIN SWITCHBOARD
· ENG. CONTROL DESK
· GAUGE PANEL
· GROUP STARTER

WORKSHOP
· UNIVERSAL MACHINE
· ELECTRIC WELDER
· TOOL GRINDER

CLASS ROOM
TWO, ONE EACH FOR DECK AND ENGINEER CADETS
· EACH CLASS ROOM: 100 DESKS, BLACKBOARD
AND TEACHER'S TABLE

CARGO HOLDS
· FIVE ALL CELLULAR
· CONTAINER STOWAGE: 440 TEU
· CONTAINER SIZE: 20' × 8' × 8'6"
  40' × 8' × 8'6"
· ON HATCH COVER: 3 TIERS
· IN CARGO HOLD: 5 TIERS

ENGINE ROOM
· MAIN ENGINE 9,400 BHP × 144 RPM
· GENERATOR ENGINE (3 SETS)
· AUX BOILER
· FW GENERATOR (2 SETS)
· SEWAGE TREATMENT (3 SETS)

GYMNASIUM
· TABLE TENNIS TABLE (2 SETS)
· BICYCLE MACHINE (2 SETS)
· BAR-BELL (1 SET)

PARTICULARS OF FULL CONTAINER VESSELS

No.	Ship Name	G.T.	D.W.T.	3-Tiers (T.E.U.)	4-Tiers (T.E.U.)	Service Speed	Built	Builder	Main Engine Type	H.P.	Draft (M)
1.	Ever Guard	36,500.00 T	43,401.00 K/T	2,390	2,728	20.5	Jun. 1983	IHI	IHI-Sulzer 6RLB90	24,000	11.60
2.	Ever Guide	36,500.00 T	43,401.00 K/T	2,390	2,728	20.5	Jul. 1983	IHI	IHI-Sulzer 6RLB90	24,000	11.60
3.	Ever Going	36,500.00 T	43,401.00 K/T	2,390	2,728	20.5	Sep. 1983	IHI	IHI-Sulzer 6RLB90	24,000	11.60
4.	Ever Grade	36,500.00 T	43,401.00 K/T	2,390	2,728	20.5	Mar. 1984	IHI	IHI-Sulzer 6RLB90	24,000	11.60
5.	Ever Giant	36,500.00 T	43,401.00 K/T	2,390	2,728	20.5	Jun. 1984	IHI	IHI-Sulzer 6RLB90	24,000	11.60
6.	Ever Grace	36,500.00 T	43,401.00 K/T	2,390	2,728	20.5	Jul. 1984	IHI	IHI-Sulzer 6RLB90	24,000	11.60
7.	Ever Glory	36,500.00 T	43,401.00 K/T	2,390	2,728	20.5	Feb. 1984	Onomichi	IHI-Sulzer 6RLB90	24,000	11.60
8.	Ever Globe	36,500.00 T	43,401.00 K/T	2,390	2,728	20.5	Jun. 1984	Onomichi	IHI-Sulzer 6RLB90	24,000	11.60
9.	Ever Greet	36,500.00 T	43,401.00 K/T	2,390	2,728	20.5	Aug. 1984	Onomichi	IHI-Sulzer 6RLB90	24,000	11.60
10.	Ever Grand	36,500.00 T	43,401.00 K/T	2,390	2,728	20.5	Oct. 1984	Onomichi	IHI-Sulzer 6RLB90	24,000	11.60
11.	Ever Gather	36,500.00 T	43,401.00 K/T	2,390	2,728	20.5	May 1984	CSBC	TMMC-IHI-Sulzer 6RLB90	24,000	11.60
12.	Ever Garden	36,500.00 T	43,401.00 K/T	2,390	2,728	20.5	Jul. 1984	CSBC	TMMC-IHI-Sulzer 6RLB90	24,000	11.60
13.	Ever Genius	36,500.00 T	43,401.00 K/T	2,390	2,728	20.5	Jul. 1984	CSBC	TMMC-IHI-Sulzer 6RLB90	24,000	11.60
14.	Ever Gentry	36,500.00 T	43,401.00 K/T	2,390	2,728	20.5	Aug. 1984	CSBC	TMMC-IHI-Sulzer 6RLB90	24,000	11.60
15.	Ever Gentle	36,500.00 T	43,401.00 K/T	2,390	2,728	20.5	Sep. 1984	CSBC	TMMC-IHI-Sulzer 6RLB90	24,000	11.60
16.	Ever Gifted	36,500.00 T	43,401.00 K/T	2,390	2,728	20.5	Feb. 1985	CSBC	TMMC-Hitachi-Sulzer 6RLB90	24,000	11.60
17.	Ever Growth	36,500.00 T	43,401.00 K/T	2,390	2,728	20.5	Apr. 1985	CSBC	TMMC-Hitachi-Sulzer 6RLB90	24,000	11.60
18.	Ever Golden	36,500.00 T	43,401.00 K/T	2,390	2,728	20.5	Jun. 1985	CSBC	TMMC-Hitachi-Sulzer 6RLB90	24,000	11.60
19.	Ever Gleamy	36,500.00 T	43,401.00 K/T	2,390	2,728	20.5	Aug. 1985	CSBC	TMMC-Hitachi-Sulzer 6RLB90	24,000	11.60
20.	Ever Govern	36,500.00 T	43,401.00 K/T	2,390	2,728	20.5	Sep. 1985	Onomichi	Hitachi-Sulzer 6RLB90	24,000	11.60
21.	Ever Goods	36,500.00 T	43,401.00 K/T	2,390	2,728	20.5	Sep. 1985	Onomichi	Hitachi-Sulzer 6RLB90	24,000	11.60
22.	Ever Guest	36,500.00 T	43,401.00 K/T	2,390	2,728	20.5	Jan. 1986	Onomichi	Hitachi-Sulzer 6RLB90	24,000	11.60
23.	Ever Group	36,500.00 T	43,401.00 K/T	2,390	2,728	20.5	Apr. 1986	Onomichi	Hitachi-Sulzer 6RLB90	24,000	11.60
24.	Ever Given	36,500.00 T	43,401.00 K/T	2,390	2,728	20.5	Jul. 1986	Onomichi	Hitachi-Sulzer 6RLB90	24,000	11.60
25.	Ever Linking	24,802.00 T	28,916.00 K/T	1,566	1,810	21.0	Jun. 1983	CSBC	Hitachi-Sulzer 7RND90M	22,260	11.23
26.	Ever Loading	24,802.00 T	28,849.00 K/T	1,566	1,810	21.0	Aug. 1983	CSBC	Hitachi-Sulzer 7RND90M	22,260	11.23
27.	Ever Lynic	24,804.59 T	28,900.00 K/T	1,566	1,810	21.0	Oct. 1979	Onomichi	Hitachi-Sulzer 7RND90M	22,260	11.23
28.	Ever Level	24,804.59 T	28,898.00 K/T	1,566	1,810	21.0	Jan. 1980	Onomichi	Hitachi-Sulzer 7RND90M	22,260	11.23
29.	Ever Living	24,804.59 T	28,902.00 K/T	1,566	1,810	21.0	May 1980	Onomichi	IHI-Sulzer 7RND90M	22,260	11.23
30.	Ever Laurel	24,804.59 T	28,904.00 K/T	1,566	1,810	21.0	Sep. 1980	Onomichi	IHI-Sulzer 7RND90M	22,260	11.23
31.	Ever Valiant	14,402.15 T	18,834.27 K/T	1,008	1,174	21.0	Apr. 1977	Hayashikane	IHI-Sulzer 6RND90M	20,100	10.02
32.	Ever Valor	14,949.52 T	20,186.55 K/T	1,048	1,214	21.0	Aug. 1978	Onomichi	Hitachi-Sulzer 6RND90M	20,100	10.32
33.	Ever Value	14,949.52 T	20,157.70 K/T	1,048	1,214	21.0	Nov. 1978	Onomichi	Hitachi-Sulzer 6RND90M	20,100	10.32
34.	Ever Vital	16,358.06 T	20,025.05 K/T	1,048	1,214	21.0	Apr. 1979	CSBC	IHI-Sulzer 6RND90M	20,100	10.32
35.	Ever Vigor	16,358.05 T	20,025.05 K/T	1,048	1,214	21.0	Jun. 1979	CSBC	IHI-Sulzer 6RND90M	20,100	10.32
36.	Ever Spring	12,413.28 T	15,752.23 K/T	754	878	20.0	Jul. 1975	Hayashikane	Mitsui-B & W 8K67GF	15,000	9.32
37.	Ever Summit	12,413.28 T	15,752.23 K/T	754	878	20.0	Oct. 1975	Hayashikane	Mitsui-B & W 8K67GF	15,000	9.32
38.	Ever Superb	12,413.28 T	15,752.23 K/T	754	878	20.0	Jan. 1976	Hayashikane	Mitsui-B & W 8K67GF	15,000	9.32
39.	Ever Shine	12,413.28 T	15,764.10 K/T	754	878	20.0	Apr. 1976	Hayashikane	Mitsui-B & W 8K67GF	15,000	9.32
40.	Ever Pioneer	7,806.98 T	11,875.35 K/T	522	522	16.0	Aug. 1973	Tohoku	Hitachi-B & W 6K62EF	8,300	8.81
41.	Ever Promoter	7,806.98 T	11,857.11 K/T	522	522	16.0	Dec. 1973	Tohoku	Hitachi-B & W 6K62EF	8,300	8.81
42.	Ever Breeze	6,900.00 T	9,600.00 K/T	510	510	14.0	Jan. 1984	Hakodate	Hitachi-B & W 8L35MC	5,440	7.80
43.	Ever Bridge	6,900.00 T	9,600.00 K/T	510	510	14.0	Feb. 1984	Hakodate	Hitachi-B & W 8L35MC	5,440	7.80
44.	Ever Better	6,900.00 T	9,600.00 K/T	510	510	14.0	Feb. 1984	Hakodate	Hitachi-B & W 8L35MC	5,440	7.80
45.	Ever Fortune	12,900.91 T	18,828.20 K/T	832	956	17.0	Sep. 1978	Narasaki	Hitachi-Sulzer 7RND68	10,500	9.75
46.	Ever Forward	12,900.91 T	18,821.10 K/T	832	956	17.0	Dec. 1978	Narasaki	IHI-Sulzer 7RND68	10,500	9.75
47.	Ever Forever	12,869.50 T	18,813.80 K/T	840	964	17.0	May 1979	Narasaki	Hitachi-Sulzer 7RND68	10,500	9.75
48.	Ever Humanity	11,289.43 T	17,806.40 K/T	680	680	15.5	Nov. 1975	Narasaki	Hitachi-B & W 7K62EF	9,400	9.33
49.	Ever Handsome	11,317.66 T	17,821.20 K/T	680	680	15.5	May 1976	Narasaki	Hitachi-B & W 7K62EF	9,400	9.33
50.	Ever Moral	12,000.00 T	16,900.00 K/T	818	818	16.0	Dec. 1984	Hayashikane	Mitsu-B & W 7K62EF	9,400	9.30
51.	Ever Modest	12,000.00 T	16,900.00 K/T	818	818	16.0	Nov. 1984	Narasaki	Hitachi-B & W 7K62EF	9,400	9.30
52.	Ever Master	12,000.00 T	16,900.00 K/T	818	818	16.0	Oct. 1984	Narasaki	Hitachi-B & W 7K62EF	9,400	9.30
53.	Ever Mercy	12,000.00 T	16,900.00 K/T	818	818	16.0	Nov. 1984	Hayashikane	Mitsui-B & W 7K62EF	9,400	9.30
	Sub Total:	1,297,085.10 T	1,589,465.57 K/T	84,682	95,956						

This page and overleaf: The Evergreen Line Fleet.

PARTICULARS OF BULK CARRIERS

No.	Ship Name	G.T.	D.W.T.	Service Speed	Built	Builder	Main Engine Type	H.P.	Draft (M)
1.	Ever Ocean	14,743.30 T	29,346.61 K/T	15.0	Feb. 1982	Hakodate	Hitachi-Sulzer 6RND68M	10,800	10.67
2.	Ever Oasis	14,743.30 T	29,290.07 K/T	15.0	Apr. 1982	Hakodate	Hitachi-Sulzer 6RND68M	10,800	10.67
3.	Ever Order	14,743.30 T	29,314.10 K/T	15.0	Jun. 1982	Hakodate	Hitachi-Sulzer 6RND68M	10,800	10.67
4.	Ever Onward	15,993.24 T	31,193.87 K/T	14.8	Oct. 1982	Hakodate	IHI-Sulzer 6RLB66	11,100	11.00
5.	Ever Orient	15,993.24 T	31,189.55 K/T	14.8	Jan. 1983	Hakodate	IHI-Sulzer 6RLB66	11,100	11.00
6.	Ever Obtain	15,993.24 T	31,187.48 K/T	14.8	Mar. 1983	Hakodate	IHI-Sulzer 6RLB66	11,100	11.00
	Sub Total:	92,209.62 T	181,521.68 K/T						

PARTICULARS OF TRAINING VESSELS

No.	Ship Name	G.T.	D.W.T.	3-Tiers (T.E.U.)	4-Tiers (T.E.U.)	Service Speed	Built	Builder	Main Engine Type	H.P.	Draft (M)
1.	Ever Training	2,683.20 T	2,084.00 K/T			14.5	Mar. 1960	Sanoyasu	Mitsubishi 7UET45/75	3,150	5.30
2.	Ever Trust	9,079.73 T	15,276.46 K/T	440	440	16.0	Jan. 1972	Hayashikane	Mitsui-B & W 7K62EF	9,400	8.90
	Sub Total:	11,762.93 T	17,360.46 K/T	440	440						

	G.T.	D.W.T.	3-Tiers (T.E.U.)	4-Tiers (T.E.U.)
Grand Total: 61 Vessels	1,401,057.65 T	1,788,347.71 K/T	85,122	96,396

competitive and restrictive practices which were then being forced on the larger operators.

Eventually however, from the original tramp service between the Far East and USA, Evergreen expanded into a position whereby their continued existence could not go unnoticed. The oil boom in South West Asia was the stepping stone that Evergreen needed, and by being in at the ground floor and offering highly competitive tariffs, the commencement of Middle East–Far East and Far East–South America liner operations rapidly picked Evergreen up from their inauspicious start. By the end of 1973 Evergreen

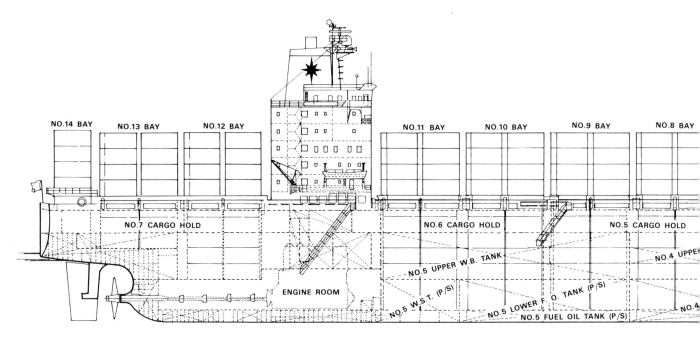

Ever Linking is one of six 1,810 TEU container vessels deployed by Evergreen Line on their Hong Kong–Taiwan–Pacific coast service in mid-1984, offering sailings every six days. Four smaller ships provide a Japan–Korea–US Pacific coast link at nine-day intervals. (*FotoFlite, Ashford*)

had 14 ships in operation, including their first newbuilding the 10,442 grt *Ever Safety*, and had taken the decision to containerise all their liner services.

The next major milestone for Evergreen occurred in July 1976, when the 12,413 grt *Ever Spring* made her debut on a new Evergreen line service between the Far East and US East Coast. Once again, by inaugurating the service between the Far East and US *East* Coast rather than following the major operators into the trade to the *West* Coast, Evergreen managed to avoid too much confrontation with competitors. Also significant was that *Ever Spring*, built by Hayashikane in Japan, was the first fully cellular container ship to join the Evergreen fleet.

By the early 1980s however, Evergreen's policy of non-confrontation had, by virtue of the size and continued expansion of the company, brought them into conflict with other lines. Their policy of under-cutting competition had put a sour taste in the mouths of some of their rivals who could not, and did not want to match the low rates then being offered. Evergreen,

MIDSHIP SECTION

General arrangement drawing of the new 'G' class ships. Having been constructed during a period of relative recession in the shipbuilding industry, the 'G' class vessels were able to be secured relatively inexpensively in capital terms, at $29.2 million each. Per TEU, this is on a par with the 12 US Lines ships which should, theoretically, be cheaper by comparison. Further savings are achieved as, following an Evergreen trend, they are slightly under-engined for this ship type, bearing a Sulzer 6RLB90 developing 24,000 bhp which will operate at 19.5 knots on the RTW service, giving a daily fuel consumption of around 62 tonnes. The last four ships will, however, be powered by the even more economic Sulzer 6RTA84.

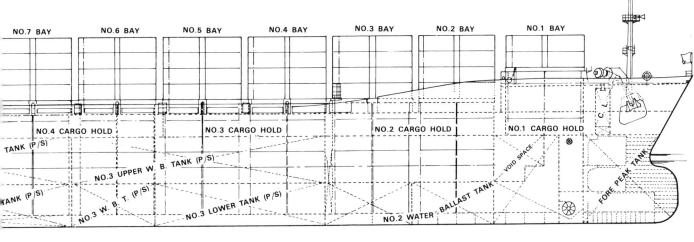

always considered something of a noisy outsider by some of the longer-established lines, were offered Conference membership. In return for a reduction of 300,000 TEU per year based on an Evergreen lifting totalling 1.3 million TEU, the Far Eastern Freight Conference offered Evergreen a form of associate membership in which both parties were destined to agree a realistic schedule of loading rates and tariffs. However, it soon became clear that all was not in order with this agreement and, at time of writing, the disagreement between the FEFC and Evergreen seems likely to end in a court battle, and thus Evergreen's future relationships with the Conference do not look rosy to say the very least!

With the inauguration of the new Round-The-World service in July 1984, Evergreen are embarking on their most ambitious plans to date. Twenty-four new ships were ordered for this venture, which represents a lot of additional capacity in anyone's language, although the transition from existing services into a two-way RTW service is not quite the spectacular growth or increase in business that it seems to be. In fact, it represents a rationalisation of existing route networks to a very large degree.

Ports of call on the Round-The-World service are largely those hitherto served by Evergreen on their pre-1984 route network. Some sailing schedules, such

One of Evergreen's other trading practices is to buy ships sized to the available business and extend them later as trade improves. This is the case with the early 'G' type vessels including *Ever Guard, Ever Guide* and *Ever Going* which were built to accommodate 2,240 TEU and are now to be enlarged to carry 2,728 TEU. The later 'G' class were built, and are to be built, with this higher capacity.

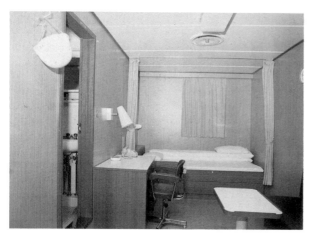

as that of the former Far East–US East Coast route, have in fact had their frequency reduced. However, the inauguration of both-way sailings has for all practical purposes increased the shipboard slots actually available between those points in any given time span, and the present 10-day frequency of sailings

The 'G' class have a high standard of accommodation for their crews, which consist of only 17 persons. Small crews, low wages (compared to equivalent Western operations), low capital-cost ships, fractionally slower operating speeds and consequent bunker savings, are among the hallmarks of the Evergreen operation. The crew of 17 however, is temporary apparently, as Evergreen now wish to *reduce* this number to 14!

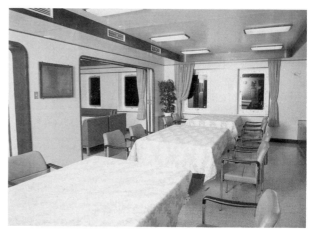

Evergreen also operate a fairly respectable fleet of six bulk carriers. However, in 1984 it was decided that these 'O' class ships would be converted into container ships. The six 15,933 grt ships are named *Ever Onward*, *Ever Orient*, *Ever*

Obtain (*Below*), *Ever Order* (*Above*), *Ever Oasis* and *Ever Ocean*. i (*Skyfotos*), ii (*FotoFlite, Ashford*)

Ever Gather, seen at Felixstowe in July 1984 during her maiden voyage, was the first of Evergreen's 'G' type vessels to be built in Taiwan. In September 1984 Europe came under the umbrella of the RTW Services.

in both directions will, when the remaining eight 'G' class vessels enter service, be increased to a weekly service frequency anyway.

The impact of Evergreen's RTW service will be most noted on the sectors where prior to 1984 no (Evergreen) service was offered. Two significant new sectors are the North Atlantic, where Evergreen will commence sailings between Le Havre and New York west-bound, and Baltimore and Hamburg east-bound. Here, Evergreen will face their greatest opposition and competition in what amounts to a head-on attack to the operators already established in these trades.

Mr Chang, however, does not feel this to be so, anticipating increased trade on this route for the future rather than attempting to win a tariff-cutting battle and taking trade from the existing North Atlantic liner companies. Evergreen state that they are not dependant on attracting business from competitors on this leg, and that the link up between Europe and America is valuable in many other ways as a rationalisation of former route networks. They also state that rates will not be cut and that they will be 'on a par with the majority'. Furthermore, they have no intention, apparently, of offering cut-price rates on the east-bound leg out of the US, although load factors in that direction are far from the usually good pickings to be obtained between Europe and the US on the west-bound sailings. However, the passage of time may well hold revised strategies in store.

It is certainly far from clear as to what precise effects the commencement of these ambitious sailings will have on the majority of operators. Only time will tell. But one can rest assured that effects there certainly will be, and that interest in this still expanding organisation will hold the attention of many in the shipping world, as this significant Corporation moves ever onward, into the second half of the 1980s.

US Lines' Big 12

by A J Ambrose

The christening ceremony of the container ships *American New Jersey* and *American Alabama* on 31 May 1984. (*D H Mann*)

The container-shipping sphere of activity has provided much in the way of significant news and developments in 1984, not least of these being the two new fully cellular services of Evergreen and US Lines. Both differ in concept however, and particularly in the tonnage which each has chosen to operate their Round-The-World services. It will be interesting, therefore, to monitor the development of the respective operations, and see which concept comes out on top. The US Lines venture will be particularly interesting, as prophecies of doom seem to have plagued the plan right from the beginning. It is towards the ships (the largest container ships in the world) that much of the criticism has been directed, alleging that economic viability in today's over-tonnaged market simply cannot be achieved with these vessels.

However, if these 12 ships of the *American New York* class can obtain loadings of greater than 50 per

American New York and *American New Jersey* (*far right*), under construction in No 1 drydock at Dae Woo Ship-buildings yards in South Korea. (*D H Mann*)

cent, it is difficult to actually comprehend them making a loss. If they achieve load factors of 80 per cent or more, then it seems clear they will make a handsome profit, as their actual operating costs per TEU are exceedingly low! With a deadweight of 57,800 tonnes, they have a capacity for 2,129 FEU or 4,380 TEU. Of this total 897 FEU are carried on the deck hatches, and 1,232 FEU in the ship's 20 hold compartments. Only 146 of these can be refrigerated units. (Apparently, reefers are not in demand in the RTW trade – Evergreen offer none!) Predominantly, the US Lines' ships cater for 40-foot units, but 20-foot units can also be carried. The ships' dimensions are 289.5 m (overall) × 279 m (between perpendiculars) × 21.5 m (depth) × 32.22 m (beam) × 11.65 m (maximum draught) × 10.67 m (design draught).

Power is provided by a single Sulzer 7RLB90 developing an output of 28,000 bhp at maximum continuous rating, driving a single screw giving a service speed of 18 knots. Designed by C R Cushing & Co of New York, the hull form, which was limited to Panamax due to the canal-transiting requirements of the Round-The-World service, is both efficient and, coupled to the Sulzer RLB, most economical, giving a daily fuel consumption of 72.5 tonnes and allowing a standard range of 30,000 nautical miles. As such, this gives the vessels a *very* economical fuel usage rate as low as 38 grams fuel per TEU mile, (or 2.9 gftm).

Added to the fuel economies are the crew savings. Whereas the Evergreen 'G' type use 17 crew for a 2,240 TEU vessel, the US Lines vessels have only 21 crew for 4,380 TEU. This is another considerable economy. Although 1½ times the size of the next largest container ships afloat, the crew is exactly half on the American vessels.

Originally, US Lines plans called for a series of 14 ships to operate a two way Round-The-World service, but due to finite capital availability, the order when placed in 1982 was reduced to 12 ships. Even then, the $570 million (£413 million) order still represented the largest single peacetime merchant shipbuilding contract and expansion in the US merchant fleet in the history of American shipping.

The first five vessels in the series were financed by a consortium headed by Citibank, and with the exception of Hull 4,005 were all launched on 28 May 1984, and named in a ceremony on 31 May 1984. The first, *American New York* followed by *American New Jersey* entered service a few weeks later, with *American New York* sailing on her maiden line service from Hong Kong on 21 June 1984, bound for Japan and the US East Coast. The next two vessels *American Maine* and *American Alabama* joined the fleet later in the year.

On 31 May 1984, on the day the first four ships were named, the builders Dae Woo Shipbuilding announced that delivery dates of the remaining vessels were all to be advanced in response to requests from US Lines, with the last now due for handover in May 1986.

The Round-The-World service actually went into operation in 1984, but will not maintain its full weekly sailings until the remaining seven ships enter service in 1985 (four) and early 1986 (three). The last seven ships (financed by the Korean Development Bank) when all operational, are then expected to herald a complete change of service pattern, details of which are presently another USL guarded secret, but could include a two-way service with ships sailing from both US East and West coasts, omitting the Panama canal.

American New York, the first of the 12 to be completed, on sea trials. She entered service on 21 June 1984. (*D H Mann*)

The 14,001 grt/16,443 dwt *Mormacaltair*. US Lines' apparent planning with the Moore McCormak operation was to secure connecting feeder services for their Round the World services. (*World Ship Society Photo Library*)

Whether the future of the container trade will be based on massive Very Large Container Carriers such as these, or the more conventional style such as Evergreen's 'G' type, cannot be predicted with certainty. But, having said that, for the reasonably predictable flows on the major liner routes, the lowest cost/TEU is the factor which in the final analysis, is the one that must count.

The United States Lines Round-The-World service is a project conceived by none other than former Sea Land head, Malcolm McLean. Widely regarded as the man who pioneered containerisation and brought about the box revolution in the first place, he took over US Lines in 1978. Thus, the project is in good hands and is unlikely to falter, even though many have said it will.

American Alabama, launched on 28 May 1984 and the second of the 12, is seen here in the English Channel after having called at Rotterdam and bound for the south of France. (*FotoFlite, Ashford*)